ONDON to DARWIN FLIGHT
ctober 14th, 1927 - March 19th, 1928

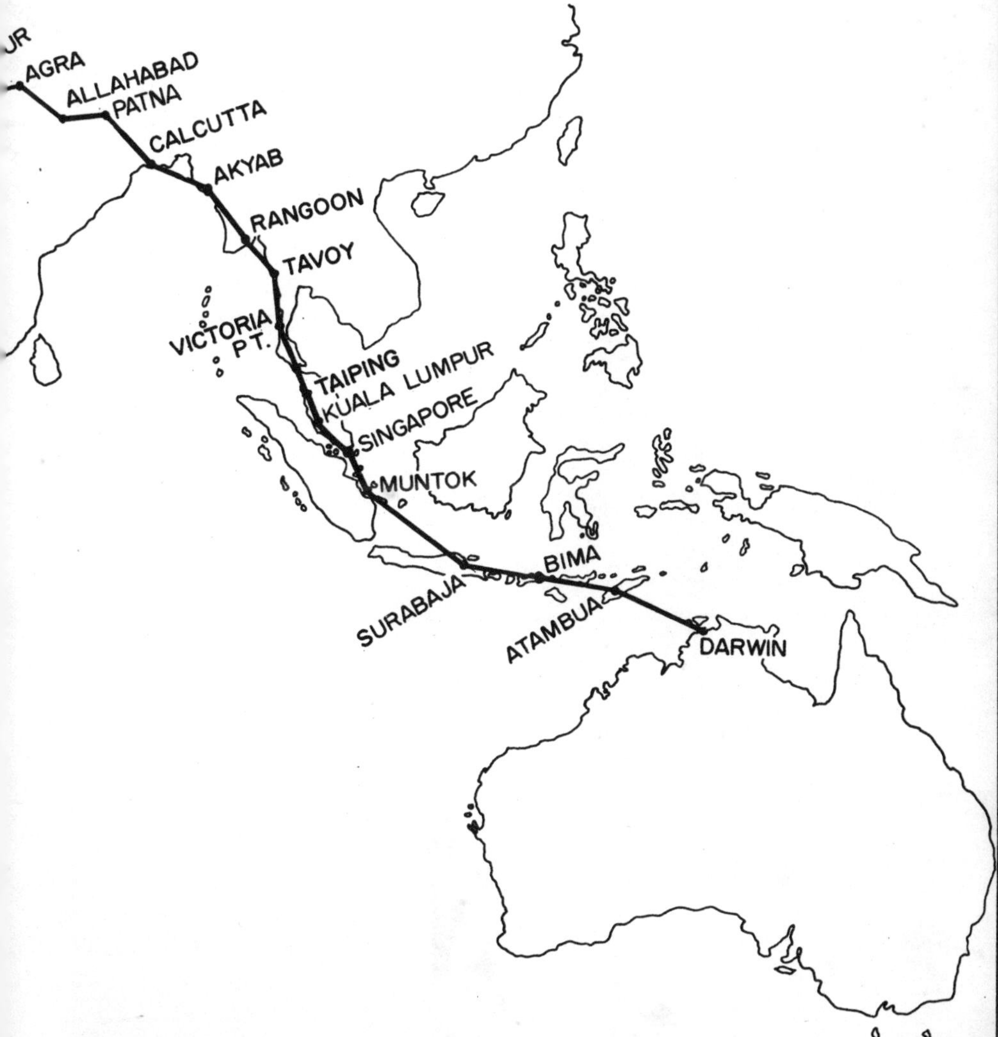

# Verdict on a Lost Flyer

RALPH BARKER

Verdict on a Lost Flyer

The Story of Bill Lancaster

ST. MARTIN'S PRESS
New York

Copyright © 1969 by Ralph Barker
All rights reserved. For information write:
St. Martin's Press, Inc., 175 Fifth Ave.,
New York, N.Y. 10010
Printed in Great Britain
Library of Congress Catalog Card Number: 70-135523
First published in the United States of America in 1971

AFFILIATED PUBLISHERS: Macmillan & Company, Limited, London – also at Bombay, Calcutta Madras and Melbourne – The Macmillan Company of Canada, Limited, Toronto.

Contents

Chapter		Page
	Prologue	9
I	The Man without Fear	13
II	Towards Australia	23
III	Setback at Muntok	33
IV	America: Failure and Success	44
V	Hope fades for Chubbie	57
VI	The House in Miami	67
VII	Destination Mexico	76
VIII	Chubbie falls in Love	89
IX	Lancaster Returns	99
X	"Did you do this?"	108
XI	Building a Defence	117
XII	The Evidence is Circumstantial	128
XIII	The Prosecution rests its Case	139
XIV	Lancaster on the Stand	152
XV	Cross-examination	163
XVI	Of Haden Clarke and the Medical Evidence	175
XVII	The Final Speeches	189
XVIII	Consider your Verdict	199
XIX	The Last Flight	206
XX	The Diary	218
	Epilogue	236

Illustrations

PLATES IN HALF-TONE

Edward Lancaster	*page* 24
Bill and Kiki, 1919	24
Kiki, Pat, and Nina	24
Dressed for the Australia Flight, 1927	*between* 24 *and* 25
In the Tandem Cockpits of the *Red Rose*	*between* 24 *and* 25
Bill kisses Kiki Goodbye	25
Pat writes "Good Luck" on the Fuselage	25
Bound for Australia—the Take-off from Croydon	96
Chubbie packs before Take-off	96
Forced Landing at Rutbah	96
Test-flying the *Red Rose*	97
A Curtiss Robin	97
Lancaster with the *Southern Cross Minor*	97
Reunion at Nassau after Chubbie's Disappearance	112
A Recent Photograph of the House in Coral Gables, Miami	113
Lancaster with the Famous Flyers who testified at his Trial	168
Chubbie on the Witness Stand	168
Lancaster with his Counsel	*between* 168 *and* 169
Cross-examined by the State Attorney	*between* 168 *and* 169
Acquittal	169
Lancaster before leaving New York	208
Entries by Bill Lancaster and his Parents in the Visitors' Book at Lympne	209
Lancaster says Goodbye to his Mother	209
The French Patrol finds the Wreck of *Southern Cross Minor*	224
A Montage of the Wallet and Documents found with Lancaster's Body	225
The Wallet	225
Lancaster's Pilot's Licence	232

The Aircraft Log-book	232
"That is my constant craving. WATER."	*between* 232 *and* 233
"I have stuck to my guns re sticking by the ship and I have stayed the course for a week."	*between* 232 *and* 233
"The chin is up right to the last."	233
"So the beginning of the eighth day has dawned."	233

MAPS AND DIAGRAMS

Principal Points of Call for Lancaster's Caribbean Flight, March–April 1929	53
Havana to Miami, November 28th, 1930 —Chubbie's Intended Track	65
Lancaster's Flight from Miami to Mexico, March 6th–29th, 1932	94–95
Layout of the Sleeping-porch	173
London to Darwin Flight, October 14th, 1927– March 19th, 1928	*front endpaper*
Lancaster's Last Flight, April 11th–12th, 1933	*left-hand rear endpaper*
The Discovery of Lancaster's Aircraft by a French Patrol, February 12th, 1962	*right-hand rear endpaper*

Prologue

THE three heavy trucks which comprised the motorized platoon of the *Groupe Saharien Mixte du Touat* had turned off the trans-Saharan motor-track at Bidon Cinq in the central Sahara two days earlier, on February 10th, 1962. The patrol's purpose was to carry out a reconnaissance of the area in the region of Signal du Tanezrouft, one hundred miles west of Bidon Cinq, in the heart of the Tanezrouft desert. This was the parched, forsaken plain three hundred miles south of the French atomic station at Reggan over which the first French atomic bomb had been exploded two years earlier.

The platoon bivouacked for the night of the tenth, reconnoitred the Signal du Tanezrouft area on the morning of the eleventh, found nothing but a few prehistoric tombs, and then turned north, striking across the flat, featureless desert, on a course roughly parallel with the trans-Saharan motor-track a hundred miles to the east. After motoring eighty-five miles north of Signal du Tanezrouft they bivouacked again for the night.

The Tanezrouft, the very core of the Sahara, is a desert within a desert. Waterless, trackless, bereft of all plant and animal life, shunned by travellers, dreaded by explorers, it is avoided even by the Sahara's own nomadic tribes, who call it the "Land of Thirst". Here the desert is absolute.

The adjutant and *méharistes* of the motorized platoon carried their own food and water; the dry, dehydrating, desiccating heat demands at least two gallons of water per man per day. To start walking in the Tanezrouft at sunrise without water is to be dead by nightfall.

On the morning of February 12th the patrol was ready to abandon the uncharted hinterland of the Tanezrouft and return to the reassurance of the motor-track north of Bidon Cinq. But between them and the track lay an area of *fech-fech*—soft sand which even their heavy-duty tyres could not safely negotiate. They therefore continued their progress due north, hoping the sand to their right would improve.

They had travelled a further twenty-five miles when the *fech-fech* gave way to hard sand. Shortly afterwards they turned due east to pick up the motor-track. Otherwise the terrain was unchanged—flat and featureless as far as the eye could see.

They had travelled exactly a hundred kilometres due east when they noticed a tiny black speck in the distance, very slightly off their course, and they steered towards it. In the Sahara, and particularly in the Tanezrouft, every isolated feature deserves to be investigated, its nature recorded, and its position charted, as a possible future aid to navigation.

The shape of the object they were peering at was difficult to define. It was not until they were less than two kilometres from it that they realized it was a crashed aircraft.

At once they thought of the bomb. Perhaps, unknown to them, a plane had been lost at that time, forced down by the explosion, or by radiation.

When they were about a hundred yards from the wreck, the patrol adjutant ordered his platoon to draw aside so as to avoid any risk of contamination. Then he got down from his truck and approached the plane on foot.

From what he could see of it, it was a small, single-engined biplane, lying on its back, buckled and skeletal, its fabric covering perished. The nose of the plane, its propeller blades broken off at the shaft, was pointing towards the east, as though the pilot had been trying to reach the road. Perhaps, after the crash, he had done so. Yet it seemed from the wreckage that he must have been badly hurt.

Before the adjutant could attempt any closer study of the wreck his eye was held by an object which lay under what had been the lower starboard wing. It was the object he had been looking for. It was a human skull.

The body was lying on its left side, partly covered by a thin layer of sand. The state of preservation was good, and in the light of the discovery that the adjutant was about to make, extraordinary. Those parts which had been exposed to the air had become mummified in the dry desert atmosphere; they were like parchment. The right arm was slightly bent, with the fingers clutching upwards, perhaps towards the throat, in what must surely have been a dying gesture. The injury the man had received in the crash was clearly visible as a scar above the right eyebrow. The clothes were ragged but recognizable.

On the wings of the plane the dead pilot had tied his principal belongings. They included a thin metal case holding his passport and other documents, and a large waterproof envelope into which he had fitted his aircraft log-book. A glance at the log-book revealed that aircraft and body had lain undisturbed for twenty-nine years. The date of the flight that had ended in tragedy was April 12th, 1933.

After the crash, while he waited first for rescue and then for death, the pilot had kept a diary, using the empty pages of his log-book. It told a great deal about the man, and about the flight on which he had crashed. But above all it told of his love for a woman.

It was a love that had taken him away from wife and children, a love because of which, less than a year before his disappearance, he had stood trial for murder in an American court. It was a love which had buoyed him up with hope and courage in his last hours. Yet it was a love which, in the eyes of the world, had destroyed him.

Now, with this chance discovery by the French motorized platoon, the truth about this man, and about the woman he loved, might at last be known. His name was Bill Lancaster.

CHAPTER I

The Man without Fear

THE party in the Baker Street studio was generating a frenzy of chatter and animation. The open windows that allowed an attenuated echo of the din to escape into the street admitted just enough of the June night air to save the smoke-laden atmosphere from becoming suffocating. Presently the volume of sound ebbed as the vibrant notes of a grand piano struck an introductory chord. Then all was silence save for the music. The voices that sang were the most famous voices in London: the year was 1927, and two of the guests at the party were the American Negro singers Layton and Johnstone.

"It ain't gonna rain no more," they sang, and the guests at the party almost believed it. These were the roaring twenties, the era above all others that seemed made for the young. If the world was not exactly at their feet, London at least was only three storeys down. Life was heady, gay, emancipated; above all, life was Twentieth Century. Invention, discovery, exploration, excitement, enchantment—the ingredients were all there to be sampled, unsullied and unspoiled. "I can't get over a girl like you," sang the voices, beautifully modulated. One war was forgotten, another not yet imagined. "Ain't she sweet?" came the refrain. It was the most carefree, intoxicating of nights.

That, anyway, was how it seemed to two Australian girls who shared the flat below—a one-room bed-sitter on the second floor of the Pleyel, Lyon (piano manufacturers) building, 15 Baker Street, a quarter of a mile from Oxford Street and only a few yards north of Portman Square. Soon after they moved in they had run into George, the artist who lived in the studio above them; later they were thrilled at being asked to look over his studio. Were all Australian girls as naïve as they were, he wanted to know?

The walls of the studio were lined with paintings; but apart from a single divan, a small table and chair, and a pile of cushions for visitors, there was no furniture. For the party, though, George had asked their help. Could they get some lamp-shades and some cheap glasses from Woolworth's, and a few more cushions? The party was building up. Then came the day when George appeared at their door looking distraught. Layton and Johnstone were coming, and other well-known artists and musicians, and he would have to get a piano. The Pleyel people downstairs were asking a deposit of £15, and George was temporarily short of cash. . . .

Now here they were, their first party in London, meeting famous and fascinating people. "I want you to meet . . ." "Come and say hello to . . ." "Who brought you? No? Well, what do you know . . ."

"Chubbie" Miller, twenty-five, dark and petite, five feet one and weighing only seven stone, had been in England for several months. She had lived with an aunt before teaming up with another Australian girl in the Baker Street bed-sitter. Her nickname dated from early childhood—she had grown into a slim, attractive young woman. Now George was holding her wrist, leading her across the studio to meet a man of average build and medium height, compact and muscular, hair brushed down on his scalp, with an open, oval face and an attractive, bubbling laugh. She decided he was about thirty. "This is Flying Officer Bill Lancaster," said George. "He's flying to Australia. That should give you something in common—you ought to get together."

Lancaster did most of the talking. He was full of his plans for a solo flight to Australia. It was to be in a light aeroplane—the first such attempt ever made. What did she know about the route? What were the landing fields like in Australia? What were the weather conditions, especially at Port Darwin, his arrival point in Australia? He explained that he had spent a few months in Australia as a young man but had seen little of the country, and he plied her with questions, few of which she could answer; in any case they could hardly hear each other above the din. But the fact that she had lived in Australia all her life seemed to convince Lancaster that she could help. "Come and have tea with me tomorrow," he suggested. "At the Authors' Club, in Whitehall Court. Then I'll show you the route and the plans I've made so far. I'm sure you'll be able to help."

He was a famous flyer—or anyway, he was going to be famous, if he wasn't already. She didn't think she could help him, but if he felt she could, well, all right. Tomorrow at four o'clock.

Already she had had an idea.

Bill Lancaster had left the Royal Air Force just over twelve months earlier, in April 1926, at the end of a five-year term on the active list. He had learnt to fly back in 1917 during War service, but as a Service pilot he seems to have been no more than average, and there is no record that he accomplished anything outstanding during the War. He was born on February 14th, 1898, at King's Norton, Birmingham, but his family was a Croydon family, and they moved back to South London within a year or so of his birth.

Lancaster's father, Edward Lancaster, was a distinguished civil engineer; he had three children by his first marriage, and three more, Elizabeth, William Newton (Bill), and Jack, by his second, to Maud Lucas, a first cousin. "Billee", as Maud Lancaster called her eldest son, went to boarding-school at Ardingly as a junior and later as a senior to Stafford College; otherwise he lived with his parents in South London.

By some yardsticks Maud Lancaster would be adjudged a crank; certainly she was unorthodox and eccentric. And like many eccentrics she enjoyed the limelight. But she was artistic, self-taught in several languages, and of a sympathetic nature; in marrying her cousin she took on a ready-made family of three young children in addition to the family she later produced herself. She wrote a book, *Electricity in the Home*, which sold well as a textbook for housewives, besides showing her to be a capable woman with a practical bent; but she devoted most of her time to a charitable society known as the "Mission of Flowers", an association formed to do good works for the needy in which the members assumed the names of flowers. Maud Lancaster, inevitably, was "Sister Red Rose". The password of the mission was "Kindness", and the motto the oft-quoted (and misquoted) lines beginning, in this version, "I shall pass this way but once . . ." Mrs Lancaster also dabbled in the occult and was a practising Spiritualist.

Although often acting possessively towards her sons in later years, Maud Lancaster allowed them to go to Australia as very junior members of a Dominions Royal Commission when the opportunity came in the summer of 1914. They were to live with an uncle until they joined the Commission. But by the time they reached Australia the Commission had been abandoned because of the War. Lancaster worked for a time at Hay, New South Wales, as an electrician—a skill he clearly inherited—and he also worked as a "jackeroo" on a sheep station. Then in 1916, at the age of eighteen, he joined the Australian cavalry, quickly developing into a first-class horseman. He also displayed a flair for mechanical things, and when the chance came to go overseas he transferred to the engineers and embarked for Europe in November 1916.

Like many young men of this period, Lancaster looked with envy, after a few months in the trenches, on the comparative freedom of the lives of the men of the air forces, and in July 1917 came the real turning-point in his life: he transferred to the Australian Flying Corps as an air mechanic second class. Within a few weeks he was training to be a pilot, and he was commissioned as a second lieutenant on November 1st, 1917. He had not long begun his operational career, however, when he crashed in a snow-storm, and he was in hospital for the next three months. He seems to have spent only short periods on operational squadrons after this, probably for medical reasons, because on October 14th, 1918, shortly before the armistice, his appointment with the Australian Flying Corps was terminated through medical unfitness. Five days later he enrolled as a student at the Royal Dental Hospital in London. But within a fortnight, his medical troubles apparently over, and his dental career forgotten or shelved, he was given a temporary commission as a second lieutenant in the newly-formed Royal Air Force, in which he served until he was demobilized with the honorary rank of captain in February 1920.

Meanwhile, in April 1919, he had married a young war widow named Annie Maud Mervyn-Colomb. Widowed at nineteen, she was now twenty-three. Lancaster was just twenty-one. Maud Colomb—Lancaster for some unexplained reason always called her "Kiki"—was a woman of great poise and moral strength, tactful, tolerant, and unselfish, yet with a keen sense of humour, and her serenity and steadfastness seemed ideal qualities to offset against the restless, immature phase that Lancaster was passing through.

When Lancaster left the Service in February 1920 he returned for twelve months to London University to continue his studies as a dentist. But it didn't last. He applied to get back into the RAF on a short-service commission, and this he eventually achieved, rejoining on April 30th, 1921, and being posted to No. 25 Squadron at Folkestone for flying duties. One of his fellow-pilots on 25 Squadron was James Fitzmaurice, later to make, with two German airmen, the first east-west crossing of the Atlantic, and Lancaster's ambitions as a pioneer flyer may well have been fired by this contact.

After five months at Folkestone Lancaster volunteered for service in India, and he was sent on a short refresher course on Bristol fighters at Kenley before being posted to No. 31 Squadron. This squadron, based at Peshawar, was commanded at the time by "Bert" Harris, better known in later years as "Bomber" Harris. In spite of a shortage of aircraft due to economies practised by the Government of India, they were rapidly gaining a reputation as the outstanding squadron in India. The pilots were mostly serving on permanent commissions, and they were dedicated professional airmen, jealous of squadron reputation and *esprit de corps*. To them, Lancaster seemed not a particularly good flyer, and his background they regarded as uncertain. The man in charge of the photographic section, however, remembers him as a keen and able pilot with a special interest in aerial photography.

In a world of studied reticence and under-statement, Lancaster sometimes seemed brash and almost boastful. He had inherited as a characteristic a slight tendency to show off, and he had not yet acquired the maturity to suppress it. This, to the officers of 31 Squadron, was anathema. Another crime in the eyes of his fellow-officers was the fact that he was married and living out; socially he was thus a stranger, divorced almost entirely from Mess life. This was rendered the more unacceptable because Lancaster, at twenty-four, was too young to qualify for marriage allowance, and getting married in these circumstances was generally felt to be beyond the pale. In fact, of course, Lancaster had married before his short-service commission was granted.

Within a few weeks of the Lancasters' arrival in India a daughter, Patricia Maud, was born, and Lancaster, with a wife and child to support on his single, officer's pay, found it difficult to pay his way. Sometimes bills went unpaid, at least for a time. This was not a matter on which he could expect much sympathy, and none was forthcoming. His financial difficulties, like his marriage and his short-service commission and his unorthodox behaviour and background, were held against him. But he was not the worrying kind. He saw to it that Kiki had an *ayah* to look after the child, of whom he was very fond, he bought a horse, on which he rode to and from the RAF station, and he played polo for the squadron, rode at point-to-point races, and generally exercised his talent for horse-riding. Maud too rode well, and riding became the Lancasters' chief compensation for a disappointing social life.

Towards the end of 1922 the squadron moved to Dardoni on the North-West Frontier, but Lancaster did not go with them. This, and his subsequent repatriation, may have been partly due to illness; but the conclusion is unavoidable that his days with 31 Squadron were numbered anyway. Whether one regarded the squadron as an *élite* corps or merely as a clique, the effect was the same: such was the pressure exerted by this sort of inbred comradeship that it was quite capable of getting an officer posted if his face didn't fit. Whatever the reason, early in 1923, after little more than twelve months in India—the average tour was four to five years—Lancaster was posted back to England.

It was five months before Lancaster received his next appointment, and he was apparently non-effective sick for most of that time. His new posting was to No. 1 School of Technical Training (Boys) at Halton for administrative duties, and he arrived there early in August 1923. He still retained his flying category, however, and like all general duties officers he flew regularly while he was at Halton. From being a somewhat shadowy figure, a mystery to his acquaintances and an enigma to his friends, Lancaster's personality developed more fully in the broader atmosphere of Halton. Although as untypical as ever, and alternately irresponsible and immature, he was accepted at Halton as a character.

Lancaster's short-service commission was due to expire in April 1925, so it was natural that he should begin to think ahead to what his future was to be when he left the Service. His assets were a cheerful disposition, some mechanical knowledge and aptitude, and a father who was prepared to invest in a business. He decided on the motor trade, and where better than at Wendover, the town near Halton camp, where a regular supply of customers was assured and where a bus and taxi service might be operated with advantage to all? Lancaster senior paid a visit to Wendover, and a site was chosen in the town and a partner found who could run the business while Lancaster completed his service. Lancaster meanwhile would become a director and would play his part in building up a connection. Such an activity might not be encouraged by the RAF, but there were no regulations to prevent it, and towards the end of 1923 the new business began trading in High Street, Wendover, under the name, predictably, of the "Red Rose Garage".

From this point on Lancaster became typical of the car salesman in that he turned up in a different car almost daily, and his escapades in these cars, generally of the £20–£30 variety, became common gossip. The old flamboyance too was still there, and few of these escapades lacked a touch of showmanship. When one of his cars broke down on the way into Halton from the house where he was living-out near Princes Riseborough, he commandeered a horse from the nearest field and rode into the camp on that. On another occasion he drove straight into a clump of rhododendrons and appeared on the far side minus car but wreathed in blooms and clutching the starting handle. He would get a party together to drive to London, spend the evening at the RAF Club, then run out of petrol on the way back, disappear into a blacked-out garage, and emerge with enough petrol to get home. How he got it, and whether he paid for it, were questions no one asked. But all Lancaster's passengers agreed that he was an adventurous driver and that they were always glad when the ride was over.

The incident that really established Lancaster at Halton came in June 1924, at the time of the Wembley Exhibition. As part of the entertainment that summer C. B. Cochran, the impresario, staged an International Rodeo at Wembley Stadium which lasted three weeks. Roping, steer-wrestling, and riding of the bucking broncho produced wonderful displays of horsemanship from the contenders in the various competitions, most of whom were American cowboys but some of whom came from Canada and Australia. In addition there was an open challenge to spectators to stay on a bucking broncho—if they could—for two minutes and win a prize of £10 (equivalent to about £50 today). The challenge was taken up by the occasional spectator, among them expert horsemen, but no one succeeded in riding the broncho for more than a few seconds, so the promoter's money looked safe. Five spectators who tried for the prize on Wednesday, June 18th, all suffered injuries, some serious. "Any man who can sit such an animal", said *The Times*, "must have the qualities of a limpet." But when this was read out in the Mess at Halton, Lancaster was rash enough to say that he could probably do it.

No one at Halton knew much about Lancaster as a horseman, but from what they had read in the papers they were quite certain that he would be thrown within seconds. Above all, they were anxious to see it happen; that would cut short the fellow's boasts for ever.

Lancaster drove up to Wembley to make his challenge, and for once there was no shortage of passengers. Those who couldn't find room in the car went by train. One man, afterwards an air marshal, went by motor-bike. A study of the newspapers of the period does not disclose a single other instance in which a challenger was successful. But Lancaster did it, staying on in spite of the violent gyrations and joltings to which the 'bronk' subjected him, and a dozen retired RAF officers confirm the story. According to one of them, he performed the feat in bowler hat and pin-striped suit. He duly received the £10. Although many people at Halton still thought him a bit of a show-off, he had made good his most extravagant boast, and he was taken much more seriously from then on.

Lancaster's short-service commission had meanwhile been extended to five years, and in October 1924, possibly to separate him from his business activities in Wendover, he was posted to the School of Technical Training (Men) at Manston in Kent. Here he quickly won a reputation as a sportsman, a man game for anything, unpredictable but fearless. In the final of the RAF team boxing championship, Manston against Uxbridge, Manston found themselves without a representative in the welter-weight class, and Lancaster was asked to fill the gap—"which he readily did," according to a fellow-officer. Not having had any preparation for the fight, against a much taller and fitter opponent, he was not surprisingly knocked out in the first round, but the point he gained by entering the contest helped Manston to a narrow victory.

In the Station swimming sports that year he performed something even more spectacular. He got into a sack, the open end of the sack was sewn up, and he then jumped off the high board and disappeared under the water with a huge splash and a gasp from the spectators, reappearing half a minute later to enthusiastic cheers. He had, of course, armed himself with a knife, and the sack was sewn up with darning wool, but it looked secure enough, and the incident was typical of Lancaster. He would have a go at anything.

When, in April 1925, the RAF finally decided to go in for parachutes, stations were asked to put forward the names of volunteers for a ground parachute course at Henlow, followed by a series of practice jumps with No. 12 Squadron at Andover. "As there was no great eagerness at Manston for such training," recalls an officer stationed there at the time, "the obliging Lancaster was the obvious choice."

The RAF had clung too long to the suspicion that if you gave a man a parachute he was less likely to do all he could to save his aircraft. The Germans had used parachutes as early as 1916, and the Americans had regarded them as standard equipment since 1919. Early in 1925 the RAF sent an officer named Flight Lieutenant F. C. Soden to America to study their methods, and when he got back he became the leading exponent of parachuting in England, acting as an instructor on the course at Henlow and again at Andover.

By the end of May 1925 some sixty practice jumps had been made from the Fairey Fawn two-seater bombers of 12 Squadron, resulting in one fatality when a corporal air gunner apparently failed to pull the rip-cord and fell to his death from 2000 feet; that, anyway, was the finding of the court of inquiry, though the corporal, poor fellow, was not there to testify. Soon afterwards, from a large number of volunteers, the three outstanding men from the two courses were selected to take part in the first-ever public display of parachuting by the RAF at the Hendon Air Display on June 27th. The first man to jump would be Soden himself. The second would be Lancaster.

The method of jumping was for the pilot to fly over the airfield at 2000 feet, signalling to his passenger in the front seat of the Fawn when the moment came for him to climb down the external ladder, which reached to the base of the fuselage. The pilot then throttled back and signalled the appropriate moment to jump.

The event had been prepared for in absolute secrecy lest something should go wrong in practice, and also, perhaps, lest pressure should be applied to leave the item out. Not even Lancaster's own commanding officer knew that one of his men was involved. Lancaster, however, had confided in Kiki, and she went to Hendon on the day.

"Early in the afternoon," wrote C. G. Grey of the *Aeroplane*, "a rumour had gone round among the knowing ones that three pilots were to do parachute drops just to show that the RAF really had got parachutes." After expressing the opinion that parachuting in public was unwise because of the shock to many thousands of people if there was an accident, Grey went on: "When the machines came over the aerodrome people with glasses could see that men were standing on what looked like ladders outside the fuselages of the machines. Then word went round that this was the parachute show. And as soon as the machines were well over the far side of the railway bank the three passengers rolled off the machine almost simultaneously."

Lancaster was in trouble when he got back to Manston; his commanding officer had been at the display and had been astonished to read afterwards that one of his own men was involved. "I can imagine many circumstances which would account for such arrangements being made by the ever-obliging Lancaster," writes a contemporary, "also for his natural casual forgetfulness in not informing his station commander...."

Although Lancaster's duties at Manston were entirely on the administrative side, as a general duties officer he was required to complete a prescribed number of flying hours each month, and this he did with enthusiasm. Assessments of his flying ability vary, but it would seem that although he was a skilful pilot in many ways he was still not a particularly safe one, his ventures into the air often causing alarm. Yet he had one outstanding merit—confidence. It was the confidence of a man who had been trained as a mechanic, knew something about engines, and was not afraid to get his hands greasy. It was also the confidence of a man without fear. Landing after his engine had misfired badly in the circuit, convincing everyone within earshot that he was about to crash, he would protest that everything had been fine, tinker with the engine for a minute or so, and then take off again quite unperturbed. He thus acquired the enviable reputation of being ready and able to fly anything that he could get off the ground.

At Manston, Lancaster and his family lived in married quarters on the station, and neighbours recall that he was good-natured, hospitable, and accommodating. He played a sound game of bridge and was always ready to make up a four, even at some personal inconvenience. When his dog and the dog next door got into his car and tore the upholstery to pieces, he waved aside his neighbour's apologies and insisted that his dog had talked the other dog into it. As to his characteristic casualness, he is reliably reported never to have owned an alarm clock at Manston, depending on the one next door, with unexpected results when his neighbour happened to be orderly officer, or on leave.

Thus Bill Lancaster passed his last months in the Royal Air Force, still slightly immature and irresponsible, the life and soul of the party on Mess occasions, to all appearances happily married, the subject of many good stories, and looked upon with a kindly tolerance. What lay ahead of Lancaster was as unpredictable as the man himself; but whatever it was, none of his Air Force associates would be surprised by it.

Chubbie Miller was a young woman of uncompromising directness, practical, adaptable, and determined, but also gay and mischievous. Beneath the surface Australian hardness lay a woman of absolute femininity. Married at eighteen, virtually straight out of school, she was naïve and unsophisticated in many ways in spite of her status as a married woman of seven years' standing. Up to the age of eighteen, and even for much of her marriage, she had led a sheltered life.

Chubbie's father was an Englishman who, stopping off in Australia on a trip round the world, had met the woman who was to become Chubbie's mother, married her, and settled there. A banker himself, he was a clergyman's son, and the grandson of a bishop, and Chubbie's mother was a clergyman's daughter. Chubbie's uncle—her father's brother—had gone into the Church and had served as a padre during the War and as a missionary in Samoa before settling in Australia with a parish in Melbourne. Thus from an early age Chubbie was surrounded by clergymen and the ghosts of clergymen. Brought up with narrow, Victorian strictness, she was interminably being driven off to church. When she got married and was able to choose for herself, her attitude not surprisingly was "no more church for me".

The marriage, to a young journalist named Keith Miller, was not a success. Although five years older than Chubbie, he was as raw and unsophisticated as she was; it had been like two children getting married. This might not have mattered if they had developed common interests, but their characters and temperaments grew further apart as time passed. They were completely maladjusted, and the children they both wanted did not come. Chubbie lost one baby born prematurely at six months, and after two other serious miscarriages she was advised not to go in for child-bearing. It was a double tragedy as it was the one thing that might have held the marriage together. Both parties made the best of it and the marriage jogged along, but the breaking point came when Chubbie lost her only brother, Tommy, three years her junior, the only real friend and confidant she had ever had.

Ever since she could remember, she and Tommy had discussed and planned their futures. They had wanted their lives to be adventurous, they had meant to see the world. Now Tommy was dead, and none of their dreams had come true. Heartbroken at the loss of the one person who she felt really knew and understood her, Chubbie saw that it was a loss she must learn from. She decided she must earn some money to enable her to plan some sort of personal future, and she took a job as a part-time saleswoman, secretly, without telling husband or family. When her husband found out what she was doing, and the showdown came, she told him exactly what she intended to do. Her ideas, in fact, were no more outrageous than to save up enough money for a trip to England.

With a wife as unsophisticated as Chubbie, journalist Keith Miller could not be unaware of the emotional experience she was going through, and eventually he agreed to her plan provided she saved enough money to buy a return ticket. And after the initial quarrel, he relented to the extent of allowing her £3 a week while she was away—the equivalent of perhaps £15 today. The arrangement was that she should stay six months.

CHAPTER II

Towards Australia

IN the rarefied literary atmosphere of the Authors' Club, Chubbie studied the route that Lancaster had mapped out for his flight. "No light plane has ever attempted it," he told her. Ross and Keith Smith had done it in a Vickers Vimy—the type used by Alcock and Brown—and Parer and McIntosh had got there in a D.H.9a, but such a flight by a light aeroplane was undreamt of. He spoke of a new light plane that had just been introduced on the market—the Avro Avian. That was what he was after. He would really be proving something if he could fly it to Australia.

"What's so special about it?"

First, said Lancaster, was the engine, an 80 horse-power A.D.C. Cirrus. It was a marvellous engine, he told her, destined to revolutionize light-aeroplane flying. Then there was the plane itself, a two-seater with an all-up weight of 900 lb., virtually capable of carrying its own weight. It cruised at 80 miles an hour, had a range of 900 miles, and was exactly right for his purpose.

"Can you get one?"

In her direct Australian way, Chubbie began to pin Lancaster down. His father had refused to help financially, but he hoped to win him round. Casual promises of help from various sources that Lancaster had taken at their face value had proved illusory when he tried to follow them up. Even one or two apparently firm offers had been withdrawn. It was soon apparent to Chubbie that Lancaster's plans for the flight were no more than embryonic, even vague. He knew what aeroplane he wanted, yes, but he had no immediate hope of getting one. There was the problem of laying down caches of petrol and oil en route. RAF stations east of Suez would be a help but there was practically nothing beyond India. The fuel, like the aeroplane, would have to be paid for. So would the maps. Landing fees, licences, visas, servicing, spares—all these would require money. And Lancaster didn't have any. But in spite of his obvious unpreparedness his enthusiasm for the flight was unbounded. She had no doubt he was capable of doing it. She liked him and trusted him, and decided he would make a satisfactory business partner. The idea that had been forming in her mind had seemed crazy at first, but she was beginning to see it as the perfect practical answer for them both.

"You said the plane was a two-seater?"

"Yes."

"If I can raise the money, say fifty per cent of the total outlay, can I come with you?"

Lancaster seemed staggered by the proposal. He had clearly never suspected that she might be thinking on these lines, and she liked him for his guileless sincerity. A certain unwillingness to face facts—that, she thought, he was probably guilty of—but he wasn't a schemer. She would have to do the scheming herself.

Recovering himself, Lancaster began to list the objections to her going. "In the first place there's the extra weight. Speed and range would both be seriously affected. And you can't imagine what the flight would be like —you'd have to rough it everywhere. I'll be landing at remote airfields where there's virtually no accommodation at all, and it's just not on for a woman. Besides, it's dangerous. I'm confident for myself but I couldn't take on the responsibility of a woman passenger."

To Chubbie the flight seemed to crystallize everything she had ever wanted. It was just what she had been looking for. She had never flown, never even thought about it, but it had suddenly become her life's ambition. It was practical, it was adventurous, it was dangerous, and it had the irresistible attraction of the unknown. Going back to Australia by sea was something she could no longer contemplate.

"No go, no money."

Chubbie had no clear idea of where the money was coming from either, but she backed her tenacity and powers of persuasion to get it. She had got the money for the sea voyage over, she would get it for the flight back. And she knew she had put her finger on Lancaster's essential weaknesses—lack of money, and lack of organizing ability to get it. She did not press the matter any further that day, but they agreed to meet again. And the time came, a week or so later, when Chubbie decided she would have to be brutal.

"Look, Bill," she said, "you've been talking about this flight for months, planning it for months, or so everyone tells me, and where have you got? When are you going to start? The truth is that you haven't a hope of getting started without money. Soon someone else will beat you to it. I've got Australian contacts who'll help with money, and I'm a woman, which will help with publicity. It seems to me that it's a case of either you take me or you don't go at all."

It was difficult for Lancaster to admit that he wasn't capable of organizing the flight himself. And from the achievement angle, nothing would be quite so satisfying as a solo flight. But Chubbie's argument was overwhelming, and reluctantly he gave in. It would be purely a business

Edward Lancaster
Photo Mrs P. Hayes

Bill and Kiki, 1919
Photo Mrs P. Hayes

Kiki with Pat (*right*) and Nina
Photo Mrs P. Hayes

Dressed for the Australia flight, 1927
Central Press Photos, Ltd.

In the tandem cockpits of the *Red Rose*
Central Press Photos, Ltd.

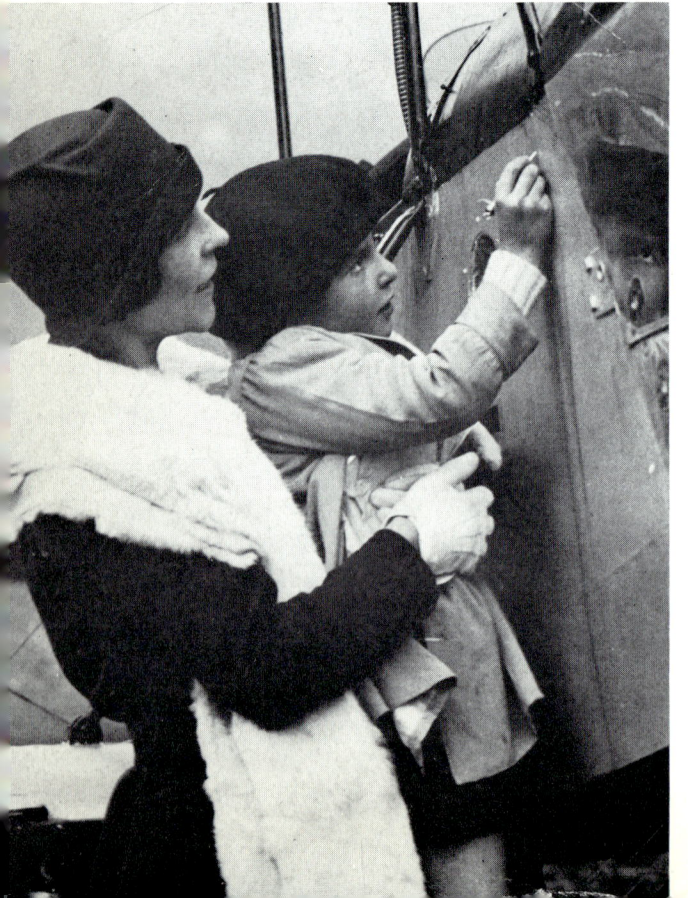

Bill kisses Kiki goodbye
Photo Mrs P. Hayes

Pat writes "good luck" on the fuselage
Photo Mrs P. Hayes

partnership. Both had revealed from the start that they were married. They shook hands on the deal and arranged to meet at Stanford's next day to inquire about maps.

Stanford's told them they would make a set of strip maps to cover the entire route, which totalled about 13,000 miles, and have the courses and distances marked out by a specialist navigator. The maps would cost £40. Chubbie paid this sum at once out of her savings, feeling that this cemented the deal. There would be no turning back now for either of them.

The route that Lancaster planned to take was the obvious one and there was nothing original about it. Croydon to Paris, south to Marseilles, then via Rome, Sicily, and Malta across the Mediterranean to Tripoli; then Cairo, Baghdad, down the Persian Gulf and east to Karachi, across India to Calcutta, then south to Rangoon and Singapore. The last stages would take them through Sumatra and Java and finally across the Timor Sea—the longest sea crossing of the flight—to Darwin. That leg across the Timor Sea would be the most hazardous of all, and they would need to fill right up with fuel. If they succeeded it would be the first crossing of this sea in a light plane.

When the maps were ready, Lancaster took them to show his parents at their home in Crystal Palace Road, South London, taking Chubbie with him. Their reaction to the idea that their son might be accompanied by a woman passenger was predictably hostile, but like everyone else they were impressed by Chubbie's forthrightness and candour, and the strip maps, beautifully prepared, and the receipt that accompanied them, showed she meant business. Edward and Maud Lancaster were won over, and they agreed to go into the question of helping to buy the plane. A condition was that a quantity of pamphlets be distributed in the course of the flight, which would be provided by the "Mission of Flowers". The plane was to be called the *Red Rose*.

For a woman with no business experience, Chubbie showed remarkable acumen in seeking the right backing. She went with Lancaster to see Sir Sefton Brancker,[1] the monocled Director of Civil Aviation, who took an immediate liking to her, entered into the spirit of the flight, suggested possible contacts, and listed the permits they would need to over-fly foreign territory, promising all the support within his power. Lancaster had already sounded all the obvious promoters of this kind of flight—the oil companies, instrument makers, and so on—and Chubbie, accompanied by Lancaster, visited them again. Shell and B.P. promised to supply the petrol, laying it down where necessary, and Wakefield's supplied the oil. All this help was given free in the hope that the flight would be successful and that valuable publicity might accrue.

Chubbie also introduced many ideas of her own. A flight to Australia

[1] Killed in the R101 disaster in 1930.

was clearly of interest to Australians too, and she called on a number of Australian businessmen. The response was not over-generous, and a good many promises were broken when it came to putting up hard cash, but the total mounted slowly. Two Australian newspapers gave her small contracts, and the editor of the *Daily Express* gave her an advance on the strength of her promise to cable a story to him from their stopping-place each night. The spectacle of this small, determined woman setting out to become the first of her sex to fly to Australia evidently impressed him.

The Avian that Lancaster finally bought from Avro's, at a reduced price, was taken from the Avian II production line in September 1927 to be modified and fitted with overload tanks to become the first Avian III. Its registration letters were G-EBTU. Apart from a slim tubular-steel interplane and centre-section struts the airframe was identical to the Avian II, and the main difference lay in an improved design for the installation of the Cirrus II engine. The modifications increased the all-up weight and meant that luggage and spares would have to be kept to a minimum. Avro's were more than ready to co-operate when they realized that the flight was not just a stunt: Lancaster consistently denied any intention of racing, describing the flight as a reliability test that would be spread over several weeks.

One other thing Chubbie was determined to make no mistakes over, and that was Lancaster's wife. He had told her that they were not living together, and that his parents were looking after their children—a second daughter, Nina Ann, had been born in February of that year—but what the precise situation was between them she didn't know. This was another matter on which she must pin Lancaster down. "What about your wife?" she asked him, when the preparations for the flight began to go forward and there seemed every chance that they might go. "Are you sure she won't object?"

"Quite sure."

"Hadn't we better discuss it with her?"

"She isn't in London. She's down on the south coast, acting as a hostess at a private hotel for vegetarians."

"Let's go down and see her."

For the first few months after leaving the RAF, Lancaster had lived with his family in a cottage at Whyteleaf, near Princes Risborough, and run a local bus service from the Red Rose Garage at Wendover. The business, however, could not fully support him once he was out of the Service, and he flew as a free-lance civil pilot when the opportunity arose. As their financial situation deteriorated, Lancaster became more than ever drawn into flying as a career, but he had no qualifications as an airline pilot, and it was in this period that he appears to have conceived the idea of a solo flight to Australia. He gave up the cottage at Whyteleaf, Kiki's mother looked after the children, and while he canvassed support for the flight Kiki took a job. Of a gentle, sensitive nature, she was passionately fond of animals, and this had led her to espouse the causes of vegetarianism and anti-vivisection. She was to work in these fields to the end of her life.

An RAF friend of Lancaster's agreed to drive them down to the coast, but because of his duties he could only make the journey at night. The car was an open Morris Cowley—the old bull-nosed Morris—the night air was chill, and Chubbie, sitting in the back of the open car, was frozen. To put her further out of temper, the new hat she was wearing blew off and the men refused to turn back to look for it, assuring her, with a good deal of mirth, that in the darkness they would never find it. They got to the hotel at two o'clock in the morning and were put straight to bed by the staff.

Chubbie was still asleep next morning when she felt someone shaking her to wake her up, and when she roused herself she found it was Lancaster's wife. With Kiki Lancaster smartly dressed and made up, Chubbie felt at a disadvantage, but the two women were soon on friendly terms and the meeting went well. During the morning the three of them went for a walk, and when they got tired they sat down at the top of a grassy slope. Suddenly Lancaster got up and shouted, "Come on, I'll race you to the bottom." It was the sort of unpredictable, impulsive thing he was fond of doing, and Chubbie responded at once. But Kiki simply wasn't built in that tomboyish fashion. "I'd be terrified," she said. "I wouldn't dream of trying to race." So Lancaster and Chubbie ran down to the bottom of the slope together. When they had climbed back to the top and got their breath back, they sat down again and lit a cigarette. It was time, Chubbie thought, to put the final question.

"Look, Kiki," she said, "you're quite sure you don't mind if I go with Bill on this flight? He's agreed that I can go provided I can raise a half-share in the expenses."

"My dear," said Kiki, "I don't care who he goes with as long as he makes some money."

On October 7th Lancaster went to Woodford, Cheshire, to test and take delivery of the Avian. The morning was misty and autumnal, but Lancaster made a smooth take-off and landing and the machine behaved perfectly in the air. He expressed himself delighted with the Avian's performance, and he flew it down to Croydon the same day. Meanwhile, Chubbie had had her first flight, and they were both relieved to find that she suffered no air-sickness and seemed perfectly at home in the air. Lancaster was to fly the Avian from the rear cockpit, but dual control could be fitted in the front and Chubbie certainly hoped to do some flying after they got away.

In the next few days all outstanding problems resolved themselves except one—the question of insurance of the plane. Lancaster senior had promised to take care of this, but he was finding it difficult to get any British company to give a quotation. Meanwhile the plans for the flight had been announced and Lancaster and Chubbie were waiting to get away. One of the difficulties was that Lancaster, unlike most of the long-distance pioneers of the twenties, was completely unknown as an aviator. Men like Scott, Mollison, Lindbergh, and Kingsford-Smith were established flyers when they turned to record-breaking, but Lancaster had no reputation as a pilot and no prior achievements to give credence to his plans. In the eyes of the aviation world he was an amateur, and the idea of a woman passenger was regarded as little more than a cheap stunt. Rumours of the dropping of religious pamphlets, too, encouraged an amused scepticism among professional airmen. "For some reason or another," wrote C. G. Grey in the *Aeroplane*, "this particular flight does not seem to be taken very seriously by those who have seen the preparations for it being made at Croydon." Yet Lancaster and Chubbie were quite determined to go.

On the evening of October 12th, Sir Sefton Brancker gave a farewell dinner-party for them at Murray's Club. "What are you taking in the way of luggage?" he asked Chubbie. "I hope you're taking an evening dress." Chubbie certainly hadn't thought of doing so: all she planned to carry was a small handbag with pyjamas, tooth-brush and tooth-paste, a clean pair of socks, clean shirt and clean set of undies, and the minimum of make-up. "I strongly advise you to take an evening frock," said Sir Sefton, "no matter how flimsy and diaphanous. And a pair of evening shoes. Otherwise you'll feel perfectly terrible whenever you're invited out at the various night-stops en route." Next morning she rushed into town and bought a black chiffon evening gown and a pair of black satin slippers before hurrying down to Croydon for the take-off. For the flight itself she planned to achieve a tactful masculinity by wearing tight-fitting breeches and a collar and tie.

The insurance problem was still unresolved, however, and neither Lancaster nor Chubbie felt like taking off uninsured on the 13th of the month, so they decided to wait one more day and then go, insured or not. Kiki had come up from the coast to see them off, every day they stayed in England the bills were mounting, and the Press too were getting impatient. The High Commissioner for Australia had passed a letter to them for delivery to the Australian Prime Minister, and his wife, Lady Ryrie, had promised to come and see them off and was asking for news. The important thing, Lancaster felt, was to get away from Croydon. Once they had shown their determination to go the insurance company might relent.

"We can't stay another night here," he pleaded with his father. "Everyone will lose faith in us. We'll have to get away today. We'll land at Lympne and ring you from there." When no word had come from the insurance company by midday, Lancaster senior agreed.

Lady Ryrie was summoned, and on the small square of tarmac in front of the airport building she handed Lancaster the letter. Lancaster said a few words to the Press about his route and the nature of the flight, reiterating that it was a reliability test and not a stunt, and then they climbed into their open cockpits, Chubbie in the front, Lancaster in the rear. Kiki Lancaster was there, with a kiss for Bill and another for Chubbie, and Pat, Lancaster's five-year-old daughter, was lifted up by her mother to write a good-luck message on the fuselage. Then with a final wave they taxied out to the grass runway. They took off at two-forty that afternoon, October 14th, 1927, and headed for Lympne.

An hour later, Lancaster telephoned his father from Lympne to inquire about the insurance. "You can't go," said Lancaster senior. "They won't insure you. I'll have to try another company."

"We're going anyway. We can't call it off now."

Lancaster senior protested, but his protests were in vain. There was nothing more he could do now but keep pressing the insurance companies. He was eventually successful in taking out life cover, but the premiums asked for insuring the aeroplane were prohibitive.

It was four o'clock that afternoon before they took off from Lympne, and the light was already failing as they crossed the Channel. When they reached Abbeville it was almost dark. Lympne had sent a departure signal but it had not yet reached Abbeville, so the airfield was unlit. After searching for it for several minutes Lancaster put the Avian down in a field on the outskirts of the town. They were soon surrounded by French peasants, who were able to point out the direction of the airfield—it was only two miles away. But the field they had landed in was so small that Lancaster doubted if he would get off again with a full load, and he decided to unload his passenger and some loose luggage to reduce the weight. He got off all right, landed safely at Abbeville, and waited there for Chubbie. Accompanied by two Frenchmen, and carrying her own luggage, she walked the two miles to the airfield. Flying to Australia, she was discovering, called for unexpected qualities of philosophy and endurance.

Paris, Marseilles, Pisa, Rome, Naples—these were among their stopping-points in the next few days. Lancaster was in no hurry; he was more concerned for the moment with getting thoroughly acquainted with the aeroplane, both in the air and for servicing on the ground. His aim all the time was to nurse the engine and to keep it at maximum efficiency. A first-class mechanic himself, he soon taught Chubbie the rudiments, and wherever they landed she had her jobs to do—straining the aviation spirit through a chamois leather, cleaning the plugs and checking the clearances—so that she soon got used to getting her hands greasy. They had no radio, and Lancaster was content to plan the flight in easy stages, while Chubbie, for her part, was pleased to feel more than a mere passenger. Lancaster had taught her to fly the plane, and although he did not allow her to attempt landings or take-offs she was able to give him a rest on the longer hops or relieve him when he was map-reading.

They reached Malta on Saturday, October 22nd, and were persuaded to stay the week-end. "Machine and engine perfect," Lancaster cabled to Avro's, "leaving for Tripoli Monday." At most of their stops they had been entertained in the evening, and Chubbie was grateful for the prescience of Sefton Brancker: she had already worn her evening dress several times, and Malta was no exception. She was aware, however, of a certain antipathy there. The reaction of the Service wives was a reminder that she was doing the unconventional thing.

Despite low cloud and strong headwinds they crossed the Mediterranean safely on October 24th; the 225-mile flight took nearly four hours. Next morning they took off for Benghazi, 425 miles distant and their longest hop so far. Lancaster felt that the preliminaries were over; they had given the plane a thorough test over land and completed their first major sea crossing, and the aeroplane had performed well. Headwinds were again forecast on the route to Benghazi, and the flight would probably take about seven hours, but this was well inside their endurance.

After an hour's flying visibility deteriorated and they realized they were running into a sandstorm. The headwind stiffened, and soon the coastline beneath them was blotted out. Lancaster eased the plane down to 150 feet, but they could still see practically nothing. What little they did see showed that the headwind had reached gale force and that they were making very little progress. They would certainly never reach Benghazi. Lancaster estimated the wind as 45 miles per hour and their ground speed as not more than 25. The best hope seemed to be to hug the coastline and look for the town of Sirte, rather more than half-way between Tripoli and Benghazi. If they failed to find Sirte they would be in real trouble, but Lancaster kept this to himself. (They had no means of direct communication, but there was a tiny trap-door between the two cockpits, and when he wanted to speak to Chubbie he would attract her attention by tapping her head and then pass a note through the trap-door.) As soon as they glimpsed Sirte Lancaster came down low over the coast, and presently they spotted a wind-sock. Lancaster landed at once, and they found they were on the main Italian military aerodrome. Next morning the weather was clear and they flew on to Benghazi.

On the flight from Benghazi to Sollum they ran into another sandstorm, and they were shot at by tribesmen, but they reached Alexandria on October 28th, and next day they flew on to the RAF station at Heliopolis, Cairo. A fortnight for a flight to Cairo was certainly no record even for those days, but it constituted the first such flight carrying a passenger, and the Press were beginning to show interest, realizing at last that the project was the biggest thing ever attempted in a light aeroplane. The attainment of Cairo had convinced everyone that the flight was worth while after all.

The next stage of the flight, across the Syrian desert through Ziza and Rutbah to Baghdad, with few landmarks and no coastline to follow, was the worst so far, and the commanding officer at Heliopolis insisted on giving them an escort of a Vickers Vernon, for which they were grateful when they ran into another sandstorm. Half-way between Ziza and Rutbah Chubbie smelt fire, and she wrote a note to Lancaster: "Something is on fire. What is it?" "Hanged if I know," replied Lancaster. "Wait and see." Nothing in fact developed and they landed safely at Rutbah.

After a delay of twenty-four hours they flew on to Baghdad, arriving at the RAF airfield at Hinaidi in appalling weather, the rain being so heavy that all other aircraft were grounded. The flooding of the airfield became so bad that they were held up for five days. While they were waiting Lancaster arranged for an additional tank of 13 gallons to be fitted by the RAF, making a fuel capacity of 56 gallons in all, giving an endurance of about 10 hours. He was anxious to have this margin for some of the longer and more desolate legs of the route that lay ahead. Chubbie also decided on some modifications; she was finding breeches and woollen socks unbearably hot, and the Iraqi tailor at Hinaidi made her some shorts.

When they finally got away from Baghdad on the afternoon of November 8th, all the RAF aircraft were still grounded by the floods, but Lancaster was able to find a clear run for the tiny Avian as the flood-water went down. The late start, however, meant that he was uncertain of reaching Shaibah, the RAF airfield at Basra, before dark. He made for an intermediate landing ground at Wasiriyah, and when this proved to be covered in a layer of soft mud he followed the railway line to Ur Junction, 100 miles north of Basra—the legendary Ur of the Chaldees.

They spent two nights at Ur Junction while Lancaster tried to clear a magneto fault, and eventually, with the help of two RAF mechanics sent from Baghdad, he patched it up well enough to fly on to Shaibah, which they reached on November 10th. The diagnosis at Shaibah was that they would need a new magneto, and since they would have to have one sent out from England this meant a wait of several days. To make matters worse they were put into quarantine for a week because of a cholera scare.

In all they spent sixteen days at Basra, Chubbie staying with the British Consul and his wife while Lancaster stayed at Shaibah. But at last, on November 26th, they pushed on to Bushire, on the Persian side of the Gulf opposite Bahrain. "We advise you to follow the coast round instead of crossing the Gulf," the RAF told them. "The water is shark-infested and you'd have no chance if you came down." But as this would have almost doubled the distance, Lancaster decided to go direct across the Gulf. They wished they hadn't when the new magneto began to give trouble and they looked down at a gleaming stretch of water in which they could see literally dozens of sharks. Chubbie began talking to the engine, begging it to keep going, and she was limp and exhausted when they finally got to Bushire. She had been quite sure they were coming down, and she had never known such fear.

There was no one to meet them when they landed at Bushire except a squad of menacing-looking soldiers who brandished rifles complete with rusty but apparently serviceable bayonets. They gave the soldiers all their cigarettes, and Lancaster asked for petrol, oil, food, and accommodation, but he could not make them understand. The heat was intense, they were tired and hungry, and Chubbie was almost in tears. Eventually a Persian officer appeared and led them to an unoccupied barrack block, where he left them. A meal was brought to them, but it was swimming in oil and they were unable to eat it.

It was six weeks since they had left England, and during that time their partnership had been consolidated by that most durable of adhesives, the sharing of common danger. Then during sixteen days of inactivity at Basra they had seen each other hardly at all. The flight across the Persian Gulf had brought them face to face with the prospect of death in what seemed the most unpleasant form imaginable. Safe for the moment, but utterly alone, they seemed to have neither past nor future, their minds and bodies numb, drained of all feeling and emotion except that which they might express together. With the gentle ferocity of complete exhaustion, they fell into each other's arms.

CHAPTER III

Setback at Muntok

TO the adventure of the flight was now added a new dimension—they were deeply in love. They both realized it and tacitly accepted the implications, though this was made easier by the fact that for the moment these implications didn't have to be squarely faced. Chubbie had always known that Lancaster was not living with his wife when she met him, though what their precise relationship was she was naturally unaware. For her own part she did not conceal from him that her own marriage had been a mistake. If there was any deception on Lancaster's part she was unaware of it; but he evidently encouraged her to believe that his marriage had broken up. The home, certainly, had broken up for economic reasons, and Kiki Lancaster had been forced to take a job out of London where she could not personally care for the children. She maintained afterwards, however, that she had always loved her husband and had never had any intention of giving him up. She had understood his restless ambition and was prepared to give him the necessary freedom to pursue it.

When Kiki was confronted with the proposition of her husband flying to Australia with Chubbie Miller, the possibility that they might fall in love didn't occur to her. Moral standards, while covertly perhaps not much different from today, were vastly different overtly. It was possible for the uncynical to imagine a man and a woman thrown into the closest and loneliest proximity without succumbing to physical attraction.

The edifice of public morals, façade though it might be, certainly exerted an inhibiting influence. For the remainder of the flight, and indeed for the foreseeable future, Bill and Chubbie would be obliged to maintain in all their behaviour and attitudes what had now become the fiction that theirs was purely a business partnership. Each would have to pay lip-service to a public image—she to her husband, he to his wife. Except when there was no danger of their being observed they would have to keep studiously apart. Any other mode of conduct, besides ruining Chubbie's reputation—in those days a negotiable asset—would have put them outside the society of the very people whose help they would need to get to Australia.

The harshness of their initial reception at Bushire was forgotten when the British Resident invited them to his home, and they stayed in his house for the next few days while the magneto trouble was cleared. Then on December 2nd they took off for Bandar Abbas, at the foot of the Persian Gulf. It was a wild day, with high winds and fast-moving cloud sweeping across the sky, and the little Avro was tossed and jerked about unmercifully. After a most unpleasant four hours they finally reached the small telegraph station of Bandar Abbas and landed safely. They were accommodated for the night at the telegraph station and took off for Karachi at nine o'clock next day.

After the long delays in Baghdad and Bushire Lancaster was keen to make up for lost time. And he was flying now towards an area with which he was familiar. Thus, with a single stop for refuelling at Chah Bahar, on the Gulf of Oman, he intended to cover the seven hundred miles to Karachi in a day. There would be a flare-path available at Karachi if they needed it, he knew; but with the engine running beautifully they reached Karachi just before dark in a total of nine and a half hours flying. Since leaving England they had been airborne for ninety-two hours and had flown over six thousand miles; they were almost half-way.

The RAF gave them a wonderful welcome at Karachi, and soon they were sitting on the verandah of the Officers' Mess, sipping whisky and soda. After the long flight they were both tired and grubby, and Lancaster disappeared into the Mess and emerged fifteen minutes later, washed and brushed and wearing a clean, borrowed shirt. Chubbie, who still looked like a tramp, asked if she too could have a wash, an expression which in those days embraced other toilet necessities. The commanding officer, offering his regrets, replied that it was strictly against Air Force regulations for a woman to enter the Mess. . . .

Their arrival in Karachi had really established the flight as worth while and a success, and both Wakefield's and Avro's advertised their products on the strength of it and cabled them funds, totalling £250. They had taken longer than they had planned, but Lancaster was satisfied. And a stay of a few days in Karachi became inevitable when the RAF, who were putting on a big display at Sind for the King of Afghanistan, asked them to stay for the display and show what a British light aeroplane could do. RAF help and hospitality had been absolutely indispensable to them all along, and in Karachi Lancaster was staying in the Mess while Chubbie was a guest of an RAF doctor and his wife, so they could hardly refuse; and in any case Lancaster felt he should lose no chance of demonstrating the Avian. They stayed in Karachi for the next ten days.

Their route now took them across northern India, and they left Karachi on December 15th on the 700-mile flight to Agra, continuing next day to Allahabad, where to Chubbie's amusement a woman attached herself quite shamelessly to Lancaster, parading before him at every opportunity in various stages of provocative dress and undress, and she insisted on seeing them off. But when they got to the airfield Lancaster couldn't start the engine; he swung the propeller for two hours before the engine caught. Such a marathon in the tropical heat was utterly exhausting. After they had finally taken off he passed a note forward to Chubbie.

"Wasn't she a bitch?"
"What was the matter with her?"
"Mixture too rich—needed backing up."
"What are you talking about?"
"The engine, of course—what did you think?"

When they reached Calcutta on December 19th they had flown 8500 miles since leaving England and had beaten the 8000-mile flight of Flight Lieutenant R. P. Bentley to Cape Town—the record in a light plane until then. They left Calcutta on the 21st, taking off at 4.30 in the morning to get the best flying conditions, and their immediate object now became to get to Singapore for Christmas. But an hour after they had taken off Lancaster remembered that he had left all their cash, amounting to over £200, under his pillow back at Calcutta. They went back, but the money had gone. From comparative riches they were once again flat broke. They took off again and after another five hours' flying reached Akyab, in the Arakan. There were no recriminations from Chubbie; it had happened, and she accepted it. But she resolved to look after their finances herself from then on. Meanwhile she cabled her family for money.

The flight down the Burmese coast and across the Irrawaddy towards Rangoon was uneventful except for some engine over-heating caused by the air temperatures in which they were flying. Then, approaching Rangoon, they had their first real scare. Lancaster, as always, was in the rear cockpit, Chubbie in the front. Chubbie had been flying the plane and her dual control stick was fitted in place. The additional petrol tank installed at Baghdad had been fitted in the front cockpit, and the installation prevented the control stick from being pushed fully forward: thus, when Lancaster was flying the plane, and always before coming in to land, he checked with Chubbie to make sure she had removed her stick, so as to allow full movement for his own. This time he had neglected to do so, and Chubbie had forgotten it. Letting down on the approach to Rangoon, Lancaster pushed the stick forward to lose height and the dual control stick in Chubbie's cockpit jammed under the auxiliary tank. Unless she could release it, a crash at high speed was certain.

Chubbie could feel Lancaster banging her on the head and could hear him shouting above the roar of the engine. "Get that stick out! Get that stick out! I'm rigid, I can't move my stick!" Chubbie took the locking pin out but this didn't help—the stick was still held firmly in position by the tank. She pushed and pulled but couldn't get it out. Meanwhile they were down to 500 feet, diving straight for the ground.

There was nothing Lancaster could do to help matters other than throttle back. He could see Chubbie was doing all she could to free the stick. For several seconds they were silent as the ground rushed up towards them, resigned to the fact that a crash was inevitable. Then Chubbie gave the stick another tremendous clump and it came out.

They had barely recovered from this experience when, about ten minutes later, with Rangoon harbour coming into view, the over-heated engine gave a sickening jar and packed up altogether. Fortunately Lancaster had regained just enough height to allow him to glide over the jungle-covered mountains and across a river until an area of rice-fields lay beneath them, a few miles short of Rangoon. He made a smooth landing in the rice-fields without damaging the plane.

In the blistering sun he stripped off his shirt and examined the engine. The cause of the stoppage was a broken piston, which meant a cable to Calcutta for spares and a wait of a week or ten days.

The RAF engineers came out from Monkey Point to pick them up and to look at the machine. "We don't advise you to leave the plane here any longer than you can help," they said. "We have kraits here and their bite is fatal." But they soon realized that Lancaster had no alternative; until the spare piston arrived the plane couldn't be moved. "Close everything up before we go, then," the engineers advised, "so that the snakes can't get in." It was a week before the spare piston arrived and Lancaster was able to patch up the engine, and meanwhile they spent Christmas in Rangoon.

Ten days later, on January 2nd, after more grim warnings about kraits —which they tended to treat as a leg-pull—they finally got away from Rangoon. After heading out across the Gulf of Martaban, they aimed to follow the Burmese coast south for Tavoy. The flight would take about three and a half hours. They were safely across the Gulf and were settling down to a pleasant but bumpy flight, the Andaman Sea to their right and the flat Burmese jungle to their left, when Lancaster sensed a movement behind him. Looking down at his feet he saw something wriggling its way forward; it was a snake. He ground at it with his heel but the snake coiled forward towards the front cockpit.

"Snake—look out!"

Lancaster knew that Chubbie couldn't hear him above the roar of the engine so he throttled right back, put the Avian in a gentle glide, and shouted again. "Snake, snake! It's coming under your seat!" Chubbie laughed—Bill must be having a joke. Then she looked down and saw the head of the snake emerging from the small flap near the floor through which they passed their notes. It was quite small, with a blunt nose and tail, whitish belly, and dark back. It was just as they had been described to her at Rangoon. It was a krait.

Instantly Chubbie swung her feet off the floor and tucked them underneath her on the cockpit seat. In the same moment she wrenched at the control stick—the only weapon to hand—and was relieved when it slipped easily out of its socket. Then, as the Avian sank through the sky, engine still idling, she concentrated her aim, screwed her eyes up with tension and fear, and began thrashing wildly at the head of the snake. Blood spurted all over the cockpit, yet the snake still writhed, and she went on striking at it with frenzied strength. At last she realized she had killed it. She was still too terrified to put her feet to the floor.

Several times while he had been working on the engine in the ricefields, Lancaster had had to open inspection panels and leave them open for a time. The snake must have got in then.

Their jangled nerves had still not recovered when they landed on the beach at Tavoy. They filled up with fuel and continued to Victoria Point. Still hugging the coastline, they flew on next day to Taiping, in northern Malaya, and then on to Kuala Lumpur. Then at last, on January 6th, 1928, they reached Singapore. After being welcomed by the acting governor they were entertained and accommodated by the Singapore Flying Club; there was no RAF station as yet in Singapore. Next day, at a ceremonial lunch in Raffles Hotel, the meal included Omelette Lancaster, Roast Partridge Miller, and Tournedos Red Rose.

The attainment of Singapore was acclaimed on all sides. "Their effort thoroughly deserves to succeed," wrote C. G. Grey. "They have already done far more than has ever been done by any light aeroplane. Their expedition was started under the greatest difficulties. . . . Mrs Miller raised the necessary finance by sheer pluck and persistence—and never lost her sense of humour. The flying people at Croydon, where they made their meagre preparations, treated their scheme as a joke and refused to believe that they would get much farther than France. But in spite of it all they have made good."

The last stretch of the flight, via the Dutch East Indies—Sumatra, Java, and Timor—to Port Darwin, some 2500 miles, lay ahead of them. They were still taking the flight in easy stages, flying mostly in the morning, then checking the plane over and resting in the afternoon, and the machine was still behaving perfectly. They took off from Singapore at seven o'clock on the morning of January 9th and reached Muntok, on Bangka Island, 300 miles to the south-east, at 11.30, landing on a clear piece of ground that sloped downhill. The next leg would take them another 300 miles to Batavia.

Their take-off time next morning was again seven o'clock. The Avian ran downhill for some distance, but Lancaster had no real difficulty in getting off, and they had reached 150 feet when the engine suddenly cut out. Lancaster had insufficient height to get back to the landing field, but ahead the country was broken and uneven. He tried to side-slip to lose height quickly, but they hit the ground heavily, starboard wing first, and then somersaulted on, tearing off the undercarriage and strewing debris behind them as they went.

Momentarily stunned, Chubbie recovered to find herself hanging from her straps in the cockpit, upside down. Petrol from the tank in the wing was pouring over her and she could hear it dripping and hissing on the hot engine. Her eyes were hurting and her nose was broken and she was trapped in the cockpit, imprisoned in a mesh of wreckage and stay-wires. The plane would surely burn at any moment. There was no sign of Lancaster.

The sun helmet she was wearing may have protected her in the crash, but now it was preventing her from forcing her head through the stay-wires. She began to wriggle out feet first, forcing her body past obstructions, ignoring the pain as she tore the skin off her legs. At last she got clear.

The cockpit behind her was empty. Lancaster had not been strapped in and he was lying on his back about twenty feet away, limp and lifeless. She staggered across to him and was appalled at what she saw. Blood was pouring from his mouth, suggesting severe internal injuries. Then she saw that his teeth had been forced right through his lower lip. She bent down and unhooked them, then gently slapped his face to bring him round. By that time a Dutch soldier had appeared and she sent him to get help.

They were taken to the local hospital, where Chubbie's injuries were treated and Lancaster's lip was stitched. Chubbie had to have a peg in her nose. Next day, still feeling badly shaken, they were driven to the landing field to see the plane; they found it in even worse condition than they had imagined. It looked like a complete write-off. If the crash had happened on an RAF station there might have been some chance of rebuilding it; but here, on this remote Dutch island, lacking even so much as a flying club, it was hopeless.

Lancaster was able to diagnose the fault; it had been his own. A sudden stoppage in the fuel supply had caused the engine to cut out. He found that he had failed to make his fuel switches before take-off; they were still in the 'off' position. No wonder the supply had dried up.

No pilot of that period could have flown a plane that far without considerable ability, and it was particularly galling that their downfall should be due to carelessness. Yet the merit of what he and Chubbie had achieved was not completely debased. "The Avian had put up a splendid flight of greater distance than any hitherto made with a machine of such low power," said the magazine *Flight*. "And moreover, it was carrying a passenger, so that, what with the extra weight, a large quantity of fuel, luggage etc., it must have been very heavily loaded. In spite of this it had been making good progress, and to have got as far as it did is a very fine performance."

C. G. Grey wrote in the *Aeroplane* in similar vein—but he knew Chubbie too well, from the one or two occasions on which he had met her, to assume that the flight was necessarily over. "They have yet the possibility," he noted, "of being the first to reach Australia in a light plane." A danger to them, he added, was the Australian Bert Hinkler, who was proposing, now Lancaster was apparently out of the hunt, to attempt the full journey in under a fortnight.

A radio message to the acting governor in Singapore brought an invitation to return at once, and they travelled back in a small cargo boat on the deck of which they also transported the wrecked Avian. Back in Singapore, Lancaster was put up in the police quarters of Government House, and Chubbie stayed with an Australian member of the Singapore Flying Club, Keith Bon, and his wife. But the most urgent need was to get someone to assess the damage to the Avian and see if it might be possible to work out a repair schedule. And overshadowing everything else was the fact that they had no money. Then a man named Sam Hayes, boss of one of the biggest rubber-broking businesses in Singapore, offered to finance them. He was determined, he said, to give them the chance of completing the flight.

Success, however, still depended on two things—getting Avro's and the A.D.C. engine company to send the necessary spares, and getting someone to rebuild the plane. Both firms had acquired good publicity out of the flight so far, but neither firm would consider sending spares without seeing an expert technical report on the aircraft state. This and the repair job were beyond the competence of the Singapore Flying Club. But by great good fortune, a flight of RAF Southampton flying-boats which had left England on October 17th on a long-distance cruise was now in the Far East. A base engineering party had preceded them by sea, disembarking at each flying-boat port of call to service and maintain the machines, and this party was now in Singapore.

Squadron Leader Sydney Freeman, the officer in charge, was an ex-naval warrant officer who had transferred to the RAF on its formation in 1918. He had heard about the flight of the *Red Rose*, and when he met the crew he found them a pathetic pair, both scarred as a result of their crash, with Mrs Miller sporting two gorgeous black eyes. But he was impressed by their determination to continue the flight, and he agreed to ferry the plane to Seletar, on the Johore Strait, where a concrete platform and a slipway had been built to accommodate the flying-boats. (This was the beginning of the first Singapore air base.) Normally Freeman would have considered the plane a write-off, but his sympathies had been engaged, and he advised Avro's that the machine was repairable, adding a long and detailed list of the spares he would require. He also undertook to overhaul the engine. Sam Hayes promised to meet the repair bills.

The spares had to be sent to Singapore by sea and it was several weeks before they arrived. Meanwhile Freeman and his men stripped the Avian and prepared everything as far as they could. It was a difficult time for Lancaster and Chubbie, still without money and still dependent on other people's kindness for almost everything. For a time they were lionized, and Lancaster was able to do the occasional service for the civil or military authorities, such as refereeing a boxing tournament, but to some extent they inevitably wore out their welcome. Freeman did not lose his sympathy for Chubbie, but he was resentful of Lancaster's apparent lack of interest in the progress of the repair work. In Freeman's view, Lancaster would have been better employed helping with the plane than wasting his time with the British colonial set. But Lancaster's position was not easy. The guest of Government House, and dependent for the cost of repairs on Sam Hayes, he may well have found it difficult to escape the daily round. In any case Seletar was fourteen miles out of Singapore and it may have been impossible for him to get to and fro. It may have been no more than his characteristic thoughtlessness. Or it may simply have been that he was in love.

Lancaster and Chubbie were too much in the public eye to live together in the conventional atmosphere of pre-war Singapore, nor could they risk being lovers. But they remained deeply in love. Chubbie, of course, was moving towards a reckoning with her husband; but what was in Lancaster's mind about his wife and family is not clear. Perhaps he was able to put uncomfortable thoughts from his mind.

That Lancaster had a moral sense is clear from his attitude to the threat posed by Bert Hinkler. This threat duly developed, Hinkler leaving London on February 7th—also in an Avro Avian—and reaching Singapore on February 19th. Sam Hayes, Keith Bon, and other sympathizers with the Lancaster/Miller venture were so incensed at the way Hinkler was attempting to steal Lancaster's thunder that they hinted that Hinkler's plane would not get beyond Singapore. Lancaster, realizing that Hinkler had waited until his own attempt with Chubbie foundered, bore no resentment, and his reaction was to give Hinkler all possible help. Fearing that his supporters meant business, he sat in the cockpit of Hinkler's Avian all night while Hinkler rested, to make sure that no attempt was made to delay him. Poignantly, Hinkler delivered a letter to Lancaster from his wife.

Hinkler left for Bandung on February 20th, and two days later, on February 22nd, he landed at Port Darwin, fifteen days after leaving London, to become the first man to make the flight in a light plane. It was a distinction that must have fallen to Lancaster and Chubbie but for the setback at Muntok.

Setback at Muntok

Not until the first week in March was the *Red Rose* ready, and then it had to be transported by lorry to the racecourse; Seletar was still nothing more than a flying-boat base. The repair work had been beautifully done, and early on the morning of Monday, March 12th, exactly two months after leaving Bangka Island by sea for Singapore, the *Red Rose* and her crew took off again for Muntok. This time they passed through Muntok without incident, flew south to Batavia, and then worked their way eastwards across Java and Sumatra, finally reaching Atambua on the island of Timor on Saturday, March 17th, after flying through a fierce rainstorm. Only 500 miles from their goal, they still faced the longest sea crossing of the entire flight.

There was no airfield at Atambua, just a clearing with reeds and scrub growing on it which served as a landing ground, and it was badly waterlogged by the rains. Although they got down safely Lancaster knew it would be impossible to take off again with the fuel load they would need for Port Darwin until the ground dried out. The field was also dangerously small. The only European residents at Atambua appeared to be two Dutch officers, but Lancaster told them the position and an hour later a gang of prisoners from the local gaol, still shackled at the ankles, arrived and began digging trenches to drain the water and cutting the grass and scrub to smooth and lengthen the run. Strip after strip of locally made matting was then produced and laid over the surface, making quite a passable runway. They would be able to get away next day—Sunday—after all.

Next morning a cable was received at Atambua from the Shell Company representative in Melbourne, who had arranged their fuel supplies over the later stages of the flight. 'Telegram received from our agent at Darwin advises that the landing ground is boggy, and that there have been heavy and continuous rains since Friday. The weather forecast shows no signs of the rains abating, and visibility is very bad." The Shell man recommended a postponement of the flight, and Lancaster decided on a twenty-four-hours' delay. But in fact, although part of the field at Port Darwin was indeed waterlogged, a section had been prepared on which Lancaster could have landed. The authorities at Port Darwin knew nothing of the Melbourne cable, so Lancaster and Chubbie were expected all that day. Virtually the entire population of Port Darwin turned out that Sunday to welcome them, waiting into the late afternoon with a mixture of disappointment and concern.

Lancaster sent a cable that evening advising Port Darwin that he would be taking off at seven o'clock next morning, Monday, March 19th; and receiving no reply he concluded that all was well. A further cable confirming their departure was sent by the Dutch as they left. But soon after takeoff they again ran into torrential rain. Neither of them had ever seen anything like it, and it got worse as they continued. They were flying at 1000 feet and visibility was practically nil. Below them, they knew, was the dreaded Timor Sea. They were less than half-way across when the engine started popping and spluttering and they began to lose height.

The *Red Rose* was alternately running smoothly and climbing steadily and then coughing and missing and losing height until they were dangerously near the water. Lancaster could find nothing that might explain it, unless the rain was getting into the fuel. When the trouble had continued intermittently for ten minutes and had still not cleared itself, he began to realize that their chances of reaching Port Darwin were slim.

He went on struggling to maintain height, but another period of coughing and missing would almost certainly bring them down. Then the engine spluttered again, and in spite of all his manipulating of the throttle and switches they again began to lose height. Chubbie, in the front cockpit, was only too well aware how desperate their situation was. Then she realized that Bill was passing her a note.

"I don't think we're going to make it, old girl," she read, "but it's been a damn good try."

The tone of the note, the underlying assumption of comradeship, and the complete absence of self-pity, struck a responsive chord in Chubbie. She undid her safety-belt, knelt up on her seat and reached over the windshield, and they shook hands.

Back at Atambua the Dutch had just received a cable from Melbourne. It told of further severe flooding of the landing ground at Darwin; on no account was the *Red Rose* to come.

Oblivious of what lay ahead of them, Lancaster and Chubbie were still sitting it out a few hundred feet above the Timor Sea. Hour after hour the nerve-racking switchback went on. Once they got right down to the wave-tops. The sea was fairly calm but there would be no hope whatever for them if they came down. In these desperate circumstances any pilot might have been forgiven for losing his nerve, if only for a moment, for giving way briefly to panic or despair. Yet throughout these interminable hours it seemed to Chubbie that Lancaster remained perfectly calm. If anyone could coax the *Red Rose* to dry land, he would. Aware of his faults of thoughtlessness and carelessness, she was conscious too of his immense strength in a crisis. Whatever his feelings, he never showed fear. She began to wonder, indeed, if he knew what fear was.

He was passing her another note. "Seventy miles to go and we're losing height again. But we might just do it."

At last, after seven and a half hours' flying, with the rain still torrential and the engine still performing uncertainly, they sighted Port Darwin. When at last they were overhead they could see that the conditions were appalling. The landing ground was flooded and deserted; no one was expecting them.

After a preliminary circuit to pick the driest area, Lancaster got the plane down safely in two inches of water. Nervously exhausted, they slumped in limp relaxation as the Avian splashed to a stop. They were dying for a smoke, but neither of them had any matches. They sat completely still for several minutes. Then at last someone appeared.

They got out of the plane and waded towards him, up to their ankles in water, but he waved them away. "I can't come near you," he shouted. "You've got to be checked by the health inspector first. You weren't expected but he's on his way." On appeal he threw them a box of matches.

It was hardly the welcome they had expected at the end of their flight to Australia.

CHAPTER IV

America: Failure and Success

AUSTRALIA did its best in the next few days to make up for its uncharacteristic welcome of the *Red Rose* and her crew. A civic reception was given for the two flyers at the Town Hall in Darwin the night after they landed, and a cable from the Prime Minister's department in Canberra invited them to an informal reception and luncheon at Parliament House. Chubbie's dreams of a few days' relaxation, however, enjoying the fêting and the interviews, were quickly dispelled when Lancaster arranged for them to be out at the airfield before six o'clock on the day following the civic reception. He was anxious to overhaul and decarbonize the engine in preparation for the long flight across Australia; it was 2000 miles to Brisbane, across millions of acres of sparsely populated territory, and then another 700 miles down the coast to Canberra, so the plane had to be right. The trouble they had had crossing the Timor Sea he diagnosed as severe oiling up of the plugs.

Back in England, Avro's were mounting a big advertising campaign to capitalize on the success of their aircraft, and the sales of the Avian leapt ahead, so that they were able to reduce the price to £600. "This means that you can now obtain a similar machine to those used by Mr Bert Hinkler and Captain Lancaster for their flights from England to Australia," said the advertisement, "at a price which makes it the most remarkable value in the aeroplane world." A special tribute came from a journalist who had always shown faith in them—C. G. Grey. "The arrival of the Avian *Red Rose* at Port Darwin", he wrote in the *Aeroplane*, "marks the success, though not the end, of one of the pluckiest flights in the history of flying.... Moreover, the *Red Rose* set up two new records, in that it is the first aeroplane to take a woman to Australia, and the first light aeroplane to take two people there. And this is the longest flight ever made by a woman." Grey thought the greater credit was perhaps due to Chubbie; in his opinion it had been her enthusiasm and drive which had made the attempt possible. But Lancaster, by piloting the aeroplane the whole way, and keeping it in running order, had proved himself, in Grey's view, to be an aviator of the first class.

Although she had gone as a passenger, Chubbie had learnt almost all there was to know about flying and maintaining a light aeroplane in the course of the journey, and her achievement, as a woman of her era, was certainly no less remarkable than Lancaster's. Three months later, in June 1928, Amelia Earhart was to become a household word simply by flying the Atlantic as a passenger, an achievement not to be compared with Chubbie's.

The world Press, in recognizing their joint achievement, made pleasant reading, but it did nothing to make their fortunes, and Lancaster's impatience to get going again was more than justified economically. Avro's, the A.D.C. company, Wakefield's, Shell, the newspapers—all who had backed the flight in any way—were ready to come through with useful cash payments, but the big money was in newspaper contracts and personal appearances in the cities, especially in Sydney and Melbourne, and a long delay in getting there might considerably reduce their impact. Their potential earnings in any case would be diminished through the prior arrival of Bert Hinkler.

Two months earlier Lancaster's father, hearing that the *Red Rose* was going to be repaired at Singapore and would fly on to its destination, had sailed for Australia to see his son. When they finally met in New South Wales at the end of March 1928 after the flight across Australia, Edward Lancaster urged his son to break off his association with Mrs Miller, to cash in on the flight as far as possible, and then to return to his wife and family in England, where his reputation was made. But Lancaster refused to consider ditching Chubbie. "She's come through all the hardships," he told his father, "and she's taken all the risks. I wouldn't dream of it." But the truth was that, so far as Australia was concerned, the boot was on the other foot. Although the credit for the successful completion of the flight was entirely Lancaster's, as Chubbie was the first to admit, it was Chubbie, the first woman to fly to Australia, and herself an Australian, who was in demand and for whom the offers and contracts were pouring in, and it was Chubbie who was shortly to be signed up, at a fee of £150 a week, for a two-month lecture tour of Australian capital cities and principal towns. If any ditching was to be done, it was Chubbie who was in a position to do it. But she was very much in love with Lancaster, and there were occasions now, after the first wave of publicity had died down, when they were able to be alone together, for the first time since that night in Persia. And besides their physical attraction to each other, they had entered into partnership together, not in the legal sense but morally and spiritually. Apart from a brief meeting when she first arrived in Sydney Chubbie had seen nothing of her husband, and she was aware that her marriage was over in all but name. She certainly had no intention of leaving Lancaster out of her plans for the future, and she had in fact arranged with him that a third of their combined earnings should go to his wife.

Lancaster played an important part in the fulfilling of the lecture contract by flying Chubbie everywhere in the Avian—and the distances involved were often vast. He took on other flying contracts to swell their finances, made personal appearances with Chubbie, and introduced her when she lectured. It was a thoroughly successful partnership, and although their hotel and travelling expenses were high they were able to save.

One contract Lancaster got was to fly a photographer up to Brisbane to meet the Australians Charles Kingsford-Smith and Charles Ulm, with their American crew, navigator Harry Lyon and wireless operator James Warner, when they completed the first air crossing of the Pacific in their Fokker *Southern Cross* on June 8th, 1928. It was the greatest trail-blazing flight of the period, by perhaps the greatest of all pioneer flyers, and a quarter of a million people turned up to greet them when they flew down to Sydney next day.

The arrival of the *Southern Cross* was the second watershed in the partnership of Bill Lancaster and Chubbie Miller, if one counts as the first the chance meeting in the Baker Street flat. Unlucky though they had been to be overtaken by Hinkler, they had at least arrived in time to share the limelight with him before the emergence of any major counter-attraction. But with the arrival of the *Southern Cross* public interest in the *Red Rose* and her crew, already on the wane, finally evaporated. Lancaster and Chubbie were thus receptive to anything that offered a fresh challenge.

No doubt Lancaster should have accepted his father's advice and gone back to England. There would have been many opportunities open to him there. But his love for Chubbie had grown until life without her was unthinkable. His father had already given up the task of persuading him and gone home. Now, when the fuss of the arrival of the *Southern Cross* had died down, Harry Lyon, the American navigator, showed Lancaster a cable he had received from Hollywood offering $75,000 for the crew's help in making an aviation film. Kingsford-Smith and Ulm had decided to stay for the present in Australia, so there was room for Lancaster and Mrs Miller to take their place. After that, said Lyon, he had plans for an Atlantic flight.

Lyon was a big, hearty character who was immensely popular in Australia; he always introduced himself as "Mrs Lyon's son, Harry". He was thoroughly enjoying his sudden fame, and the three of them got on well together and would make a colourful team. Warner had been included in the project originally, but he and Lyon didn't get on and he had dropped out.

America, as an escape from personal problems in England and

Australia, had attractions for both Lancaster and Chubbie, and with Lyon in their team the prospects looked good. It didn't take them long to decide to throw in their lot with the convivial and warm-hearted Harry Lyon, and once the decision was made they moved quickly, selling the Avian and booking a passage with Lyon on the *Sonoma*, in which they sailed for San Francisco on June 23rd, giving themselves no time for conventional goodbyes. Thus Chubbie did not see her husband again before she left.

The send-off they were given on the *Sonoma* was a boisterous one; when they came out on the bridge just before the ship sailed, the cheering lasted for several minutes. And as the ship moved out, ferry-boats hooted in shrill farewell and the clamour was deafening. But it was overshadowed when they got to San Francisco in mid-July. The welcome was largely for Lyon and Warner, in recognition of their part in the trans-Pacific flight, but the Englishman and his Australian co-pilot, as Chubbie was known in America, were included in the ceremonies. The ship was given an air escort through the Golden Gate—there was no bridge then—and they were driven through the streets of San Francisco in open cars to a ticker-tape welcome, Lyon and Warner in the first car and Lancaster and Chubbie in the second. When they got to the Town Hall they were asked what they would like to drink. "I thought you had prohibition in America," said Chubbie. This was greeted with howls of laughter, and the sliding doors of a cupboard were swept back, revealing a complete wall lined with bottles and glasses, with refrigerators underneath. Their only problem was that the jovial Harry Lyon seemed reluctant to cut celebrations and get down to business.

From San Francisco they flew down to Los Angeles and then drove to Hollywood, but the aviation film project proved to be a wash-out. In view of the distance they had travelled on the strength of the cable they felt the company's defection ought to be actionable, but they were advised to forget it. Fortunately good progress was made with the Atlantic flight project, a firm called Hall Aircraft Corporation signing them up on a contract to fly a newly-designed three-engined monoplane of all-metal construction across the Atlantic and back, from New York to London and return. The machine was to be powered by two wing motors of 220 horsepower and a central motor of 550 horse-power, and wireless would be installed. The manufacturers hoped to have it ready for testing within a few weeks.

"Mrs Lyon's son" was kept on a fairly tight rein for a time by Mrs Lyon herself, who had crossed the continent from her home in Maine to meet him; but when she went back, Harry Lyon was not so easy to control. Eventually Lancaster and Chubbie decided they must get him back to his home in Maine as soon as possible. But Lyon refused to go unless they went with him.

At first they resisted; there was nothing to attract them to Maine. But after discussing it they changed their minds. It would keep the team together, it would be better for them to lead a quiet life and get fit for the Atlantic flight, and they could live cheaply with Harry Lyon and his mother. So early in August 1928 they all went to Maine.

After the excitement of the previous months, a few weeks in Maine was more than enough for them all. They began to get restless, the more so because the Hall Aircraft Corporation wrote almost daily with news of delays and setbacks in the production of their Atlantic machine. Unable to stand the Maine backwater any longer, and feeling that they might be making money elsewhere, they left for New York.

Socially their arrival in New York was a success, but financially it was a failure. They moved into the Biltmore Hotel, where the management offered them free accommodation, and waited for the contracts to come rolling in. Nothing happened. Plenty of parties and lionizing by the smart set, yes, but nothing more tangible. They made the rounds of the agents and the lecture bureaux and wasted hours talking to them, but not a single contract was forthcoming. And they soon found that living in a luxury hotel, even with free accommodation, was an expensive proposition. They found themselves slinking out of their impressive suites and making for the "Automat"—the eating house a few blocks away where they could get a packaged meal for a nickel or two. Their worst moment came when the bellhop from the Biltmore came into the same automat. Lancaster saved their faces by putting on his best Oxford accent. "Quite an experience," he said, "to eat in a place like this. Frightfully interesting." They finished their meat pies and left. After that they ate in another automat two blocks farther down.

But whatever economies they practised their money would not last for ever. They had made between £3000 and £4000 out of the Australia flight, but a great deal of this had gone on expenses in the previous few months, some of it had been sent to Kiki, and they would have to keep something in reserve. So when the Hall Aircraft Corporation wrote to say that owing to finance difficulties there would be a delay in completion of at least another three months, they determined to find some other project to keep them going.

The only man of substance they had met in New York with any interest in aviation was George Putnam, the publisher, later to marry Amelia Earhart; Lancaster and Lyon had tried to interest him in a flight from New York to Bermuda. No one had yet made a flight of any kind to Bermuda, and Putnam eventually agreed to finance such a flight provided he could accompany them. The machine chosen was an Ireland Neptune amphibian.

Bermuda, 800 miles from New York, a small island with thousands of square miles of sea around it, was the sort of target that they felt ought to be within their compass while still being worth while from the publicity angle. They would need a specialist navigator, so with Lancaster and Putnam that meant a crew of three. The amphibian would have to be fully loaded with fuel to make the distance, so there would be no room for Chubbie. Indeed, when they began the load tests in New York they found that with a full load of fuel and a crew of three the amphibian wouldn't take off at all. The only way they could reduce the fuel load was to reduce the distance, so in the middle of October 1928 they flew the amphibian down to Hampton Roads, Virginia, intending to set off from there. They stayed at the U.S. naval station at Hampton Roads while Lancaster made further tests, but he soon found that even the 700 miles from Hampton Roads to Bermuda would necessitate a heavily overloaded take-off and would leave an inadequate margin. The sensible thing was to get a plane with a longer range. By this time George Putnam had had enough, and he abandoned the whole idea.

One thing that was resolved in this period was the future of the Lancaster–Miller–Lyon partnership. They were fond of Harry Lyon, and they shared his liking for a party, but they found him altogether too difficult a partner. Eventually Lyon agreed that when the plane was ready the Atlantic venture should go forward without him, and they parted company.

The Hall Corporation were still in almost daily contact with them on the progress of the plane, and in November they asked Lancaster to go to Los Angeles to discuss such matters as cockpit lay-out and ancillary equipment with them; it looked as though the plane might soon be ready. But Lancaster had been having discussions with a firm of New York bankers over the possible manufacture in America under licence of the Cirrus engine—the engine which had taken him to Australia. At the end of November the deal went through and Lancaster was offered the job of chief test and demonstration pilot. It was impossible in these circumstances for him to leave New York, and Chubbie, after a careful briefing from Lancaster, went instead.

"Do you know anything about wireless?" Chubbie was asked when she got to Los Angeles. "It would save weight if you could act as co-pilot and wireless operator."

"No," said Chubbie, "but I'll find out." She took a tiny apartment in Los Angeles and began the course at the YMCA radio school, learning radio theory and how to carry out fault testing and running repairs, besides slogging away at the tedious business of sending and receiving in Morse code. She was the only woman in the class.

Kiki Lancaster had followed the reports of her husband's flight to Australia with a deep and unselfish interest, content for the time being to continue to be the bread-winner for herself and her children. Cuttings, articles, and letters had all been carefully preserved. She had moved back to London from the coast to take the job of secretary to the Anti-Vivisection Society, a cause dear to her heart, and she was living in a small Fulham flat. Money was short at first, but then she began to receive quite substantial sums from her third share in the fees earned when the *Red Rose* reached Australia.

It was easy, in the drab surroundings of Fulham, to envy the exciting time that she imagined her husband and Mrs Miller must be having in America, and a note of wistful reproach crept into her letters to Bill. She knew too of his plans for an Atlantic flight, and while she was looking forward to seeing him at the conclusion of that flight she was anxious for him, and wanted to see him beforehand. What she knew or guessed of his relationship with Chubbie is uncertain; they had been discreet in their behaviour and there had been no scandal. But Lancaster's parents were naturally keen to preserve the marriage, and Edward Lancaster, on his return from Australia, may well have encouraged Kiki to take the initiative. Ostensibly, though, her attitude was that she didn't see why she shouldn't join Bill for a short holiday in America and share some of the fun.

Bill agreed that she should come to New York, the Anti-Vivisection Society gave her a long Christmas leave, and she left England in mid-December, arriving in New York on the 19th. Chubbie was still in Los Angeles, so if there was any prospect at all of a reconciliation the way was clear for it.

America under prohibition was a land of Gilbertian absurdity. Lancaster had asked Kiki to bring with her the compass he had used on his flight to Australia; when he sold the *Red Rose* he had retained it and sent it back to the makers for overhaul. He trusted this compass implicitly and wanted to use it for the Atlantic flight. But when Kiki attempted to pass through the Customs in New York, they announced that they would have to confiscate the compass under the Eighteenth Amendment (Prohibition) because it contained alcohol. Either that, or they would have to break it open and pour the alcohol away. Kiki demanded that they send for her husband, and eventually Lancaster was able to persuade the Customs inspectors that the pure alcohol in the compass was outside the terms of prohibition. This ludicrous incident made the headlines in all the New York papers.

Christmas 1928 in New York was for Kiki and Bill an empty, unreal festival. For Kiki it was strange to be away from her children. Lancaster's thoughts were of Chubbie. New Year's Eve, too, had an element of fantasy. "The Management of the Biltmore", warned a notice that was posted in every room, "notifies its guests that the Prohibition Laws must be strictly observed." It was a reminder that few seemed to heed.

Following the Cirrus engine negotiations, two Avro Avians with British-

America: Failure and Success

made engines were bought by the American company for demonstration purposes, and arrangements were made by another American company for the manufacture of the Avian itself under licence. Lancaster was the obvious man to test-fly and demonstrate these aircraft. Another British pilot who was linked with the Avian and Cirrus projects was Lady Heath, who earlier that year had become the first woman to fly from Cape Town to England. Lady Heath was flying her de Havilland Gipsy Moth down to an air meeting in Miami at the beginning of January, and the American Cirrus company decided to send Lancaster down to show off the Avian. Kiki had struck up an immediate friendship with Mary Heath, and the two women arranged to fly down together.

A flight of such length by two women was a novelty then, and the variety of incident that characterized it got good Press coverage. They left New York at midday on January 2nd, accompanied by Lancaster in an Avian, but with the faster machine they soon left him behind. Headwinds and severe cold reduced their range and they were forced to come down in a field; the farmer obligingly fetched them some gasoline. At Washington, still in intense cold, it took four hours, and much help from the U.S. Navy, to get the engine restarted. From Charleston on January 4th they missed the flying field at Savannah and came down in a field of crops, an irate farmer needing some mollifying before he would agree to get them more gasoline. At Daytona, again short of fuel, they landed on the beach with the tide coming in rapidly and the wingtip only inches from the sandhills; sympathetic inhabitants rushed into the town to get more gasoline for them as the sea crept up towards the plane. For someone who had previously done no flying at all it was an exhausting flight, virtually from one end of the States to the other, but Kiki found it exhilarating. "A marvellous trip" was how she described it in her scrapbook.

To what extent Kiki was trying to show that anything Chubbie could do she could do better is uncertain. She was not really that sort of person, and in any case she would have known that she could hardly compete with Chubbie on that level. Nevertheless, the idea may have been in her mind. If, as seems likely, she had come to America to get her husband back, she might well have felt the need to show him that she too could take a full and active part in his flying life.

Lancaster caught up with them at various stages along the route but made no conscious attempt to keep with them. As with most cross-country flyers of the twenties, he was having his own adventures with the Avian.

Over a hundred and fifty machines attended the meeting, converging on Miami from all over the continent. Mary Heath's Gipsy Moth won two events and was second in another, and Lancaster duly gave demonstration flights in the Avian. Then they returned to New York, and on

January 19th Kiki sailed for home. That her visit was a happy one seems clear from her scrap-book; but she was far too intelligent a person in any case to play the pathetic abandoned wife. Lancaster, with his capacity for putting awkward matters out of his mind, and anxious perhaps not to spoil her holiday, may not have been as importunate as he had intended over the divorce he wanted. But, from his own account given later to Chubbie, he certainly pressed her hard. Kiki's attitude was predictable and inevitable: if he could make a financial settlement that would guarantee the future of the children, a way might be found; but for the moment, on material and religious grounds, the answer was no.

Lancaster's salary with American Cirrus Engines Incorporated began at $500 a month, and this was soon raised to $600. He had fallen on his feet in America, and the decision to go there had been amply justified. He and Chubbie had each entered America on a six-months' visitor's visa, since renewed, and now Lancaster had applied for and been granted an immigration quota number. Chubbie was still getting periodic extensions of her visa.

Chubbie returned from Los Angeles with her radio licence and took an apartment on West 56th Street; Lancaster was living at the Army and Navy Club, where he remained. There was no firm news yet from the Hall Aircraft Corporation. Chubbie studied for her pilot's licence at the Red Bank school in New Jersey, secretly, because the American Press had taken it for granted after the Australia flight that she was a licensed pilot, and Lancaster felt it was not in their interests to correct that impression. Thus they still pursued their separate lives and careers, though the understanding between them remained as it had been for more than a year—that they would get married when they were free to do so.

To publicize the first American-built Cirrus engine, the American company instructed Lancaster, in March 1929, to compete for a gold medal that was being offered for the most successful light aeroplane flight over the route New York–Miami–Trinidad–Panama–Mexico–Miami–New York, a distance of some 10,000 miles, including several long sea stretches in the Caribbean. The primary object was to demonstrate the reliability of the Cirrus engine, and to show it off at all the major stops, so there was no question of record-breaking.

Lancaster left New York in the Avian on March 4th and followed the coastal route to Miami, much as he had done to the air meeting two months earlier. From Miami he crossed the Florida Strait to Havana, then headed west through Haiti and Puerto Rico, making stops on the way, before bearing south again for Guadeloupe, Martinique, and Barbados. He was the first man to land in Barbados, and the first to carry airmail from Barbados to Trinidad, which he reached on April 2nd, landing

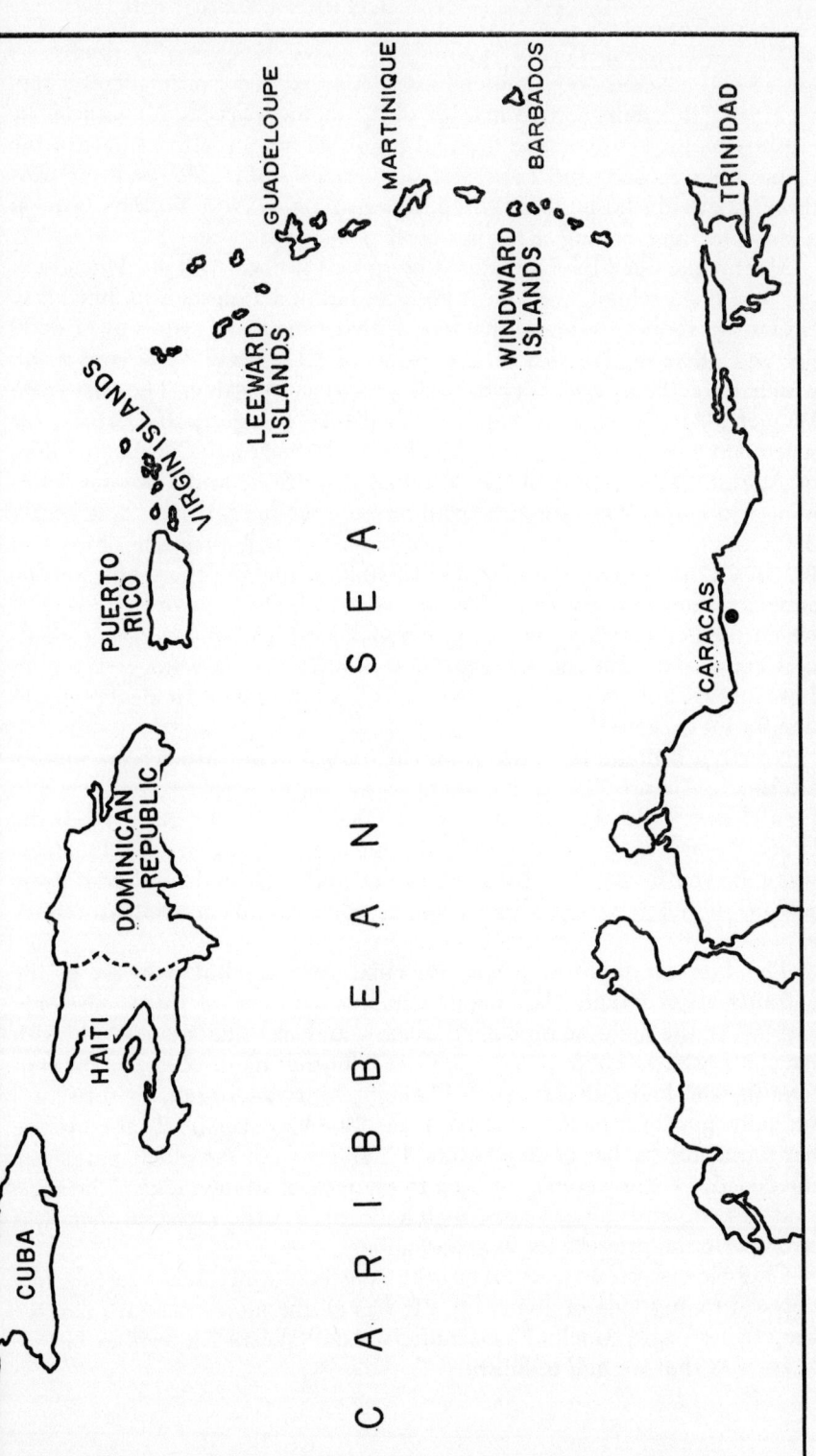

Principal points of call for Lancaster's Caribbean flight, March – April 1929

on the racecourse at Port of Spain after 3 hours' flying from Barbados. So far he had covered 4000 miles without enforced delay or incident. Then, on April 7th, taking off from Port of Spain for Caracas, Venezuela, he crashed badly, the machine finished up on its nose, the front part of the plane was wrecked, and Lancaster was seriously hurt. He spent the next three months in hospital in Trinidad, returning to New York by boat on a stretcher and having a further spell in hospital there.

Meanwhile Chubbie had gained her pilot's licence without difficulty at the Red Bank school, and with Lancaster out of action she was anxious to earn some money. Woman aviators at that time were rare: out of 4690 licensed pilots in America in the spring of 1929, only 34 were women, which gave them a scarcity as well as a novelty value. The first open Women's Air Race, immediately dubbed the "Powder-puff Derby", was scheduled to be run from Santa Monica (Los Angeles) to Cleveland, Ohio, in August 1929 as part of the National Air Races, and Chubbie determined to enter. The distance of this trans-continental route was nearly 2700 miles. She managed to convince Lawrence Bell, president of the Bell Aircraft Corporation, that she was capable of making the flight, and he agreed to supply her with a Fleet two-seater biplane, the open cockpit of which the Bell company virtually re-built round her because of her smallness compared with the average pilot. She flew in easy stages across to Los Angeles, a flight of nearly 3000 miles, and this made an ideal preparation for the race itself.

Nineteen contestants lined up for the start at Santa Monica on Sunday afternoon, August 18th, 1929, intent on averaging nearly 400 miles a day for the next eight days so as to reach Cleveland by the 26th, when the closed-circuit races were due to begin. Each day the progress of the flyers was followed in detail in the newspapers, and each night the tired flyers put up at hotels at the various stages, often sharing a room to reduce expenses.

The first overnight stop was Phoenix, Arizona, but only six of the entrants arrived there that night. Chubbie was one of them—the only arrival in the light aeroplane division—and she shared a room with Amelia Earhart. There was tragic news later that night of one of the contestants who had failed to reach Phoenix; Marvel Crossan, aged twenty-six, had spun in over the Arizona desert. She had apparently tried to use her parachute, as her body was found 200 feet from the plane, parachute unopened. People weren't yet used to the idea of women taking the same risks as men, and the news cast such a gloom over the race that there was strong external pressure for its abandonment.

Chubbie discussed the situation with Amelia Earhart. Both were fiercely opposed to any idea of giving up. "It was all the more necessary that we keep flying," said Amelia Earhart afterwards. "We all felt terrible, but we knew now that we *had* to finish."

Next day, making for Douglas, Arizona, Chubbie herself was forced down in the Arizona desert. She had run out of fuel. How this had happened was beyond her: a responsible mechanic had assured her the night before, in a signed note, that her tanks had been filled. The gauge was a primitive one, however, and she had not dipped the tank. The delay put her well behind the leaders, but she eventually reached Cleveland, finishing third in her class. The Bell company were so delighted that they entered her for the fifty-mile closed-circuit race for women, which vied with the *Graf Zeppelin* and star flyers like Lindbergh and "Batchy" Atcherley in popular appeal with the crowd. The circuit was a triangular one, marked by three pylons, and Chubbie was right up with the leaders all the way. Amelia Earhart tried to overtake her on the inside and was disqualified, and she passed everyone except Phoebe Omlie, the girl she had finished third to in the Powder-puff Derby. Mary Heath was third.[1] Then she heard that Phoebe Omlie had been disqualified for cutting a corner, and she was declared the winner. In subsequent events she got a second and a third, and Lawrence Bell gave her a generous bonus, making a thrilling start to her career as a solo flyer.

While Lancaster was still recuperating another plane manufacturer, Fairchild's, invited Chubbie to fly one of their machines in a national competition—the 5000-mile Ford Reliability Tour. Most of the aeroplane manufacturers entered one or more machines, which were flown by test or demonstration pilots. Fairchild's dressed Chubbie entirely in black and white—white kid jodhpurs, white silk shirt with black tie, white kid Norfolk jacket, white helmet, and black boots. It was a spectacular outfit. The plane too was painted white, with a black line down the fuselage. There were thirty-five male contestants and three women. It was hard flying, and Chubbie firmly established her reputation as an endurance flyer by coming eighth out of the thirty-eight starters and being the only woman to finish; the other two were forced to drop out early on. A performance like this in a national event brought her distinction as well as fame, and Fairchild's doubled her prize money, which meant that she received a thousand dollars. In addition, oil and gasoline companies showered bonuses on her, and the money poured in.

The slump in Lancaster's fortunes—he had lost his job with the American Cirrus Engine company following his crash in Trinidad—thus coincided with a remarkable surge in the flying career of Mrs Keith-Miller, as she was known all over the States. Not surprisingly it rankled a bit with Lancaster, especially when the time came, as it inevitably did, when it was Chubbie's money that was paying the bills—including a £30-a-month allowance to Kiki and Lancaster's account at the Army and

[1] Later in the meeting Lady Heath crashed through a near-by factory roof and was seriously injured.

Navy Club. But as far as Chubbie was concerned, a partnership was a partnership; and Lancaster, however sick he must sometimes have felt, gave her every possible support in her flying career, travelling hundreds of miles to be at airports to meet her. Whatever it was doing to his own pride, he was sincerely proud of her.

CHAPTER V

Hope fades for Chubbie

"I WANT two pilots to demonstrate and sell a number of aeroplane types that I'm dealing in. Have you both got commercial licences?"

The stock market crash of 1929 had thrown the expansion of American civil and sporting aviation into reverse. For free-lance pilots, making a living was becoming more and more of a struggle. The plane being specially built for Bill Lancaster and Chubbie Miller by the Hall Aircraft Corporation in Los Angeles had been finally abandoned, partly through structural weakness, partly through lack of finance. A job that Lancaster had got as a test pilot with the Victor Aircraft Corporation, at a salary of $75 a week plus bonuses, dissolved when the firm went into the hands of receivers. So when, in March 1930, a Dutchman named C. P. Stork, head of the Stork Corporation, told them of the two jobs that were going and asked if they had commercial licences, the denial that was about to form on Chubbie's lips was silenced by Lancaster's affirmation.

"Yes, we've got those all right."

"That's good, because you must have them to fly prospective customers about and demonstrate aircraft. When can you start?"

"Monday."

Bill was accepting the job on behalf of them both, but under false colours—or so it seemed to Chubbie. She kept quiet until they were going down in the lift from the Dutchman's office.

"We haven't got commercial licences, Bill. What are we going to do?"

"Get them." He reminded Chubbie of a friend of theirs named J. R. Booth who ran a flying club in Ottawa. Any time they wanted help, Booth had said, they could rely on him. "We've got about seventy-two hours," said Lancaster. "I'm going to send Booth a telegram now to say that we're catching the night train. We'll ask him to meet us in the morning and get him to fix the tests for us so we can take our commercial licences tomorrow. American and Canadian licences are reciprocal."

Booth was waiting for them on the platform at Ottawa when the train drew in at eight-thirty next morning. It was bitterly cold, so cold that they found it difficult to breathe. Booth had brought a spare racoon coat for each of them. The tests, he told them, had been fixed for that afternoon. "We'll get everything organized this morning," he said, "and then I'll take you to the Silver Slipper for lunch."

It was a good lunch—far too good for anyone facing a medical examination the same afternoon—and Chubbie had trouble with the eyesight tests. "What's the matter with you?" asked the doctor, and with characteristic directness she told him. "I had lunch at the Silver Slipper, and I'm just a little bit high."

"We'll do the rest of the examination first, then. By the time you've finished that you'll be sober."

The doctor was right, and she passed the medical without further difficulty. Then came the flying test, in a small training plane. Her rating was good and she passed comfortably. Meanwhile Lancaster was undergoing the same tests with similar success. The licences were issued at once, and that night they returned by train to New York.

They worked for Stork for the next six months, demonstrating and occasionally selling aircraft and ancillary equipment. On his list were Stinson Juniors, Great Lake trainers, Savoia Marchetti amphibians, Cirrus engines, and Irving parachutes. Whether or not Stork guessed the truth about the licences they never knew, but if he examined them—as he or one of his staff must surely have done—the truth must have been readily apparent. No doubt he admired Lancaster's resource.

The sale of an aeroplane, however, was a rare event; neither of them sold more than a couple of planes in the whole six months. But this was due more to the mounting depression all over the States than to any shortcomings on their part as pilot/salesmen. Before they were allowed to demonstrate the Stinson Junior, for instance, Eddie Stinson insisted that they both go to Detroit to qualify on the type and to carry out emergency landings. Afterwards Chubbie had a congratulatory letter from Stinson. "You fly as well as any man," he said.

By the late summer of 1930, the rapid advance of aviation in the twenties followed by the severe recession of the preceding twelve months had brought the sales of private aircraft to saturation point. The Stork Corporation were in financial difficulties, and by mutual agreement Lancaster and Chubbie resigned from the firm. All that remained to them was free-lance work, but in America there was little of this to be had. They might have done better now in England, where they were not forgotten and where aircraft equipment firms were still using their names and photographs in their advertisements—alongside those of Amy Johnson, Kingsford-Smith, Bert Hinkler, and Francis Chichester; but for personal reasons they did not consider such a move. They were back to the precarious pursuit of trail-blazing, the stunts and the record-breaking, in which, with luck, there was still money to be made.

With the Stork Corporation they had been well paid, and although they had lived well too they were by no means penniless. Yet as August dragged into September and no work came, Lancaster began to realize how desperate his situation was. For Chubbie it was different: women in aviation were still a novelty. Still excluded from the professions in spite of so-called emancipation, still second-class citizens in a man's world, they were stared at like circus animals whenever they behaved independently or attempted to compete on the same terms as men. This was even truer, perhaps, in America than in Britain; many of the best restaurants in New York, for instance, still carried notices requesting women not to smoke.

It seemed to Chubbie that the most difficult and spectacular flight left unattempted was a flight to Japan, a distance of over six thousand miles. With a route via the Aleutians and the Bering Sea, it would compare favourably with any other long-distance flight yet attempted, including Kingsford-Smith's across the Pacific. But there seemed no hope of getting a suitable plane. She decided to take it in stages—to try to get an engine first, and then an airframe to suit it; and with this in mind she went to the Wright Engine Company to ask if she could borrow an engine. When she told them what she wanted to do they were horrified; she couldn't possibly know what such a flight involved, they said. But they were ready to lend her an engine provided she planned a flight exclusively over land.

"What about a coast-to-coast record?"

"For that we'll lend you a Whirlwind. You can have it for six months."

It was a good start—and next day she heard of a plane. It was not quite what she would have chosen, but her chances of getting it seemed better on that account. Known as an Alexander Bullet, it was a low-wing four-seater cabin monoplane with a retractable undercarriage and a cruising speed of 125 m.p.h. But early flight tests had revealed bad spinning characteristics and it had a reputation of being vicious to handle. The first pilot to test it had resigned from the firm rather than continue to fly it, leaving with the parting advice that the plane as then constructed would never meet the requirements for licensing and that someone would get hurt if they kept on trying. The next pilot to fly it baled out in a spin after staying with it through thirty-five turns. His replacement was killed in the second prototype. A specialist in spin-testing was then brought in for the next prototype—and he was found dying in a half-opened parachute near the wreckage.[1] The plane had thus never been granted a type certificate. But there was one available at the Alexander factory at Denver, Colorado, and although it was in a neglected state Chubbie refused to be put off. Towards the end of September she got a lift to Denver and went to see the plane. "You can't have it," she was told. "It's never had a type

[1] All the above details appear in *Popular Aviation*, July/August, 1967.

certificate." "Look," said Chubbie, "I'm not going to do any aerobatics in it, I just want to fly it straight and level from A to B." They let her have the plane, installed the 165 h.p. Wright Whirlwind in it, and gave the airframe a thorough overhaul and repaint. She had got the plane for nothing.

While all this was going on, a well-known woman flyer named Laura Ingalls was beating Chubbie to the flight; she took off from New York and got to Los Angeles in thirty and a half hours' airborne time. But the flight got good publicity, and Chubbie decided that the record was there to be broken; in some ways this was a good thing. After working out her own maps and courses she took off from New York on October 12th and headed west. Bad weather over the Alleghanies and in the Mid-West did not hold her up, and with only five stops en route she reached Los Angeles on October 16th, 1930, after 25 hours 44 minutes in the air. She had beaten Laura Ingalls's time by 4 hours 43 minutes.

While Chubbie was flying westwards, Laura Ingalls was passing her on the return flight to New York, which she completed in 24 hours 55 minutes, but Chubbie beat this in turn a few days later with an eastward flight of 21 hours 47 minutes to become undisputed champion, holding the record both ways. There was no prize for such a record, but she collected substantial sums afterwards from advertising and from newspaper articles and interviews. Bill Lancaster, acting as her manager, negotiated the contracts.

A further chance to cash in on her record came when Harvard R. Smith, president of a firm called Aerial Enterprises Incorporated, offered $1000 and expenses for a flight from Pittsburgh to Havana, a distance of 1300 miles; and on November 22nd she took off from Pittsburgh for Miami and Havana, carrying an illuminated scroll from the Mayor of Pittsburgh to the Cuban President. Lancaster was there to see her off. Climbing again over the Alleghanies, she battled against strong headwinds down the Atlantic seaboard until she was forced down by shortage of fuel at Charleston; she had hoped to fly non-stop to Miami. She stayed the night at Charleston, reached Miami for lunch next day, and then took off for Cuba, which she reached late that afternoon. She was fêted in Havana, but she was given no time to relax. Harvard R. Smith wanted her back in Pittsburgh as soon as possible.

Day after day the weather at Havana was bad and the forecasts pessimistic, and Chubbie waited. Day after day Smith cabled her to hurry. If she wasn't back soon, he said, they would lose valuable publicity. Eventually, on Friday, November 28th, with a slightly more favourable weather report—although there were warnings of poor visibility and strong easterly winds—she decided to go, planning a single stop at Miami on the way.

Chubbie had been scared of the reputation of the Bullet at first, but she had got used to it, it had proved reliable, and she had developed complete confidence in it. Urged now to wait for the northbound Pan-American civil plane so as to have some company, she refused because it would mean further delay. She had no blind flying instruments and no radio, but she did not see how she could well miss the Florida coast.

The flight to Miami was a comparatively short one, less than three hours' flying in the Bullet, and Chubbie had not taken on a full load of fuel. But now, as a concession to the forecast of powerful cross-winds, she delayed her take-off in order to fill her auxiliary tanks right up, giving her an endurance of nine hours. She finally took off at eleven minutes past nine. Half an hour after she took off, a Pan-American Airways pilot approaching Havana saw her plane at low altitude. She was not seen again, and she did not arrive at Miami.

When she was reported overdue, two planes took off from Havana and searched throughout the afternoon, returning to Havana with the approach of darkness. Six more planes took part in an intensive but fruitless search from Miami. All shipping in the area was warned by radio, and a steamer plying the route was specially alerted but reported seeing nothing. "As nightfall obscured the waters of the Florida Straits," wrote the *New York Times* correspondent in Miami, "hope for the safety of Mrs J. M. Keith-Miller, Australian aviatrix, faded until searchers here conceded her no more than a thousand-to-one chance of a safe landing." The search was to be resumed in the morning; but by then hope had almost gone.

Bill Lancaster, who was waiting for Chubbie in Pittsburgh, left by plane for Washington to try to persuade the U.S. Navy to organize a search. Pilots on scheduled flights along the Havana–Miami route were still scanning land and sea, and the Keys—the islands skirting the southern Florida coast—were being thoroughly explored by seaplane from Miami. But as darkness descended on the second day the futility of further search was accepted by everyone—or almost everyone. There were, in fact, two exceptions, one of whom was Laura Ingalls, who happened to be in Miami. "It would be a grievous mistake to give up the hunt for her," she said. She thought Chubbie might have been forced down on some isolated reef or remote spot on the mainland. The other exception, of course, was Bill Lancaster. After much persistent lobbying in Washington he had finally persuaded the Navy, in spite of adverse weather, to lend him a plane to fly down to Miami, where he proposed to continue the search. For him it was unthinkable that Chubbie was dead. Yet, as he battled through atrocious weather across the mountains and south to Miami, the search was being finally abandoned, all the local airmen concluding that she had been blown out into the Gulf of Mexico by the gale-force winds that had swept in that morning from the Atlantic. "Aviation officials today agreed in expressing the belief that Mrs J. M.

Keith-Miller perished in an attempted flight in adverse weather conditions from Havana to Miami," said a Miami report of November 30th. "No plans for a continued search are under consideration."

When Chubbie took off at eleven minutes past nine on November 28th she climbed to 750 feet and set course for Miami. She was flying into the teeth of a gusting wind, the vertical currents were violent, and the plane rolled and pitched until she was bruised and shaken. The Bullet always needed firm handling, but she had never taken such a battering as this. Visibility, however, was fair, and she was able to keep below the cloudbase. The Wright Whirlwind was pulling beautifully, and from frequent reference to the white-capped sea she seemed to be making good progress. What she couldn't estimate so easily without instruments was the extent of her drift.

It would be at least an hour before she could hope for her first sight of land to the north—the necklace of islands known as the Florida Keys. The time was nearly up when she saw an ebony line across the sky dead ahead; she was racing towards a solid line squall which extended for many miles. Suddenly the great bank of cloud was upon her. The air turned cold, the wind increased to a new velocity, and the Bullet was jerked about like a kite. Before she had properly regained control she was swept into the towering blackness of the cloud.

Caught up in the vortex of the storm, unable to see sky or sea, entirely dependent on her altimeter and compass, she watched with dismay as the compass needle collapsed and then rotated violently, while the altimeter readings varied by hundreds of feet as the plane switchbacked through the storm. The only hope of keeping control and fixing her position was to get down near the water. She dived down to fifty feet, and there, storm-tossed and heaving, scarcely visible through the mist and spray, was the sea. The compass was still spinning like a whirligig, but she held her course as best she could. There was no sign of land, and she should have reached it by now. She must be heading for the Gulf of Mexico, or out into the Atlantic.

She pulled the stick back and began climbing through the storm. Perhaps she could get above it; she still had many hours of fuel in hand. But at 6000 feet the conditions were no better. She thought of turning back for Havana—but which way was Havana? Cold and numb, confused and panic-stricken by the loss of orientation and certain that she was irrevocably lost, she began to feel it would be better to die quickly than to wait until she went out of her mind. She opened the throttle and pushed the nose forward.

Diving through 6000 feet seemed an eternity. Her eye rested for a moment on the fuel gauge. Her fuel consumption had been high, but she still had two or three hours' fuel left. That suddenly seemed a long time.

A thousand feet above sea level she levelled out, and slowly her sanity returned. She would keep going as long as she could. Feeling that she must be somewhere in the Gulf of Mexico, she held her course.

Away to starboard she saw that the sea was tinged with green. Surely that must mean she was near land. Her conclusion that she had been blown westward must be correct. She turned joyfully to starboard, expecting to get a glimpse any moment of the outline of the west Florida coast, on the opposite side to Miami. But no land appeared, although the water retained its luminous green. The sea was calmer too, the wind had slackened, and the visibility was better. She was through the storm.

Her main tanks were nearly empty, and she switched to the reserve tanks. She had kept to her new course for about a hundred miles when she saw two tiny specks on the water straight ahead. They were small fishing boats. Whatever happened now, at least she wasn't going to die. She could always come down near the boats. But with this relief came a new set of conflicts—fears for the plane and for the engine, which she had struggled so hard to obtain, and fears for her reputation as a flyer. She was ashamed of having got lost, dreaded the publicity and scorn she felt she would have to face.

When she reached the boats she throttled back and circled low over the top, shouting and making signs at the occupants. They waved and pointed—to the east, as she expected. There was still a chance that she might have enough petrol to cross the Florida peninsula and reach Miami. It suddenly seemed of overriding importance to reach her destination, not just any piece of dry land.

A few minutes later she saw the coastline, and she studied her strip map and tried to identify where she was. She was surprised by the desolation of the landscape; the interior was an unbroken mass of jungle, with no space for a landing. There wasn't even a beach—the jungle seemed to sprout out of the sea. She decided to turn south and follow the coastline round. If her fuel held out, that would bring her to Miami. But she could not reconcile the contour of the coastline with the west coast of Florida. She was getting seriously worried about her fuel when she passed over a village, and she decided to attempt a landing.

There was no natural clearing near the village but she selected the area with the fewest apparent obstructions and headed for it. As she descended she realized that the wind was immensely strong—she hardly seemed to be moving as she crossed the coast on her final approach. The plane pancaked to a stop amongst bushes and undergrowth within forty yards, suffering nothing more than a few jolts from the rough ground and some damage to the fabric from the jungle foliage. She had been airborne for seven hours.

The natives from the village soon surrounded her. At first she was frightened. Then she realized they were talking to her in English.

"Where am I?"

"Andros Island."

Andros Island? Where was that? Who did it belong to?

"King George."

Dimly she began to realize what had happened. Andros Island was in the Bahamas. Instead of being blown westwards into the Gulf of Mexico she had been driven in the opposite direction, out into the Atlantic. Fortunately the storm had skirted the Bahamas, otherwise she would simply have flown farther and farther out into the Atlantic until her fuel gave out.

But for taking on that extra gasoline she would not even have made the Bahamas.

Andros Island consists of two islands separated by a channel of water three miles wide, and Chubbie had landed on the south island near a place called Kemp's Bay, where there was no means of communication. She knew she would have been reported missing, and she was anxious to get a message through to Miami; people might be endangering their lives searching for her. Bill would probably have flown down from Pittsburgh, and she knew he would do anything to find her. She would have to cross to the main island and contact the British Resident. But when she reached the Residency next morning she found that the local radio station was out of action, and it was another day before she could get a boat to Nassau. Lancaster, who had chartered a small seaplane to mount his own search, flew to Nassau as soon as he heard Chubbie was there, and eventually they returned to Miami together in the Bullet. Of the scores of congratulatory telegrams that Chubbie received, one offered her $1500 for her story, which she accepted.

The news that Chubbie was safe made the headlines everywhere; but fame turned quickly to notoriety when newspapermen, suspicious of the confidence shown by Chubbie's friends in her survival before she was found, hinted that the whole story had been a publicity stunt. "Gentlemen! Leave the room!" said Lancaster heatedly when the accusation was first made to him at a news conference in Miami. "If you believe that little lady could be capable of anything dishonourable, I have nothing more to say to you." And when the "hoax" story reached Chubbie in Nassau she burst into tears. But another and more famous newspaperman came out in support of Chubbie. "The ground marks reveal that it was a forced landing," wrote columnist Walter Winchell, "and her gas tanks were dry." Winchell added an accurate if unflattering appraisal of Chubbie: "a plain woman, but sincere."

It might have been wiser if Chubbie had abandoned the remainder of the flight; but her pride was hurt, and she was determined to get the plane back to Pittsburgh. There was also the $1000-dollar prize. She left Miami

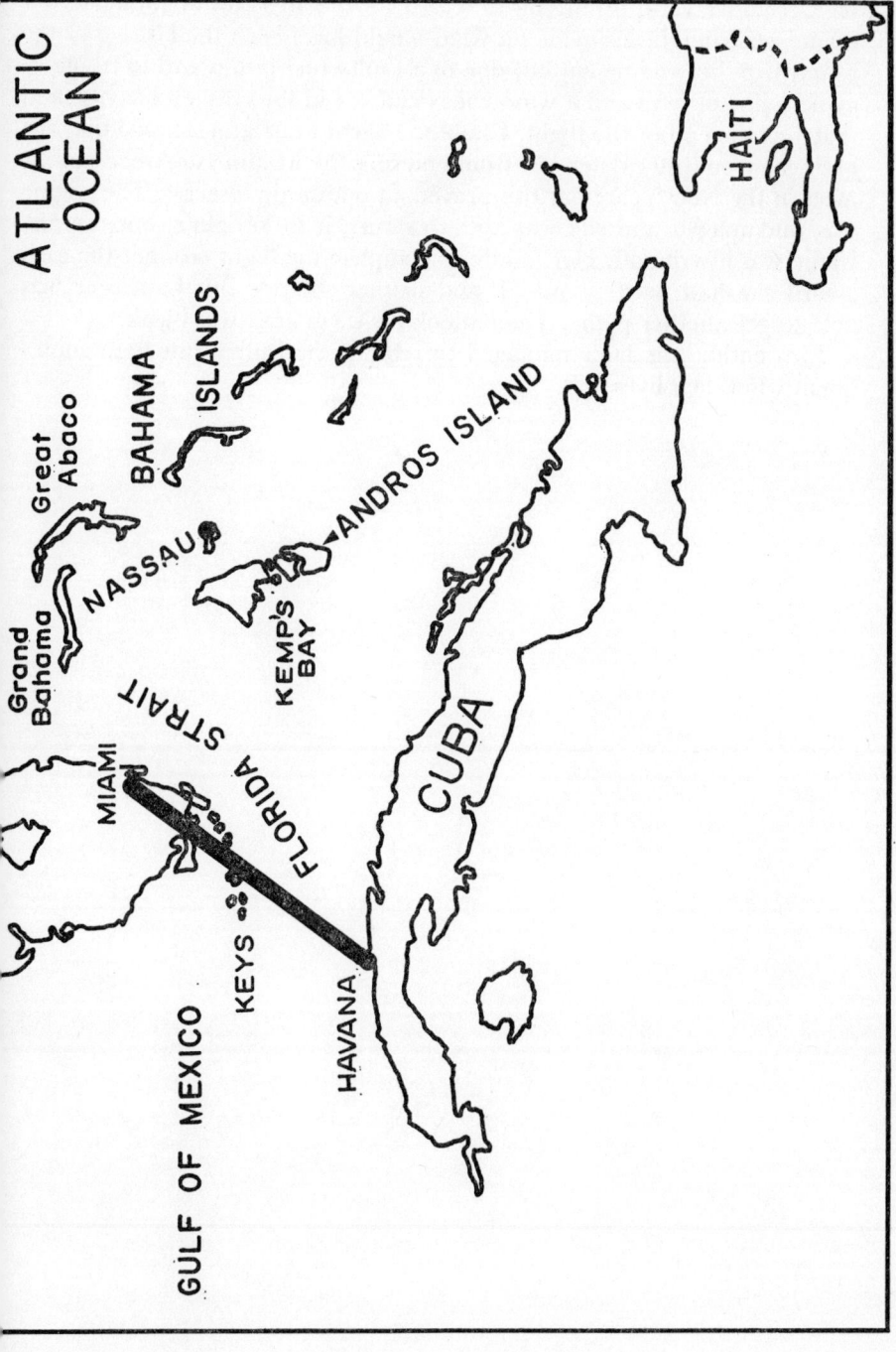

Havana to Miami, November 28th, 1930 — Chubbie's intended track

E

on December 12th, promising to return for the air races in January; but taking off from Jacksonville on what would have been the last leg of the round trip, her engine cut out due to a faulty fuel pump and in trying to avoid a line of trees and a wire fence dead ahead she crashed heavily, and that was the end of the flight. Chubbie's agent in Miami stressed that the accident would not deter her from entering the Miami All-American air meet in the New Year; but this proved an optimistic forecast. The engine was undamaged and she was able to return it to Wright's, but the airframe was a write-off. Her failure to complete the flight cost her the cash award she had been promised, and neither she nor Bill Lancaster was able to get another plane. The outlook for them both was bleak.

Two enthusiasts later managed to rebuild the Bullet, but both subsequently lost their lives in it.

CHAPTER VI

The House in Miami

"LET's go down to the air races in Miami. They'll be starting early in January and we ought to make some money there."

A year had passed since Chubbie's flight to Havana. It had been a mixed year in the fortunes of the Lancaster/Miller partnership. For some months Lancaster had held the job of personal assistant to Jack Maddox, president of Trans-Continental Western Airways in Los Angeles, but he was not happy in the role of administrator and he had come to a mutual agreement with Maddox to terminate the contract. He had been grateful for the job, but he wanted to get back to active flying; all he had done in 1931 was some limited free-lance flying and instruction. For Chubbie the best thing about 1931 was a contract she negotiated with the Redpath Chautauqa Lecture Bureau, a well-known agency which acted for political and other lecturers on American circuits. She let her apartment in New York, and for three months she flew daily from town to town to fulfil the bookings in her contract. It was an exhausting programme, and at the end of it she developed appendicitis, thus losing the chance of a trans-continental flight she had been offered.

When she arrived in Los Angeles during her convalescence, Lancaster introduced her to a young American aviator named Gentry Shelton with whom he had established a warm friendship. Shelton, of good family and background, cultured and amusing, and of an adventurous nature, had got himself into financial difficulties, and when his father refused for once to come to the rescue Lancaster had helped him out. But Shelton had other assets in addition to his charm; he owned a Lockheed cabin monoplane which his father had bought for him—although he had hired it out temporarily to a company in New York—and there was a good chance that if a sound business proposition could be put forward, his father might help still further.

What Lancaster had in mind, after the air races, was to establish a flying school in Miami, and possibly to buy an amphibian and run a charter service to Havana, the Bahamas, and the Keys. He and Chubbie were well-known in Miami, which would provide the goodwill, and they would look to Gentry Shelton and his father to furnish the aircraft, entering into partnership with Gentry. They left Los Angeles immediately after Christmas in an old black Lincoln car which Jack Maddox had given Lancaster as a farewell bonus, taking Shelton with them as far as New Orleans; there he left them to visit his family in St Louis and to go on by train to New York to get the Lockheed. There was no formal agreement between them, but they shook hands ceremonially when they said goodbye at New Orleans, and Shelton, who had become firmly attached to Lancaster, promised to bring the Lockheed down to Miami in time for the air meet due to start on January 7th, and to sound his father on the purchase of a second plane.

Meanwhile Chubbie, in the hope that Kiki would finally agree to divorce Bill, had gone ahead with her own divorce, which had come through in June of that year. Her husband had treated her with consideration, the grounds were desertion, and there was no scandal. Kiki, however, continued to resist all pleas for a divorce from Bill. According to what she told her children in later years, she still retained the hope that Bill would one day get over his wanderlust and return to them; the extent of his devotion to Chubbie she simply did not appreciate until later. The possibility that he might be able to divorce Kiki occurred to both Bill and Chubbie, and they discussed the problem many times; but they both ruled out any action which might result in hurting the children. Thus the marriage that Chubbie and Bill had looked forward to for nearly five years seemed as remote as ever.

The effect on Chubbie, who was now free to marry when and whom she chose, was greater perhaps than the effect on Lancaster. The fact that Chubbie was now free while he remained hopelessly tied was certainly disturbing; but for him, just to have Chubbie around was enough. He worshipped her, and so long as he could not get a divorce himself he was content for things to go on as they were. Because of their prominence in the world of aviation, and because of the social climate of the time, they were still unable to live a satisfactory life together, but the opportunities they found for being alone were sufficient for Lancaster. In a man's world, it was an acceptable mode of living. But for Chubbie it was different. The hopelessness of their situation depressed her, and there were times when she longed for the protection and security of married life, something she was beginning to realize she would never get from Bill. His wife, she felt sure, would never divorce him. Thus Chubbie's love, real as it was, was beginning to be blurred by disillusion; the old magic had gone. Yet her life was linked inextricably to Lancaster's, as lover, partner, and friend. And overshadowing everything else was the need to make a living; so she fell in enthusiastically with the plan to go to Miami.

The first thing they had to do when they reached Miami was to rent a house; their savings would not keep them long in a hotel. They rented a

The House in Miami

small bungalow and took in a Major Jack French as a paying guest—the man who had acted for Chubbie in Miami and who now offered himself as their business manager. In this *ménage à trois* the proprieties were satisfied, the convention of the era being that three could live as blamelessly as one. Then, on New Year's Day, 1932, their new landlady asked if they would care to move to another property which she thought might suit them better, and when they inspected it they were enthusiastic. It was a delightful place, pleasant to look at, light and well ventilated, set in an orchard of grapefruit and lemon trees, surrounded by jacaranda trees and hibiscus, with windows exquisitely framed in bougainvilia and jasmine. Situated in the residential Coral Gables area at 2321 S.W. 21st Terrace, it stood in an acre of ground, and the nearest house, which they could just see through the trees, was some distance away. They took the house in Chubbie's name for twelve months at $45 a month.

The main features of the house were a large lounge which filled the entire frontage except for an open car-port to the right of it which ran from front to back. Behind the lounge, through an archway on the left, was a small dining-room, and next to that a kitchen; at the back on the right was a good-sized bedroom and a small bathroom. An open-tread staircase wound upwards from the right-hand rear of the lounge, and a large bedroom and bathroom lay over the top of most of the lounge and dining-room. A door at the right-hand end of the landing led into a huge sleeping-porch above the car-port, again running from front to back. Chubbie had the large bedroom upstairs, Jack French the downstairs bedroom, and Lancaster moved into the sleeping-porch, where there were four single beds, two side by side at each end.

After five years of being almost continually on the move, with nothing more than hotels and a small apartment in New York to call home, Chubbie was delighted with the house, and this was reflected at once in her outlook. She was surprised at the pleasure she got from the responsibility of running her own place. A home had seemed to matter so little to her when she was flying or touring, but the feeling of substance and security that the house gave her, even with very little money to run it, gave her a new contentment. Lancaster too seemed to want to settle down and make a home for Chubbie, as an entry in his diary on the day of the move showed. "This time I really believe it will be for a lasting period . . . Chubbie and I have decided to take out American citizenship papers . . . Chubbie seems so happy over the house. She is her old sweet self again."

That night, January 2nd, there was a brief cable from Gentry Shelton to say he was in Columbus, but no news of when he was bringing the plane. "Damn Gentry!" wrote Lancaster two days later, when there was still no news of him and the Lockheed. "We telegraph him imploring him to communicate—but no reply."

Meanwhile the flying fraternity was arriving for the air races, and Bill and Chubbie met many old friends. There was a big party that night at the house. "They are here for a good time and get very tight," wrote Lancaster. Several of the party stayed the night in the sleeping-porch, which was obviously going to prove invaluable. Next day the party picked up again where it left off, and later that evening, when Chubbie was driving one of the guests back to his hotel in the Lincoln, with Lancaster sitting in the back, she bumped into a Buick. "To save Chubbie's face I declare I was driving the car, and as a result the police, acting on complaint from driver, say I was drunk. As a matter of fact I had not had a drink." Next day Lancaster was fined $50 and had his licence suspended, which, taking his perjury into account, was no more than he deserved. But he complained about it all the same. "American justice", he wrote, "is all wet."

In spite of an exciting display by Army and Navy aircraft, led by Jimmy Doolittle, the air meet was poorly attended and proved a financial failure, symptomatic of the widespread depression that was affecting the whole of America, and of an inevitable waning of public interest in sporting aviation. Bill and Chubbie were unable to borrow a plane locally, and there was still no news from Gentry Shelton. On the second day of the meeting, Lancaster read an item in the paper which explained why: the Lockheed had crashed in Pennsylvania and killed the two pilots who were flying it. Fortunately Shelton had not been one of them; he was still in New York.

The air races, the reunion with old friends, the drinks and the parties, provided an illusion of well-being in the first ten days of January that reality could not sustain. Living in Miami was cheap, and the climate was superb, which made up for a lot; but by mid-January they were beginning to realize just how far off the map they were. There seemed no prospect at all of a flying job, and the only source that seemed to offer any hope in those early days of 1932 was an old flying acquaintance of Lancaster's named Captain Frank Upton (a war-time officer in the U.S. Navy and holder of the Congressional Medal of Honor), and his wife Dorothy, whom they had met in 1928 when, as Dorothy Putnam, first wife of G. P. Putnam, she had entertained them in New York. The Uptons lived at near-by Fort Pierce and were trying to find Lancaster a job, but they did not pretend to be optimistic. Meanwhile his finances dwindled to nothing. "It's a sort of helpless feeling, this utter lack of cash," he wrote in his diary. "Chubbie still the best little sport over matters, but she is blue too." Chubbie was putting a bright face on it, but deep down she saw little hope of improvement, and no chance of breaking out of the situation which imprisoned her. She had no conscious thought of leaving Lancaster—that did not occur to her. They meant far too much to each other. It was just that her normally gay, vivacious disposition was beginning to be subdued by frustration and resentment, a resentment that she could not help directing at times against Lancaster.

In the past they had both made good money out of writing about their adventures, and they tried again now, submitting their work hopefully to the aviation and adventure magazines. Meanwhile frequent placation of their landlady became necessary; they had agreed to pay her six months' rent in advance but had so far paid her three months only. Their "paying" guest, Jack French, failed to come up with his share of the advance rental and proved to be even more broke than they were. They husbanded their remaining cash as best they could, and there were times when Lancaster actually went foraging for food in the neighbourhood. The occasional stray chicken from some near-by smallholding could be picked up without much danger.

At last Gentry Shelton phoned to say that he had acquired a Curtiss Robin aircraft; he was speaking from Floyd Bennett airport in New York, and he said he would be in Miami within two days. But after a further delay Lancaster began to feel that his best course was to go to New York and if necessary fly the Robin back himself. The possession of an aeroplane was their only hope of making money. After trying unsuccessfully to get a lift from Miami in a plane he pawned his watch to help with the fare and took the train to Jacksonville. At Jacksonville airport he drew another blank, so he took the bus for New York, arriving there two days later. He soon found Shelton, who explained that he had been held up by a number of complicated business matters. Lancaster too had business matters to take up, mostly debts which he hoped to collect; but the people to whom he had lent money in the good days proved to be even worse off now than he was. He did manage to collect on one or two small loans, enabling him to send ten dollars to Chubbie.

The morning after his arrival in New York, Sunday, January 24th, Lancaster got Shelton up early and took him out to Floyd Bennett field to try out the plane. It was a high-wing cabin monoplane, powered by a 185 h.p. Curtiss Challenger radial engine, giving a cruising speed of 102 m.p.h. and a range of 300 miles. "The Robin is not new by any means," he noted. Next day Shelton left by train for St Louis to see his father, leaving Lancaster to clear up affairs in New York, and promising to wire him some cash from St Louis to keep him going. As soon as Lancaster was clear in New York he was to fly the Robin to Miami; to help with expenses he had already found a paying passenger for the flight. But news of an accident to a famous flyer caused this passenger to lose her nerve, and she went by train. "Eddie Stinson has passed away," noted Lancaster, "crashed last night and died this morning. My promised passenger resigns on hearing of Eddie's death." It was a far more personal blow to Bill and Chubbie, who had known Stinson well.

The cash from Gentry Shelton did not materialize, but on February

3rd Lancaster received a money order for $100 from a Miami attorney named Huston: Lancaster did not know it yet, but he was being offered a job. It was a timely windfall: it would pay all his bills in New York and leave him just enough to get back to Miami. He began to feel excited at the prospect of seeing Chubbie, and when he got back to his hotel that evening he found two telegrams asking him to telephone at once. He called her repeatedly, but there was no reply.

How completely the barometer of his mind was now governed by the pressures of his relationship with Chubbie is shown by the entry he made in his diary as he waited by the telephone: "Am in a cold sweat.... What can it be? God, if anything has happened to her I shall suffer as I have never suffered in my whole life." Then he began to rationalize. "It cannot be bad, otherwise she would not be out till 1." But he continued to wait by the phone, and at last he got through. "Just talked to Chubbie. Gee! It was wonderful to hear her voice. I love her more than my very life. I think she needs me. If I did not think this I would give my life to make her happy."

Chubbie told him of a visit she had had from a representative of a small independent company called Latin-American Airways who wanted them both as pilots, and she urged him to hurry back to meet him. She also mentioned a letter she had received from a firm of New York publishers expressing interest in a book on her flying experiences, and she added that she had met a possible 'ghost' writer who was prepared to work with her. Momentous as the news was, it was dwarfed for Lancaster by the sound of Chubbie's voice and the knowledge that reunion with her was near, and he made no reference to either opportunity in his diary.

Unable to sleep with excitement, he was up at six next morning. The weather was bad, too bad to fly that day as it turned out, but he spent the morning repaying various loans accumulated in the previous ten days and phoning or visiting friends to say goodbye. Some months earlier he had sold one of his stories to *Liberty Magazine* for $250, and he lunched with the agent concerned to discuss further stories and articles. Killing time later at the Army and Navy Club, he got into a bridge four and won six dollars. Perhaps the luck really had changed. He had suggested to the Club that they cancel his membership because he couldn't pay his half-yearly dues, but they told him many of their oldest members were in the same position and to pay when he could.

He got away from New York next morning, but it was a disappointing day. The engine of the Robin was in poor shape, missing badly, and he had to make three forced landings before lunch with plug trouble. He struggled on to Washington, where he looked up old friends at the naval headquarters, and next morning they fitted a new set of plugs in the Robin at a cost of $24, which meant that he was broke again. The engine, however, ran much better, and he made a four-hour flight to Florence in South Carolina. His article had meanwhile appeared in *Liberty Magazine*, and an oil-company man at the airport who had read it made a fuss of him and took him home to dinner. It was quite like old times.

When he got into Jacksonville next day he was short of gas, with no money to pay for refuelling, but the airport manager trusted him with $10 worth. He cabled Chubbie that he was coming, and after a delightful flight down the Florida coast he was very deflated not to see her at the airport to meet him. Instead he was greeted by two strangers—a slim man in naval uniform, swarthy and hirsute, who introduced himself as Captain Mark Tancrel, formerly of the U.S. Navy, and a woman, a Mrs J. F. Russell. A lot had been happening, it seemed, while he was away.

Lancaster's first impression of Tancrel was not very favourable: he didn't measure up to Lancaster's idea of a captain in the U.S. Navy, and Lancaster couldn't help being suspicious of this claim. But the man seemed to have a firm proposition to put forward. "We want you to fly to Mexico almost immediately—in the next couple of days," said Tancrel. "We'll tell you all about it back at the house."

Next morning, Monday, February 8th, a formal meeting took place in the offices of Ernest H. Huston, the Miami attorney, attended by Tancrel, an associate of Tancrel's named J. F. Russell, Bill Lancaster, Chubbie Miller, and Huston. An agreement was signed under which "Captain Lancaster and Mrs J. M. Keith-Miller, on behalf of themselves and Captain Shelton, agree to furnish for the uses and purposes of Latin-American Airways Incorporated, a corporation, two aeroplanes of the type which they now possess, with particular reference to their use in Mexico and other points which the business of the company may require. Said planes to be used and piloted by Captain Lancaster or such other pilots as may be agreed by the parties hereto, and for such length of time as the parties hereto may deem advisable." In return, Lancaster and Chubbie, in addition to travelling and other expenses, were each to receive one-sixth of the net profits derived from trips made by them or by the use of their planes. The agreement was executed subject to the approval of Gentry Shelton Jr; in the event of his disagreement it would be void. Shelton was still in St Louis but was expected in Miami; Lancaster was confident that between them they would be able to raise the finance for a second plane. Shelton too was to receive one-sixth of the net profits plus expenses, and Lancaster was sure he would agree.

In spite of the aura of legality conveyed by the formal signing of the agreement, Lancaster was even more doubtful of Tancrel—"a terrible story-teller," he noted in his diary, "all lies." However, on Tancrel's behalf Huston came through with a payment of $25 for immediate expenses, and Tancrel, after a flight with Lancaster in the Robin, authorized certain essential repairs at the company's expense. Lancaster had confidence in

Huston, the attorney, and thought Russell and his wife were probably sound. To Lancaster's query as to what sort of passengers or freight they would be carrying, and whether any infringement of United States law would be involved, Tancrel assured him that all the flying would be done in Mexico, without crossing the United States border; but on the subject of what they would be carrying he was less specific. It would be up to Russell, he said, to work up a connection. Next day Russell left Mexico to act as Tancrel's agent and organize business. All he could do, Lancaster decided, was to string along with Tancrel and see what developed.

On the other project which had developed while he was away—Chubbie's book—he was more enthusiastic. During his absence Chubbie had met a woman called Mrs Ida Clarke at a tea-party, and Mrs Clarke, formerly a magazine editor and now professor of journalism at Miami University, had suggested her son Haden as a possible ghost-writer. The day after the meeting in Huston's office, Clarke came to the house to discuss the proposition. Chubbie, who had already met him and who had her reservations about him, left it to Lancaster to decide whether he was the right man for the job and on what basis they should work.

Charles Haden Clarke was a young man of extraordinary good looks and charm, tall, sensitive, and highly literate, with dark wavy hair and arresting blue eyes. Chubbie's reservations amounted almost to antipathy, though she liked his mother immensely; but Lancaster took to him at once. "Meet Haden Clarke, a writer," he noted in his diary. "First impression very good." Clarke told Lancaster that he was thirty-one, was a graduate of Columbia University and had an M.A. degree, that he had been on the staff of *Good Housekeeping* magazine, and that he had had newspaper experience, but that due to the depression he was temporarily out of work, and, at the moment, flat broke. It was a predicament with which Lancaster could readily sympathize. Clarke said he was married, but was awaiting a divorce. He outlined his plans for writing the book, stressing that his aim would be to write it as Chubbie herself would write it, in her own words and in the first person. To achieve this effect he would need to spend as much time as possible with her.

Lancaster for his part was equally frank about their own financial situation. It would be impossible to pay Clarke a salary or offer him an advance, he said, but if he produced an acceptable book he could have a fifty per cent share in the royalties. To relieve his present situation, and to give him the access he needed to Chubbie, he could stay at the house for nothing while the book was being written. Clarke agreed, and he moved in next day.

Meanwhile Jack French, still unable to pay his way, had moved out; and Lancaster, looking ahead to the time when he would leave for Mexico and Chubbie and Clarke would be left together, suggested to Clarke that

The House in Miami

his mother, who Chubbie had learnt was also in financial difficulties, might like to move in as well. Chubbie was keen on the idea, which had obvious advantages, but Clarke demurred; he got along all right with his mother, he declared, so long as they kept apart. So the idea was not pursued.

There was no word from Russell, but meanwhile, as Lancaster noted in his diary, there was much to be thankful for. The house was beautifully situated, Miami quickly got into the blood, and in the middle of the New York winter they were swimming in the sunshine. Chubbie, as always, was adorable. "Future unknown," he wrote, "but what the hell!"

CHAPTER VII

Destination Mexico

SUNDAY, February 14th, was Lancaster's thirty-fourth birthday, and he spent the day on Miami Beach with Tancrel, Clarke, and Chubbie. Tancrel seemed to be doing his best to please him, and the money situation had been slightly eased by the cash advances he had made, though they still owed $150 to their landlady. There was still no news from Russell, and Tancrel's money too appeared to be running out. Chubbie, like Lancaster, still distrusted Tancrel, and Lancaster decided it was time to check up on him. His friends in the naval department in Washington would surely help. He wrote and asked them to check if Tancrel's name was on the reserve list, and the reply was that there was no trace of it; it seemed likely that Tancrel was an impostor. Lancaster showed the letter first to Huston, the attorney, and then confronted Tancrel with it. "They lost my records at Washington," explained Tancrel, "when the Bureau of Records burned." Lancaster remembered hearing something about such a fire, but he remained sceptical, although Tancrel showed him letters and documents indicating that he was a lieutenant-commander—not a captain—in the U.S. naval reserve. In better times Lancaster would have pulled out; but he had accepted money from Tancrel, and he felt he couldn't sever the connection without returning the money, which he was quite unable to do.

Gentry Shelton arrived, and with nothing else to occupy his mind spent much of his time drinking. Haden Clarke especially showed a weakness for drink. Lancaster, who was test-flying the Robin, drank less than the others. Chubbie joined in the parties and drank her share, but her disillusion mounted. All she seemed to be doing was feeding a bunch of perfectly able-bodied men who were making no effort to work but preferred to lounge about the house and live virtually on her.

So the month of February passed—not entirely unpleasantly, but in a general atmosphere of suspicion and doubt, punctuated by parties whenever drink was available, interspersed with pleas and cajolery and small remittances to pacify the landlady, and enlivened by occasional fishing and swimming outings and nocturnal foragings in search of food. The main development in this period was the growing friendship between Lancaster and Haden Clarke. They roomed together in the sleep-out above the car-port. Together they discussed Chubbie's book. Together they dissected the plans and character of Tancrel and Russell and tried to make out what their game was. And together they played bridge at the Miami Bridge Club. It began with one or two boring afternoons when they cut in with other partners. Then one afternoon they played together for the first time in a set game, for stakes of a dollar a hundred. They won $32.50, and another $38 four days later, and their luck continued. When the landlady arrived one morning in belligerent mood, obviously intent on getting them out, Lancaster was able to pay off the balance of the advance rent. They were secure now for at least another four months.

All this Chubbie watched with mixed feelings. It was nice to see the rent paid off; but to her initial antipathy towards Clarke was now added a resentment at the way he and Bill attached themselves to each other and disappeared for hours on end. When was Haden going to get down to the book? That was what he was there for, that was why she was feeding and housing him, that was to be the real money-spinner. They had one or two sessions on it together, when she talked about her life and flying experiences, but Haden never seemed to do any writing, nor did he take notes. Once or twice she heard his typewriter going up in the sleeping-porch, but he never produced any drafts for her to see. Bill still showed confidence in him, but Chubbie began to have her doubts.

Clarke's behaviour, indeed, while not perhaps abnormal for an unattached young man, was not such as to reassure Chubbie. Lancaster seemed to attract and to be attracted by these slightly immature and disorganized young men, and he tolerated Haden Clarke and his misdemeanours much as he tolerated Gentry Shelton. In addition to his bouts of drinking, Clarke seemed to have several women friends, one of whom, unknown to Chubbie, stayed the night at the house more than once. This girl, called Peggy Brown, clearly hoped to marry him. And once or twice, when something annoyed him, he displayed a more than normally excitable temperament; an outstanding instance of this was when an acquaintance of theirs to whom Clarke owed money took the tyres off his car in part payment. Clarke's anger bordered on the hysterical. The fact that he couldn't get on with his mother, whom Chubbie had found an intelligent and reasonable person, was also revealing. Chubbie, however, was quite determined to pin him down to the book as soon as Bill and the others had gone. There would be all the time in the world then; and if Haden didn't get on with the book as she had a right to expect, she would find someone else.

On March 3rd, the day after Lancaster paid off the landlady, Tancrel asked Lancaster to leave at once for Mexico. He had heard from Russell, he said, and everything was fixed. But in spite of his bridge winnings Lancaster was still virtually without money. The electricity company had disconnected the supply because of an unpaid account, and he had boiled the water for the coffee that morning on a fire he lit in the back garden. There was a substantial telephone bill to pay too; that would be the next thing to be disconnected. He didn't intend to leave until these matters were settled and some provision was made for Chubbie, and he flatly refused to go. Tancrel was furious, and continued to press him to leave, warning him that they would lose valuable contracts if they delayed, but Lancaster was adamant. Eventually Tancrel promised to find a sum of $25 to leave with Chubbie; it was all he could manage, he said. Lancaster agreed to take off as soon as this sum was paid over. Tancrel also promised him a salary of $100 a week, to be recovered afterwards from his and Chubbie's share in the profits, and he pointed out that from this figure Lancaster would be able to send regular sums to Chubbie once they started work in Mexico.

On the morning of March 5th, the day before they were scheduled to leave, Lancaster had a long confidential talk with Clarke in the sleeping-porch. He was aware that in leaving Clarke with the woman he loved he was placing him in a position of trust. He had often talked to Clarke about his past adventures with Chubbie, but Clarke, so far as he was aware, knew nothing of any deeper relationship between them. Now Lancaster spelt out to Clarke his great love for Chubbie and how much she meant to him, more than his very life.

Lancaster trusted Chubbie absolutely; but he was naturally concerned at the prospect of leaving her alone for an indefinite period with someone they had known for so short a time. He urged Clarke again to ask his mother to join him, but Clarke dismissed this as impossible for him. Lancaster knew that Clarke was heavily engaged with Peggy Brown, and he also knew that Chubbie was not attracted to him, but he feared that Clarke's drinking and general way of life might be an embarrassment to Chubbie and even perhaps a bad influence. Clarke gave his faithful promise that he would behave moderately, concentrate on the book, and take the greatest care of Chubbie while Lancaster was away.

Lancaster and Clarke won another $17.50 at bridge that afternoon, and the electricity bill was paid and the supply reconnected. That night Gentry Shelton went out on a final spree. Arrangements for the trip were complete, said Tancrel, and he told them that their final destination would be Nogales, the border town where Arizona spilled over into Mexico, a distance of some 2500 miles. Lancaster estimated that the flight would take them three to four days. Next day they all drove to the airport in Lancaster's Lincoln—Lancaster, Chubbie, Tancrel, Shelton, Clarke, and Peggy Brown. There had been a heavy storm during the night and the weather was still unsettled, but they were anxious to get away.

Chubbie, although encouraging Lancaster to go, made him promise that he would have no part in anything illegal; her suspicions of Tancrel remained strong.

Soon after take-off the weather deteriorated, until Lancaster found himself flying into the teeth of a gale. After three and a half hours of hard flying they had covered only 175 miles, and Lancaster was forced to land at Sarasota, out of fuel. His muscles ached with holding the plane on course, but his passengers, sitting side by side behind him, seemed unconcerned: Shelton was sleeping off a hangover, Tancrel ate bananas and oranges and chattered incessantly, to Lancaster's growing irritation. He found he needed full engine for the landing, and when they got down he learnt that the wind speed at ground level was 50 m.p.h. He knew it would be dangerous to leave the Robin exposed to such a wind, but the airport management, fearing damage to their own property, refused to open the hangar, so Lancaster took on more gas and made for St Petersburg, 18 miles farther north. St Petersburg itself was partly under water—houses had been blown away and coast roads were being swept by the sea—but Lancaster landed safely and they got the Robin into a hangar for the night.

At the Commodore Hotel in St Petersburg Lancaster tried to telephone Chubbie, only to be told that her telephone was out of order. He sent her a cable to say where he was, and also wrote her a letter in which he reminded her to attend to one or two outstanding matters—the interest on his pawned watch, the telephone bill (which Huston had agreed to pay because Latin-American Airways had used the number as an office telephone), and the collection of the rent for Chubbie's apartment in New York. (This apartment, rented unfurnished and let furnished, provided Chubbie with a small but regular income.) In spite of his preoccupations with the flight he was methodical enough not to forget these details, which suggests that in his years in America he had developed into a much more mature and responsible person than hitherto. He was also, perhaps, more introverted: there is no evidence that he was such a confirmed diarist in earlier years. "Give my very best to Haden," he concluded, "keep sober and write the book. All my love, Chubbie, sweetest. Sending daily letter, please do the same." He asked her to address all her letters care of Postmaster, Nogales, where he would pick them up on arrival in two or three days' time.

They took off from St Petersburg at six o'clock next morning and flew throughout the day except for three brief stops to refuel, reaching Beaumont, Texas, that evening in a total flying time of eleven and a half hours. In spite of more headwinds in the early part of the flight they had covered nearly a thousand miles in the day. But the Challenger engine had been throwing a lot of oil, and they arranged to have a mechanic check it over in the morning, which would inevitably mean a later start. Lancaster wired and wrote Chubbie as before, giving her all the news. "Tancrel has only just got enough to get the troops to Nogales," he told her, "so have not been able to get any cash to send." He did, however, show willing. "Don't laugh at the dollar, but it will put five gallons of gas in the Lincoln."

The mechanic at Beaumont found a thrust bearing gone on the engine, and they were held up all next day while the repair was effected. Lancaster arranged to have the engine warmed up for them next morning for a dawn take-off, but when they got to the field they found that the mechanic had started the Robin up tail into wind with the result that the plane had nosed over and badly bent both propeller blades. They managed to borrow a replacement, and Lancaster cabled Chubbie to send direct to Nogales a spare propeller of hers that he had stored at Miami. They got away at midday and flew 400 miles to San Angelo, on the rolling Texas prairie, and next morning they were up at five o'clock and out at the airfield before daylight, but the temperature was five degrees below zero and the engine wouldn't start; they exhausted themselves turning it over. Then at midday it snowed heavily, putting flying out of the question for the day. Meanwhile Chubbie had sent the propeller to Nogales and wired Lancaster that she had done so. Lancaster wrote to her that night: "Old man Gent has been a brick; he has not taken a drink since leaving Miami. Tancrel is well subdued and not so annoying. The cold has frozen him up." In his diary he noted: "Wire from Chubbie, thank God. God bless her, how dear she is to me."

The weather next morning was still bad but Gentry wanted to push on and Lancaster agreed. They had lost far too much time already, and with money short the quicker they got to their destination the better. They covered the 100 miles to Midland, refuelled, and then set a compass course for El Paso on the Mexican border, nearly 300 miles distant. Soon after they left Midland it began to snow.

Between them and El Paso lay first the Pecos River and then the Guadalupe Mountains, rising to more than 8500 feet. They were just crossing the mountain peaks, with not very much height to spare, when the engine started to knock. Lancaster described the whole incident in a letter to Chubbie next day.

IN THE MOUNTAINS:
GUADALUPE PUMP STATION
TEXAS
March 12, 1932

MY DARLING,
   One of the American Airways ships has forced landed at the emergency field here this afternoon so I am rushing this letter to get news to you. . . .

Yesterday we took off from San Angelo, Texas, trying to get through to El Paso. It commenced snowing after we left Midland on a direct compass course for El Paso.

When we were approaching the mountains halfway the visibility became nil. Gent was flying at the time.

Just as we were approaching the mountain ridge the old Challenger belched forth all the oil in the tank. It completely covered all forward windshields in blackness and things looked very bad. Oil pressure dropped, oil temp. went right over as far as the needle would go.

The engine thumped like a thrashing machine. Revs. dropped to 1200. Gent did a masterly piece of work. Very carefully he turned, about 20 feet over a mountain peak, and commenced a 20-mile trip back to the emergency field we had just passed. Gradually we lost height. Gent was completely blind forward. I opened windows and stuck my head out one side and yelled instructions.

Tancrel lost his head a bit, and tried to jump out!

After what seemed a year we staggered into the field and landed O.K. Tancrel hired a car and drove 126 miles to El Paso, and sent a mechanic out during the night.

Today Gent, the mechanic, and I have worked on the engine. It has snowed hard all the time. We have been working in an open field and are completely frozen stiff....

Tancrel certainly has had an experience which will hold him for a while. It has been my narrowest escape since my crash in Trinidad.

Wish you were here. All my thoughts and love sweetheart.

Yours,

BILL

The mechanic sent out by Tancrel from El Paso, named Harry Middleton, proved to be a first-class man, and he worked with Lancaster on the engine for two days; but at the end of that time both men had reluctantly to admit that it was beyond them to repair it on the spot and that it would have to be dismantled and taken on to El Paso. Meanwhile Russell and a man named McKinley, an associate of Russell's, had driven back from Nogales to El Paso in a Chevrolet belonging to Tancrel; there they picked up Tancrel and drove through the mountains to the pump station. After loading the engine into the boot, the whole party then drove into El Paso, where the engine was stripped and two broken pistons, a cracked crankcase, and two cracked cylinders were revealed. Tancrel sold his Chevrolet —for $200 and an old Dodge—to help with running expenses, but repairing the Challenger would cost $450; they could get a new one for less. The only hope was for Shelton to ask his father to put up the money for a new engine, and this, to keep his part of the bargain, he agreed to do. Shelton's father was ready to help, an engine was located, and arrangements were made to have it delivered to El Paso.

While Lancaster and Tancrel stayed at El Paso to await the engine,

F

Russell, McKinley, and Shelton went ahead to Nogales to look for business. The days passed drearily for Lancaster, Tancrel getting more and more on his nerves with his chatter, stories, and stream of jokes. Suspecting as he did that Tancrel was little more than a crook, he was puzzled by his relaxed, confident air. Tancrel in fact was a curious mixture of childishness and flamboyance. Of mixed British and French blood, he had been born in Mauritius, as they later learnt; and the convolutions of his mind and character were no less difficult to trace and unravel. Yet Lancaster could not help being amused by him at times. With the manager of the Hotel Sussman, where they were staying, pressing for payment of their account, Tancrel's reaction was to try to sell him stock in Latin-American Airways. And there was a hilarious occasion in the hall of the hotel before the others left for Nogales when Tancrel suddenly pointed in disgust to a bad join in the wallpaper. "I've hanged thousands of square miles of wallpaper," he announced. When Lancaster and Shelton refused to believe him he took a card from his wallet and passed it round; it was a union card from the Wallpaper Hangers' Union of Washington, D.C., and it bore the name of Mark G. Tancrel. Clearly this was a man of many parts; but for Lancaster and Shelton the incident finally convinced them that Tancrel's pose as a former U.S. naval captain was ridiculous.

Lancaster's main concern, however, was Chubbie—the almost complete lack of news of her, and the knowledge that she was short of money and that he could do nothing about it. According to their original plan, he should have been in Mexico by now, sending her money regularly. Apart from the cable he had heard nothing from her. Shelton had promised to readdress the letters that must surely be waiting for him at Nogales, but nothing came. On March 14th he wrote to Haden Clarke. "Am terribly worried on her [Chubbie's] account. Haden, old man, the knowledge that you are 'standing by' the fort and looking after Chubbie has meant more to me than you will ever know. As soon as you get this tell me frankly if I should beg, borrow or steal my way back to Miami."

"Tonight I am more than just worried," he wrote in his diary on Friday, March 18th, twelve days after leaving Miami, "I am plumb crazy, all because of no news from Chubbie." The only thing that made life tolerable was that he had run into an old war-time RAF acquaintance named Joe Ince, who next day acted as his host. "Ince proves himself to be a real good fellow," he wrote. "Were it not for the Miami news being on my mind I might have spent an amusing evening." He was glad to be able to do a small service for Ince in return. "Ince comes along and sleeps on the floor of our room to save expenses!"

By Sunday, March 20th, a fortnight after leaving Miami, Lancaster was utterly disillusioned with Latin-American Airways. "I have completely lost faith in the ability of Russell and Tancrel to produce any legitimate business worth while," he wrote in his diary, "and I have not the slightest intention of doing anything dishonest or breaking the laws of the U.S.A." Before Russell left for Nogales he had tried to persuade Lancaster to run two Chinamen over the border in a borrowed plane, and Tancrel too had made oblique reference to similar operations. For Lancaster, in his low financial state, with the depression of his spirit further aggravated by idleness, the temptation had been real, but he had resisted it. He wrote of his concern and boredom to Chubbie. "Darling, you know how much I love you, so you must realize what a ghastly thing it is for me to have no money to send you. I was much better mentally when I had work to do such as flying here, and working on the engine. The waiting around is the worst side of life."

The uncertainty about Tancrel's plans and integrity remained his other main source of worry, but as he pointed out to Chubbie, "Until Gent and I get on the spot we can't tell whether any of these Latin-American people are speaking the truth." He would simply have to await arrival of the new engine; and in any case he could not abandon Gentry. At least his judgment had proved correct there. "Old man Gent has not taken a drink since we left Miami," he noted. "He has been splendid throughout, and I am quite fond of the old boy." But if he had had the money, nothing would have stopped him from taking the train to Miami and Chubbie and talking things over with her. "I miss you and long for you, my sweetheart," he wrote. "I lie in bed at night and pray you are not suffering too great a hardship. I want to have you in my arms again, Chub. I love you more and more each moment of my life."

Lancaster's love for Chubbie, indeed, dominated his life and thoughts so much that it was in danger of becoming an obsession, draining him of his normal personality. The carefree extrovert of Halton days had become oppressed and introspective. Suppose, because of his absence and his inability to provide for her, he should lose Chubbie altogether? Such a possibility aroused in him the bile of desperation. That night, March 20th, he went to bed but could not sleep. He had not forgotten his promise to Chubbie before leaving Miami, but desperate situations called for desperate remedies. He knew that if he mentioned to Chubbie the project Russell had put to him she would oppose it uncompromisingly; but in the long run their happiness might be better served if he took the risk. He had spoken on the phone to Gentry Shelton in Nogales, and Shelton was beginning to feel that they probably had no alternative but to fall in with Russell's plan. Thus the pressure on Lancaster was mounting. Now he decided to sound out Haden Clarke, who was on the spot and could gauge Chubbie's likely reaction without actually posing the question direct. At five o'clock that morning he got up and wrote to Clarke:

> This for you only. Haden, old man, I cannot sleep, so I have decided to express the thoughts running through my mind. . . .

You know I am devoted to Chubbie. For her I would do anything, if necessary risk anything. . . . Now we are within reach of some cash if I like to take a chance and make a little trip with an unmentionable cargo. Gent has weakened and thinks we must go ahead in the manner Russell suggests.

It appears to me that Russell has made sound arrangements to handle the ground operations. I have the necessary training and equipment to carry out the air operations.

Because of our newly formed friendship for each other, I am asking you to assist me as far as possible. Write me, as fully as possible, your ideas after going over such evidence as you have. There may be a way of your obtaining Chubbie's reaction without fully disclosing the hand.

For me, life would be very empty if I lost Chubbie. To me, she is the all-important thing. If I thought my return to Miami in a penniless condition would mean the possibility of losing the kid I would take even greater chances to return with money than might be prudent.

Again, if I felt that I could embark on an enterprise with the knowledge that should things go wrong there would be at least one true friend who would make it as easy as possible for Chubbie, I would possibly be influenced in my decision if and when the time came. . . . Whatever course I take I want to do the best for Chubbie, for by so doing I do the best for myself.

Although Lancaster was outwardly as firm as ever in resisting all Tancrel's suggestions, it is clear from this letter that the influences to which he was being subjected were becoming more than he could withstand on his own. Most surprising of all to Lancaster—and most persuasive—was Shelton's optimism. Shelton's idea was that they might perhaps have to carry out one such operation, but that they could then revert to legitimate enterprises; he still thought there were genuine possibilities in Mexico.

Shelton had also told Lancaster that the new engine was due to arrive within twenty-four hours, and that he had sent on several letters from Nogales. The letters reached Lancaster next day, three from Chubbie and one from Clarke.

Chubbie had been following Bill's progress across the continent eagerly at first, even with admiration, then with increasing disappointment. Her first letter, written soon after the start of the flight, noted how far they had flown on the second day out. "That's a marvellous flight darling and I do congratulate you. We got the map out and looked it up." But this was about all Chubbie had to enthuse over. The weather was cold, she had raging toothache, there was no money to meet the bills, and there was "not a drop of booze in the house and we can't afford to buy any". Russell's wife, she had discovered, had received funds from Russell; how was it he had been able to send so little? Her worst enemy, though, as with Lancaster, was boredom. "We are bored to sobs and have nowhere to go in the evening—it's hell!" And again: "I do hope you can come back soon, as I'm so lonely here without you." Haden voiced a similar complaint. "Chub and I have been pretty well bored since you left."

But surely, with all this time on their hands, they were getting ahead with the book? "You will probably have put in some really constructive work on the book," wrote Lancaster. Clarke's reply was frank, but he did his best to be reassuring. "I'm disappointed in the progress I have been making with the book, but mother is going up to New York about the 20th and I have promised to have three chapters for her to show publishers by then. I'll deliver." Chubbie, however, was not so sure. "Don't say anything to Haden, but I'm very sceptical about that book being written. He hasn't done one paragraph so far." She suggested he send Haden a note to say that they were all relying on the book to save the family fortunes, and Lancaster did so. "I feel this is the all-important item in the future of Miller Lancaster Haden Clarke Inc.," he wrote.

Somehow, Lancaster felt, he must send Chubbie some money. But he had precisely 40 cents, and Tancrel swore he had no more than two or three dollars. Lancaster thought he knew how Russell had managed to send his wife a more substantial sum. "The money he sent Mrs R was money Tancrel gave him for expenses to go to Nogales, Phoenix, and Tucson," he told Chubbie. "He wired Tancrel for more cash the next day and has written a cock-and-bull story about the car breaking down, etc. Tancrel is furious and even if he had any money he would not send it to Russell." Another mark against Russell was that a letter Lancaster had asked him to mail to Chubbie had not reached her; in Russell's presence Lancaster had put a $5 bill inside. "Russell, I am convinced, would double-cross anyone," he wrote. "I would rather trust Tancrel. He has shown himself to be quite generous hearted. I am sure if he gets anything I shall have a share." He assured Chubbie that if he could get his hands on any amount, however small, he would send it to her.

He had already pawned his watch, and he could think at first of no other assets. Then he remembered that Ernest Huston, the attorney, had lent him a loaded ·38 revolver before he left Miami, hinting that he might be glad to have it by him. Surely he would be able to raise money on that. But several pawnbrokers in El Paso turned him down, complaining that their stores were full of guns. Eventually a taxi-driver lent him three dollars on it, taking the gun as security. He got $1.50 out of Tancrel, and eventually managed to send Chubbie five dollars.

Whatever saving graces Tancrel might have, however, the truth about the expedition was becoming more and more apparent, although Lancaster obstinately closed his eyes to it as far as he could. Tancrel again mentioned the possibility of fording Chinamen across the Mexican border;

they would get $1000 for each one, he said. Tancrel introduced the subject as though it were something that they might consider in an emergency, something quite outside his original plan; but subconsciously Lancaster guessed that this sort of cargo had been in Tancrel's mind all along. Tancrel then dropped another hint: he said he had learnt that Russell's game was dope-smuggling and that a small suitcase filled with 28 pounds of marijuana would fetch $30,000 in San Francisco. Lancaster's reaction was much the same; clearly Tancrel was using Russell as a cloak to hide his own intentions and sound Lancaster out.

Lancaster's confidential letter to Clarke brought an answer by cable on March 25th; Clarke, not unnaturally, had consulted Chubbie. The cable read: "Both advise against contemplated move most emphatically. Abide by original decision to letter. This no time to take chances. Situation not so hot but such steps by no means warranted. You are in dog house on chain if you ignore this regardless of outcome. Writing El Paso, love, regards. Chubbie and Haden."

On receipt of this cable Lancaster again told Tancrel that he would have nothing to do with any illegal project. And a few days later a long and well-argued letter reached him from Clarke. The letter, besides being an indication of Clarke's ability to express himself, revealed a genuine concern for Lancaster. He began by saying that, since Chubbie's suspicions were already aroused to the point of conviction, he had disregarded Lancaster's instructions and put the whole project up to her squarely, and she agreed that under no circumstances should he touch the proposition offered to him. The letter continued:

> The reasons for this are multiple. The risk involved is entirely out of proportion to the gain you can anticipate. The slightest slip would result in your being deported. . . . The amount of money you would make would furnish only temporary relief at best, and would in no wise help you to become permanently established.
>
> You should not let the fact that you are in a tough spot influence you to take a step that you know to be unwise. The worst time in the world to make a foolish step is when you are down to your last stack of chips. You must play every card with the utmost care of which you are capable. . . .
>
> Regardless of what your associates say, and of how rosy the chances may seem, I know perfectly well that there is a very big chance of things going wrong. As a result of all the talking that was done around Miami, the impression is firmly established here that the whole expedition was for this purpose in the first place. . . .
>
> There is just one other thing that you might overlook. You promised Chubbie that you positively would not swerve from your original intention and I am convinced for you to do so would make her most unhappy regardless of the outcome. I appreciate that your one idea in

the whole matter is her welfare and happiness, so since the move must defeat this purpose, what possible argument is there in its favour?

After referring briefly to their own problems in Miami and how he was trying to earn some quick money by writing magazine articles and criticizing manuscripts (the latter occupation, at least, had brought them in a few dollars), Clarke concluded:

> Bill, I can't begin to express my appreciation for the friendship you have repeatedly shown for me. To say that the feeling is mutual is putting it mildly. Nothing in the world would make me happier than to do everything in my power for you and Chubbie. . . . As far as I'm concerned we are playing on the same team from now on, and whatever I have or can get goes into the pot.

It certainly seemed as though Lancaster had been right about Haden Clarke.

The new Challenger engine—it was a reconditioned one—arrived at El Paso on March 25th, but there were collect charges on it of $27. Neither Tancrel nor Lancaster had such a sum, nor could they get within reach of it. "Harry Middleton—mechanic extraordinary—pays this," noted Lancaster in his diary, "and we prepare to go to the hills to get the ship. Tancrel by some unknown means persuades the hotel manager to allow us to leave owing bill, about $95.00." Short of money though he might be, Tancrel was clearly not short of charm.

It was 126 miles by road across the mountains to the Guadalupe Pump Station, and the old Dodge broke down twice on the way, but they finally got there at four o'clock on Saturday afternoon, March 26th. There was a 50 m.p.h. surface wind, and they were unable to do much work, so they turned in early. Lancaster and Middleton got up at four-thirty next morning and worked on the installation of the engine all day. "Those Curtiss-Wright people . . . have sent us an engine—reconditioned but not run. We find the oiling system all shot. More work. Eventually get it running, oil pressure no good. Test ship. It's lousy. Work on engine until late. Turn in exhausted." But Lancaster had nothing but praise for Middleton: ". . . . one of the best field mechanics I have struck in America. Nice personality—doctor's son—bitten by bug of aviation." Lancaster flew on to El Paso across the mountains next day, while Tancrel and Middleton returned in the Dodge. Gasoline for both journeys was obtained at the pump station only with difficulty, and they left owing a bill of ten dollars.

It was a week since Lancaster had heard from Chubbie, and the letters he had received then had been at least seven days old. Whereas he had been cabling and writing her daily, and sending every dollar he could scrape together, she had been silent—apart from her cabled reply to his question about ferrying illegal cargoes, a question he had not in fact intended for her. For Chubbie, the urge to write was blunted by the fact that she could never be sure where Bill was; her earlier letters, she knew, had taken more than a week to reach him. But Lancaster's disappointment at not hearing from her was becoming progressively more bitter. "Chubbie, how are you?" "No letters—Chubbie, you wretch!" "Chubbie —you might at least write occasionally!" "Cannot understand why Chubbie does not write. This is my greatest hardship, the lack of news of her." "No news of Chubbie. She has disappointed me far more than this damned expedition." These were the heartfelt cries he committed to his diary as day succeeded day. Now, back in El Paso, news was awaiting him. First he talked on the telephone to Gentry Shelton in Nogales; Russell had had a letter from his wife, and Chubbie, according to her, was having a gay time in Miami. Lancaster didn't blame her, but it was disturbing. Then he picked up his mail. There was a letter from Chubbie, and a letter from Haden; but they did not contain the assurances for which he hungered. "Very disappointed," he wrote in his diary. "Looks as though Chub has dashed off a note as a sort of duty. Haden a little more enlightening. Hope he is keeping his promise to me, feel sure he is. But Chubbie—Hell!!!"

CHAPTER VIII

Chubbie falls in Love

WITH her practical outlook, Chubbie had tried hard to encourage Haden Clarke to get down to the hard graft of writing the book. When this failed she pointed out, gently but firmly, that she could not go on keeping him unless some progress was made. To all her pleas Haden made much the same answer; everything would be all right, the right way to tackle the book would come to him, he must wait for inspiration. But after five or six inspirationless weeks Chubbie rebelled. Ever since she had moved into the Miami house it seemed to her that she had been keeping a variety of men—perfectly able-bodied men who ought to be bringing money into the home to pay their way. She was thoroughly fed up with it.

Bill, at least, was making a determined attempt to make some money, in the only way he knew. She didn't approve of the crowd he was mixed up with, but she knew well enough that the aviation and business worlds spawned some odd people, and she recognized that Bill and Gentry had no means of testing the good faith of Tancrel and his associates without going to Mexico to see for themselves. Even so, it had been a most unsatisfactory start, and Bill's departure had deepened her feeling of depression. Out of love with him though she might be in the romantic sense, she was still very fond of him, and right up to the time of his departure they had still, however spasmodically, been lovers. Now she was left alone, the remnants of her capital almost gone, faced with the problem of coercing and cajoling a reluctant writer into doing his job.

The first few days after Bill's departure seemed to pass in a vacuum. There was the business of sending the propeller: this bristled with difficulties because the airport people wouldn't at first release it. It belonged to Chubbie, but Lancaster had stored it in his name, and authorization was demanded from him. Then she fulfilled a dental appointment, only to be faced with a bill for previous visits. The outcome of the dentistry—and perhaps of the debt—was that she was again afflicted with raging toothache. In her years in the flying world, with its peaks of excitement and tension, she had become accustomed to a certain amount of drinking. Now there wasn't a drink to be had.

As it became clear that the Latin-American Airways expedition was a wash-out, Chubbie's vexation with Lancaster grew. She had warned him against them, and she could not resist writing to him now to remind him of it. He should never have left without seeing that she was paid her share and ensuring that he had the money to get back himself if things went wrong. To infuriate her still further, garbled accounts of the activities of various members of the party in Nogales and El Paso were reaching her through Mrs Russell, Ernest Huston, and others, and they never seemed to agree with what she heard from Bill. She wrote:

> Please all get together and decide what you are going to wire us in Miami and stick to the same story. Tancrel wires one thing, Gent tells Helen[1] something different, and you tell me something different again. They all phone me up when they get a wire and I simply don't know where I stand. . . . It's very confusing. Also I have been unable to wire you for days as I didn't know where you were. I wired you twice before and the wires came back to me, as you had checked out. I am sorry to have to write such a depressing letter, but I *am* depressed. Am writing very hard so Haden will have all the material he needs for the book. He is without doubt the laziest, slowest writer I have ever seen, but for God's sake don't tell him I said so or he will walk out and leave me alone. He wrote the first chapter (which is very short) but it is incorrect, as he would not take the trouble to read over that stuff I wrote two years ago. I made him read it today and now he has to re-write the first chapter as he sees where he is wrong. The only thing seems to be for me to write the whole thing and then have him re-write it, so this I'm doing. Well, darling, I'm bored, miserable, and lonely. Hurry back, I miss you. Please write me a long, intelligent letter and tell me without exaggeration what your prospects are.

Boredom, indeed, remained Chubbie's worst enemy, and after the first few days she didn't even have a car to get about in and was virtually confined to the house. Haden's car was still minus its tyres, and the battery of the Lincoln, to use Haden's phrase, was "on the blink". He talked frequently about what he would do with the money he made from the book, but he still made little progress with it. Friends of his would call and they would spend hours discussing their work. One man, a writer named Dick Richardson, was working on a play about Rasputin, and this was the subject of endless talk. On the whole Chubbie was no more impressed with Clarke's friends than she had been with the Latin-American Airways people. On one occasion the talk turned to drugs and the smoking of marijuana. "You ought to try it," Haden told her, "you don't know what a wonderful feeling it is." But she refused.

It was nearly three weeks after Bill's departure when Chubbie finally

[1] Helen Jones, Gentry Shelton's girl-friend in Miami.

determined on a show-down with Haden. He had gone to the sleep-out to rewrite the first chapter, and for a time she heard the clack of the typewriter; then there was silence. After a time she went in to ask him what was holding him up. He was sitting back in his chair, gazing out of the window, smoking. Furious, she demanded to know what he was doing, and Clarke, no doubt just as frustrated at his failure as she was, answered with equal vehemence.

"I can't write to order. I've got to have the inspiration to get the thing going. It just hasn't come to me yet. I've got to find the right way to set about it."

The outburst resolved none of their difficulties, but for the moment it cleared the air. Chubbie, in fact, felt almost remorseful. She was subconsciously aware that Haden, although bogged down on the book, was in other respects trying to please her. The few dollars he was able to make in a bridge game or in criticizing manuscripts all went into the running of the home. And in spite of herself she had been impressed by his sincere regard for her and Bill and the thoughtful and attentive consideration he always showed her. That night they had accepted an invitation to a party, and after the boredom that had oppressed them since everyone else had left for Mexico they were looking forward to it.

"What are you going to wear?" asked Haden.

"Oh, just the old black I expect."

"I'd like you to wear the one with the rose on. I like you in that."

Chubbie had hardly known what it was for a man to take that sort of interest in her. It could be just politeness—but it sounded genuine. Bill took such things for granted; he never commented on what she wore. Perhaps he was a more manly man than Haden; but that didn't mean that Haden was effeminate. If she changed her hair style, Bill might comment, but most probably not. Haden, on the other hand, suddenly said he thought he would like her in an Eton crop; she had always worn her hair short for flying, so it was not difficult to straighten it out with water, then cut it and shape it. Haden stood back and admired it. For a woman who had rarely experienced that sort of attention it was warming and flattering.

In her life with Lancaster, Chubbie had been starved of the attention which a wife normally expects. Such attention as she had received had come from the public, the sort of fleeting adulation that left one terribly flat when it was over. There had been plenty of men who had shown that they were attracted to her; but Bill had never let them get too close. As long as Bill was there, the "hands-off" sign was firmly displayed.

There was plenty to drink at the party, and they came back in the early hours, bade each other good-night, and went straight to bed. When she awoke next morning, Chubbie was scandalized to see that Haden was asleep at the foot of her bed. She slipped out of her room before he awoke, but the incident embarrassed them the whole of the next day. That night they were asked out again to drinks with friends, and when they got back Haden said it was too hot to go into the house, and they sat on the lawn and talked. There was a moon, the scent of jasmine was in the air, and Haden referred to what he had done unconsciously the night before. They kissed, and he told her that he loved her.

Chubbie's loneliness, her boredom over the past few weeks, her sense of frustration and dissatisfaction over her life with Bill, her need for protection and security, and Haden's ardent love-making, all helped to convince her that she was in love with him. When Haden asked her next day to marry him, she said yes.

It would be a blow, of course, to Bill, she knew that. She would always be fond of him. But he had no real claim on her. Haden was a young man of good family and background, well educated, even brilliant, according to his mother. The depression was a difficult time for everyone, so she should not be surprised that Haden was no exception. He offered, or would be able to offer, all the permanence and durability of marriage and a home. And just as Lancaster had made the masculine mistake of thinking he could leave a man and a woman alone and rely vaguely on their honour, so Chubbie now made the feminine mistake of thinking that she and Bill could still continue their flying and business partnership, that there need be no question of putting him out of her life. Such an impractical plan was very untypical of Chubbie, who would normally have been the first to see that she couldn't expect to have her cake and eat it. But then she too was in love.

Lancaster's letters, with their references to his love for her, now became an embarrassment. Yet Chubbie did not feel she ought to add to his worries at the moment by telling him the truth; she was aware of the turmoil the news might cause in his mind. It would be kinder and wiser, surely, to wait for his return. Meanwhile her reasoning began to be warped by a subconscious desire to delay that return. On Thursday, March 31st, she wrote: "Having spent so much time and money, not to mention hardships, it seems an awful pity to give up now. If you come back now I don't know what the hell we are going to do. I know you are worried about me, but there is no need to be. . . . Haden simply can't work with you and Gent and all the excitement that went on before. Of course, I miss you like the very devil, but I do want to get this book out. . . . This house was a madhouse before and it was impossible to get anything done. . . . Do weigh it all up carefully, dear, and write me what you think." Later her concern for Lancaster overcame her apprehension and she wrote a second letter urging him to look out for himself, and to get Gentry Shelton to persuade his father to buy the amphibian for operations in the West Indies and South America. Poor Chubbie was hopelessly embroiled.

. . . . .

On Tuesday, March 29th, creeping away from El Paso under great difficulties because of their debts, Lancaster and Tancrel at last took off on the final leg of the flight to Nogales, which they reached after four and a half hours in the air. A journey that they had planned to complete in seventy-two hours had taken twenty-three days. For Lancaster, disillusion with the expedition was almost complete already, but he was still puzzled by the confidence shown by Tancrel, and he retained a lingering hope that the arrival in Nogales might prove his worst suspicions unfounded and that some worthwhile contract might yet be negotiated. He was looking forward too to seeing Gentry Shelton—indeed, the feeling was mutual. "On arrival at Nogales I find that Russell and Gentry have been drinking. Gent seemed so glad to see me, though, that I forgave him." His hopes for the expedition, however, were soon dispelled. "Feel any time now I shall have to put my foot down and call a showdown all round," he wrote in his diary. "Visit Mexico . . . am sure there is nothing legitimate here."

His view was confirmed next day at a conference called by Tancrel, when firm proposals were finally put forward for a programme of the smuggling of aliens carrying dope. Lancaster was to land in the Robin across the Mexican border after dark, pick up several Chinamen, and fly them to a remote spot in Arizona indicated on the map by Russell. Arrangements were complete, continued Russell, for the pick-up in Mexico. All the snags had been covered and there would be no slip-up. The market for getting rid of the dope in San Francisco was good and would remain so. Each one of them—Tancrel, Russell, McKinley, Lancaster, and Shelton—would clear $100,000 dollars within three months. So the truth was out, and Lancaster, disgusted with himself for not trusting his instincts and for being so easily fooled, turned on Tancrel. "I'm going back to Miami," he announced. Shelton backed him up, and for a moment it looked like the end of Latin-American Airways. But Tancrel and Russell still had one or two cards to play. Lancaster and Shelton were broke, Latin-American Airways owed them money, and as long as there seemed any chance of getting it they would be obliged to tag along. They couldn't even start on the flight back east without money.

"I can raise funds in Los Angeles," announced Russell. The entire assets of Latin-American Airways—apart from the Robin—now amounted to $25, which would just buy enough gas and oil for the flight to Los Angeles, but it sounded to Lancaster like a forlorn hope. Yet there seemed no alternative. In addition Tancrel had a passenger for Los Angeles, a Mrs Charles Stewart, wife of a mining engineer. "Flew Russell up as he persuaded Gent and Tancrel that he could raise some cash in L.A.," Lancaster wrote in his diary under Friday, April 1st. "Am sure he can't, though. The whole bunch, Tancrel, McKinley, and Russell, are a complete wash-out. Dope-running was the game. Had to have turned

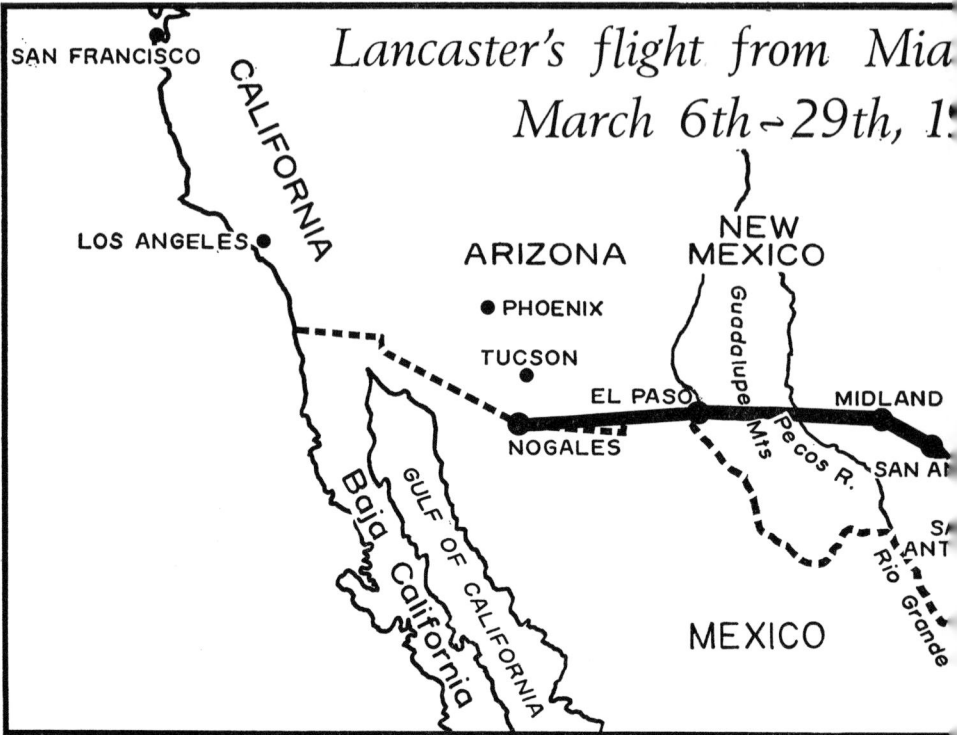

down any proposition of this nature. Money or no money. Promise to Chubbie is coming first. Would give anything for news of her." His disappointment with Chubbie was deep, but she still filled his thoughts. "I should not think of her so much. She does not deserve it."

Chubbie's decision not to add to Lancaster's mental strain by telling him that she had fallen in love with Haden Clarke, humane and considerate as it was intended to be, failed to take account of two factors: first, her complete inability, being the open, honest person that she was, to find anything else to say to him, thus leaving him in a permanent state of anxiety and suspicion; and secondly, while she herself might keep the news from him, others, out of a sense of fair play, a natural feeling for gossip, or simply to make mischief, might be less discreet. Such a sudden attachment is not easily hidden even from chance acquaintances. Thus it was that by the beginning of April Lancaster was the only one of the Latin-American Airways party who remained ignorant of what was going on back in Miami. Now, alone with Lancaster in Los Angeles, Russell suddenly realized that the information that had come into his possession from his wife's letters might be put to profitable if somewhat unscrupulous use. Producing two of the letters, he showed Lancaster the passages referring to Chubbie.

"Chubbie and Clarke came round tonight," read Lancaster. "I really

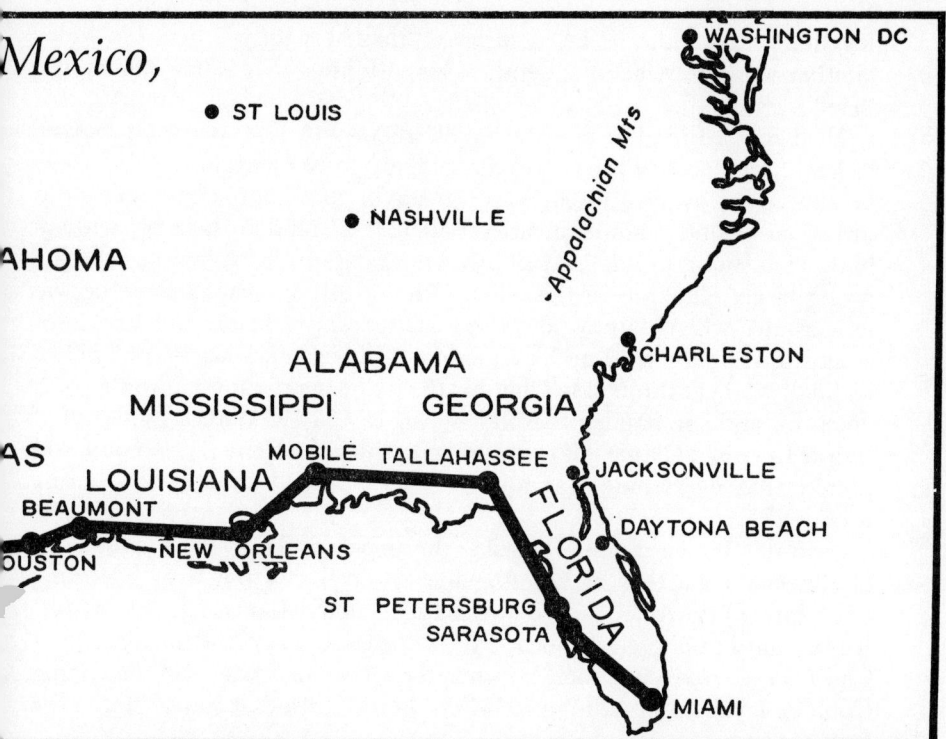

think now that Clarke has gained Chubbie's affections, and Bill lost them." There was no witness to the conversation that followed. Lancaster subsequently told one story, Russell another. But common to both versions, or anyway not in dispute, was that Russell urged Lancaster that there was no point in his going back to Miami now. His best plan was to make some quick money, then go back in a stronger position and sort things out. Russell was in a position to help him make that quick money, if necessary in a single flight, leaving out Tancrel and the others. All he had to do was fly the plane.

Lancaster had no idea how he was going to meet his hotel bill at Los Angeles. The idea of a quick flight to ease his financial worries and then a triumphant return to Miami must, on the face of it, have had strong attractions for him. But he does not appear to have given it serious consideration. Whatever his reaction to the innuendo in the letters—and it was on this reaction that the accounts of Lancaster and Russell were later to differ—Lancaster still refused to consider anything illegal. His wire to Chubbie, however, revealed his state of mind. "Flew Russell here yesterday but fruitless trip. Expect to fly Nogales tomorrow. No news from you before leaving Nogales. Terribly anxious. Tell Haden stand by I trust him." He sent her his love and wired her every cent he could raise, but the severity of the emotional shock he had suffered was clear from his diary. The phrase he used was "mental agony", and he added another word, to which the depth of his sufferings gave a new dimension: "Hell".

Next day a friend at the Metropolitan Airport, Los Angeles, promised to lend him a tank of gas for his return flight to Nogales; at least he would be able to get away. Russell, who was staying outside the city, had so far produced nothing, and Lancaster had half a mind to take off without him. That night, Sunday, April 3rd, he was up until four in the morning trying to get Chubbie on the phone. The torture he was undergoing was exacerbated when hour by hour there was no reply. "Why?" he demanded —and then he summed up his situation: "Ill with nervous worry." When he finally did get through to Chubbie the following night there was a party going on and she handed the phone over to Clarke. With a room full of people listening, Clarke felt he could do nothing but deny the rumours and protest that everything was all right. Lancaster, however, was hardly reassured.

Next day Lancaster met Russell at the airport and they flew an associate of Russell's on a tour of Los Angeles. "Russell says this man is putting $200 into Latin-American Airways, Inc.," noted Lancaster. "Poor fish! Russell finishes himself as far as I am concerned—because he talks about Chub in a nasty manner." Lancaster, it seems, was still defending Chubbie loyally and refusing to believe in the truth that stared him in the face.

So far as Russell was concerned, Lancaster had made his decision; he wasn't going to stay here any longer to help Russell with his confidence tricks. Mrs Stewart, his passenger, was ready to leave, so Lancaster announced that he would take off for Nogales in the morning. "Pick me up at Burbank Airport," said Russell, and Lancaster agreed.

When Lancaster and Mrs Stewart went to the Metropolitan Airport next morning a federal agent was waiting for them by the plane; he wanted to interview Tancrel and Russell. After plying Lancaster with questions about his movements the agent eventually left. Lancaster decided it would be best not to go to Burbank; they might find themselves involved in the arrest of Russell and be held up for days. He decided to take off without him. Mrs Stewart, who disliked Russell and had been anxious to avoid flying with him anyway, readily agreed.

When they finally got away from Los Angeles it was too late to reach Nogales before dark, so after six hours' flying Lancaster put down at Tucson, sixty miles north-west of Nogales. Mrs Stewart's husband met them and drove them into Nogales, where Lancaster, searching for Shelton, finally caught up with him across the border. Shelton readily agreed that they should abandon all contact with Latin-American Airways and head for home in the Robin.

Lancaster had also picked up his mail: "Letters from Chubbie—hard

Bound for Australia—the take-off from Croydon
Photo "Radio Times" Hulton Picture Library

Chubbie packs before take-off (*left*)
Photo "Radio Times" Hulton Picture Library

Forced landing at Rutbah (*right*)
Photo V. Bedggood

Test-flying the *Red Rose*
Photo "Radio Times" Hulton Picture Library

A Curtiss Robin
Photo Royal Aeronautical Society

Lancaster with the *Southern Cross Minor*

to analyse them." These were the two letters Chubbie had written a week earlier. "Much disturbed. Ill with worry. . . . Chubbie, darling, what is it all about?"

Next morning they sought out Tancrel and told him their decision. He tried to play for time, and when this failed he became abusive and threatening. After frustrating him in an attempt to sequestrate Chubbie's propeller they set off by road for Tucson, arranging for the propeller to be delivered to them next day. Meanwhile Shelton's father had agreed to help with their plan for buying an amphibian, and they decided to go back to Miami via St Louis. After the disappointments of the past few weeks they were more carefree now and enjoying each other's company, Lancaster especially being immensely cheered at the prospect of starting east next day.

Late that afternoon, while they were taxiing the Robin out of the hangar to give it a thorough test, a bolt sheared and the landing gear collapsed on one side, smashing the propeller and causing much other damage. Chubbie's propeller was thus going to come in handy after all, but the other repairs would be costly and might take some time. Lancaster was inevitably cast down at the delay. The work, however, was quickly put in hand, so the main worry was financial. Lancaster's impatience mounted, but he was confident that Shelton would soon get some money from his father. "On the way back east, thank goodness," he wrote to Chubbie. He explained the delay and the breaking of the propeller. "Fortunately we had yours in Nogales! We hope to take off for St Louis tomorrow, Friday, and arrive there Saturday. Russell, Tancrel, and McKinley are stranded in Nogales—serves them right! They are a bunch of crooks . . . am going to see Gent's father. . . . The Robin will be sold or given as part payment on the amphibian. Have been through hell, sweetie, but see daylight at last. Russell and Tancrel may try to be vindictive. Take no notice of anything until I get back. Mrs Russell wrote Russell, but I told Russell: 'You don't know Chubbie. To hell with what you may say or think.' Sweetheart, remember Port Darwin? We made it. Remember Andros? You made it. Well, I am going to make it this time. . . . Will wire from St Louis and telephone you."

The Robin was ready next day, and they air-tested it, but no cash arrived for Shelton and there was $89 to pay, in addition to their hotel bill, so they were obliged to wait. Meanwhile Lancaster could not keep off the subject that was always uppermost in his mind—Chubbie. Here Shelton proved himself an understanding and thoughtful companion, and, as Lancaster afterwards noted in his diary, "a true friend". He sent a wire to Chubbie to warn her that they were on their way back and that Lancaster had heard rumours about her relationship with Clarke, and he commiserated with Lancaster, preparing him as best he could for the shock he feared he would have to face. "He is anxious about Chubbie—

says Russell was *so sure*," noted Lancaster. "Never again will I go 3000 miles away on a wild-goose chase."

Day after day they waited for funds at Tucson, while Lancaster alternated between buoyant hope and bleak despair. "Wired Chubbie," he wrote on April 9th. "The reply worries me. If only she would say something nice, such as: 'Don't worry, I still love you.' " That was all he asked for—some warm message to reassure him of his special place in her affections, whatever might have happened while he was away. Encouraged by Shelton, he began to realize that he would have to pull himself together and become reconciled, if necessary, to a new situation: "Thank goodness for one thing—I have made a firm resolution to end all this mental strain —have it out! Then work for our common good. I adore her and want to see her happy. . . . Is Haden Clarke trustworthy, is my problem. . . . Chubbie, angel, it won't be long until I see you and hold you."

But the new resolve weakened under the continued frustration of waiting at Tucson. It was too much for him to cope with, as his diary entry showed next day, Sunday, April 10th. "Awakened with misgivings. Suffer the tortures of the damned. Ways and means have to be found today to get on east—east is where my life lies, everything I hold dear is there. If it's gone from me I will end this life. I can't stand the strain much longer." This showed the depths of suffering he had touched. But later he rallied: "I still have the courage to carry on. The uncertainty is hurting deep, though. Telephone Chubbie at Gentry's insistence—wish I had not. She did not make it easier for me. Am going to Miami, whatever happens, to find out first hand all about everything. . . ." Chubbie, naturally enough, had not felt it was a matter she could discuss on the telephone, and her carefully non-committal answers had sounded cruelly cold to Lancaster. She had begged him not to question her, telling him that there was a letter awaiting him in St Louis. "What is this letter in St Louis?" wrote Lancaster afterwards. "I am terribly eager to get there to receive it. Is it good news or bad news? I don't know whether I can stand any more shocks."

After a week at Tucson Shelton admitted that he had not dared to ask his father again for money in case he changed his mind over the amphibian project; he had relied on another source but it had let him down. In desperation Lancaster wired Frank and Dorothy Upton for $150—the minimum sum they would need to pay for the repairs and the hotel and get them back as far as St Louis, where they could talk to Gentry's father at first hand. The Uptons, too, proved true friends and sent the money, and on Tuesday, April 12th, the Robin climbed away at last from Tucson, heading east-north-east for St Louis.

CHAPTER IX

Lancaster Returns

AFTER the first passionate few days that had followed their realization that they were in love, Haden Clarke had confessed something to Chubbie that in all conscience he could scarcely conceal: at some time in the previous weeks or months he had contracted a venereal disease, and although he had thought he was cured he had had a recurrence of it. At first Chubbie was horrified; it was a shock she thought she would never get over. But Haden was so wretched that she soon began to feel desperately sorry for him; and as time passed she realized that if she loved him it was illogical to hold his past against him, especially as he assured her that apart from this one chance misfortune he had never had such a thing before. So she made up her mind that she must stand by him and help him all she could. Haden, for instance, had to give up drinking, and Chubbie, to make his life of self-denial easier for him, gave up drinking too. But she was adamant that they must put off any thought of getting married until he was cured.

Haden had never believed that Lancaster would give up Chubbie without a struggle, and he had tried to put the matter beyond argument by getting Chubbie to marry him at once. His divorce, he told her, was about to be finalized and they could go ahead. When Chubbie demurred he urged her at least to let him announce their engagement officially in the Miami newspapers; this, he felt, would somehow establish his claim to her. But Chubbie would not agree to this either. "Not until Bill gets back," she answered. "It wouldn't be fair." It wasn't that Chubbie had any reservations about her decision to marry Haden, apart from the obvious need for delay. She was very much in love with him. But she could not entirely rid herself of a sense of guilt where Bill was concerned. They had been such great pals and had meant so much to each other over the years that she was determined to play straight with him. All she asked of Haden was that he let her deal with the problem in her own time and in her own way.

Hearing that Lancaster had resigned from Latin-American Airways and was on his way back to Miami, Haden began to anticipate trouble.

Although he had been punctilious about the disease he had contracted, there was much in his life that he had not revealed to Chubbie. For a brief period he had been the man in possession, and this had been his greatest strength; but possession in its fullest sense was now denied him. It was the worst possible moment for Lancaster to return. The appeal of the past, the magnet of the flying background they shared, Chubbie's natural loyalty, Lancaster's comparative maturity as a person compared with himself—something perhaps that only Haden Clarke could evaluate—all these things might conspire to weaken his position and cause Chubbie to change her mind. It was Haden's turn to suffer the agonies of doubt.

Chubbie herself certainly gave him no cause for alarm. Now that Bill had resigned, she said, they must both write to him at once and tell him frankly and openly that they had fallen in love and were going to marry, addressing their letters to St Louis so that he would get them towards the end of the flight back to Miami. In all other ways she was wonderfully understanding, and they went on planning their future together. How confidently Haden Clarke believed in that future is more difficult to assess.

Lancaster and Shelton reached St Louis on Friday afternoon, April 15th, and went at once to the Shelton home. There were four letters waiting for Lancaster, two from Chubbie and two from Haden. Chubbie's letters were gentle and remorseful; she had obviously found them difficult to write. "The inconceivable has happened," she wrote. "Haden and I have fallen in love. We want to get married. . . . I know that your one thought has been for my happiness, and feel you will take it in the right way. . . . It's breaking my heart to tell you this, after all we've been through together." Haden Clarke, perhaps, had even greater difficulty; his main letter, for what it reveals of him and his mental outlook when he wrote it, is reproduced in some detail:

DEAR BILL,

You doubtless have read Chubbie's letter, so there is no necessity for my relating again what has transpired. I wish, however, to explain with absolute honesty my attitude toward the whole thing and I am hoping against hope that I may be able to justify my action in your mind and to regain in some measure at least the genuine friendship I am sure you felt for me.

When you left you put a trust and confidence in me which I appreciated from the bottom of my heart. . . . My utter confidence in my ability to fulfil this faith was gained without considering for a moment the possibility of the present situation. . . .

When this thing first dawned upon us a few days ago I weighed it carefully from every angle. . . . I did my damnedest to make friendship kill my love for Chubbie, but it was a losing fight from the very beginning. . . .

I don't know what chance of happiness you and Chubbie had before this happened, but I am sufficiently sure of my ground to know with absolute finality that now it has happened neither Chubbie nor I can ever be other than miserable apart....

You have told me many times that your one aim was Chubbie's happiness. I don't know that my word means much to you now, but I give it that I will always do everything in my power to make her the happiest girl in the world. If I ever fail in this, I stand ready to answer to you for it.... Your attitude is going to be a dominating factor in the happiness of both of us and I am extremely anxious to know what it is. I am far from hopeful in this direction, but please wire me immediately and write fully regardless....

The moment you headed East we decided to shoot the works so that you could plan accordingly.... I have communicated with my wife and have made arrangements for an immediate divorce. Chubbie and I plan to marry as soon as it is granted....

Please think it all over sanely, Bill, and try to see your way clear to help us get it over with as smoothly as possible. If you do lose your head I'm afraid I can do nothing but meet you halfway. It would break Chubbie's heart if either of us did anything violent, but the decision regarding this is entirely up to you.

Please don't fail to write upon receipt of this and communicate fully immediately.

Yours,
HADEN

However much Lancaster may have feared that something of this kind was going on, he had never faced it until now. Self-pity, a fault from which he rarely suffered, overwhelmed him, and in his own words, committed to his diary that night, he "behaved like a schoolboy". His only hope seemed to be to hurry back to Miami and try to re-establish his position with Chubbie, but how was he going to face such a confrontation? He showed Shelton the letters, breaking down unashamedly. They were so utterly final. Shelton, trying to get his mind off things, persuaded him to go out that evening, but Lancaster could not be consoled. "Drink pint of real Scotch but it does not affect me," he noted in his diary. In the course of the evening he phoned Chubbie twice.

"Do you want me to come back?" he asked her.

"Of course I do."

From the day of his return to St Louis, Lancaster's diary entries ceased. Perhaps his suffering was now so great that he was no longer able to commit his thoughts to paper. What was in his mind from this point on must therefore, to some extent at least, be a matter of conjecture. No doubt he realized that the truth he had at last been told must have been obvious to his companions for many days. Chubbie was lost to him, and he would just have to face it. The trouble was that he couldn't. She meant everything to him. Drawn to her as he was by all the ties that bind a man to a woman, he could scarcely adjust himself to a threesome as envisaged by Chubbie in which he would be the odd man out. His instinct, perhaps, was to procrastinate, to make sure that nothing irrevocable happened until he had had a chance to present himself to Chubbie in person in an effort to win her back. Surely, he must have calculated, the years they had spent together, all the vicissitudes of those years, the shared memories, the dangers, the setbacks and the triumphs, must exert a powerful influence in his favour, helping to re-establish him in her affections once he found the courage to return to Miami. Yet her letters, however much he may have read and re-read them, implicitly denied him such a hope. In going away and leaving her he had made a catastrophic mistake; now he would just have to reconcile himself to his loss. This was evidently his mood next morning when he sent a joint telegram to Chubbie and Haden:

"Am no dog in manger, but hold your horses kids until I arrive. Insist on being best man and being friend of you both for life. Happiness of you my happiness. Hope arrive tomorrow night or Wednesday latest. Love, Bill."

There is no reason to suppose that this telegram was anything but sincere. Phrases from past entries in his diary fully support such a contention. Chubbie's happiness was always his first concern. Yet in the back of his mind the idea almost certainly lingered that as long as the projected marriage was delayed it might be avoided altogether.

Exactly the same thought of course had occurred to Haden Clarke, and he continued to press Chubbie for an immediate marriage. He wrote out the announcement of their engagement for the newspapers, and tried to persuade her that the best thing for them all was to present Bill with a *fait accompli*. "When Bill comes back," he told her, "he's going to try to break down my wagon and keep you from marrying me. I won't feel sure of you until I've got you safely married." Chubbie again resisted; it was something, she told him, that she simply could not do. The result was that Clarke became more and more temperamental and emotional, his self-confidence diminished, and there were times when he gave way to depression and even despair. He loved Chubbie, he knew she was strong, and he needed her strength. He recognized the power of the bond that linked her to Bill, and he feared it greatly. He must have feared too that further revelations about his own peccadilloes were imminent; the past was catching up with him. The final blow, on April 19th, was a telegram from his wife informing him that the divorce he had supposed to be virtually final would not be absolute for a further year.

The previous day, April 18th, Shelton's father had lent Lancaster $100 to enable him to get back to Miami; Lancaster gave him a cheque for the money, apparently on the understanding that it would not be presented but would stand as a receipt for the loan. Shelton senior also promised to help with the purchase of the amphibian, but detailed consideration of business ventures was to be deferred until Lancaster sorted out his personal life.

Before leaving St Louis Lancaster attended to one outstanding matter that evidently lay on his conscience: the question of Ernest Huston's gun. Flying back as they had done direct to St Louis it had not been possible for him to redeem the original gun, so he bought a replacement in St Louis, a ·38 Colt revolver similar to the one he had borrowed, for $30. Obtaining a licence further delayed him, and he did not take off for Miami, 1000 miles to the south-east, until the afternoon of Tuesday, April 19th. He got no farther than Nashville that day, leaving him with 800 miles to go. He was determined, however, to complete the journey next day, and he got up next morning at four o'clock and was airborne soon after dawn.

Refuelling at Atlanta later that morning, Lancaster sent a telegram to Chubbie to say that he expected to arrive at Miami about four-thirty that afternoon. Chubbie and Haden were there to meet him in the Lincoln, but they had to wait over two hours; Lancaster was delayed by headwinds and did not reach Viking Airport, Miami, until nearly seven o'clock. Chubbie and Haden got out of the car and walked across to the hangar to meet him as he taxied in. Lancaster got out of the cockpit and walked towards them. There were mechanics within earshot, and although the atmosphere was strained, an uneasy cordiality was achieved.

"Hello, darling," said Lancaster. "I've missed you." He embraced her briefly. To Haden, however, his greeting was cool—a polite but distant "Hello, old man." They moved off together towards the car.

On the way back to the house they made several stops. First Haden wanted some cigarettes. He had no money to buy them, and Lancaster gave him a five-dollar bill. They then made two stops on Flagler Street, one to buy some steak for supper, the other to collect Haden's laundry. Again Clarke was unable to pay, which embarrassed him, and he protested that he could wait. In any case he was reluctant to leave Bill and Chubbie alone. After a discussion they all left the car and went into the laundry together.

"I'm nearly dead for a drink," said Lancaster as they drove home. "Let's stop and get some." Chubbie told him that Haden had given up drinking for the time being, and Haden told him the reason. Chubbie added that she wouldn't take a drink herself until he could as well. "We won't bother, then," said Lancaster. "I never drink alone."

The journey in the car to Coral Gables was not a long one, but it was sufficient for a conversation to develop on the subject that filled their minds. Lancaster broke the ice. "Chubbie, are you sure you know your own mind?"

"Yes, Bill, I am."

"Ever since I've known you my only desire has been your happiness."

"I know that."

Lancaster turned to Clarke. "Do you think you can make her happy?"

"I'm damn' sure I can."

"Why didn't you tell me about this before?"

"We didn't want to add to your troubles in Mexico. We thought you had enough to worry you already."

"On your wedding day," said Lancaster, "I'll give you a cheque for a thousand dollars. I'm only going to ask you one thing. To make absolutely sure that you're doing the right thing, I want you to agree not to get married for at least a month."

Chubbie didn't know where the thousand dollars was coming from, but she was more than grateful to Bill for taking it so well. Ever since receiving Bill's telegram her worst anxieties had been allayed; Bill had got over it quickly enough, and they could all stay good friends. That was how she wanted it, and as far as Clarke was concerned he could hardly demur at a short delay in view of his illness and the telegram he had received.

There were no scenes to begin with back at the house. After his long day's flying, Lancaster's first thought was to get into a bath. There was also a pile of mail for him, which he took upstairs. Meanwhile Chubbie and Haden busied themselves preparing a meal. Haden cooked the steak.

The meal itself went off well. There was an underlying tension, but Lancaster talked about his trip, relating much of what had happened and talking amusingly about Tancrel and Russell, while Haden and Chubbie brought him up to date with the social scene at Coral Gables. It wasn't until they'd finished eating and were sitting at the table drinking their coffee that Lancaster trod again on delicate ground. Then he lit a cigarette and turned his gaze on them sadly, rather as though they were naughty children who had been misbehaving while he was away. "Now," he said, "what's all this really about?"

"Chubbie and I want to get married," said Haden, standing his ground. "It's as simple as that."

"Haden, old man," said Lancaster, turning towards him, "I trusted you and you did this to me. You haven't behaved like a gentleman."

Lancaster's manner was calm and controlled, but the effect on the temperamental Clarke was immediate. He jumped to his feet, pushed his chair back against the wall, and towered threateningly over Lancaster. Lancaster also pushed his chair back, but remained seated.

"I resent that," shouted Clarke.

"If you two are going to fight," said Chubbie, "I'm going to bed." Clarke calmed down, Chubbie was prevailed upon to stay, and they moved through the arch into the sitting-room. All three were under heavy emotional strain. Clarke's anger turned as suddenly to remorse. "I guess you're right, Bill," he said. Chubbie went through to the kitchen to wash the dishes, and after a moment Lancaster followed. Pale and drawn, weighted down with sorrow, he contrived a smile. "This is a mess, isn't it?" And he laughed. Chubbie felt so miserable she began to cry, leaning her head on Lancaster's shoulder. He put his arm round her and began to comfort her. Meanwhile Clarke, hearing Lancaster laugh, strode out to the kitchen.

"Leave her alone!" shouted Clarke, "it's my right to comfort her now. Keep your hands off her. I won't have you trying to break down my wagon."

"I'll give you a year to make her happy," said Lancaster, "and if you haven't I swear I'll come back and take her away from you."

"Leave her alone!"

"She's always come to me in time of trouble."

"She'll come to me now." And he pulled Chubbie away. "I won't have him talking to you alone," he told Chubbie. "Anything that's said must be said in front of all of us."

"I think it's only fair," said Chubbie, "to let me talk to Bill alone."

"I won't have it."

"I've known Chubbie for five years," said Lancaster, "it's natural we should want to talk alone."

"No."

Chubbie was still in tears. "Leave me alone, both of you," she said. Realizing that she meant it, both men decided to go out to get some cigarettes. When they returned half an hour later Chubbie had gone to her room and they followed her there. Lancaster was carrying the pile of mail that had been awaiting his return, and two or three of the letters bore the stamp of a pilots' insurance company. "That company," said Chubbie, "has just gone bust." Lancaster was so shaken that Chubbie wondered why he should take the news so badly. Companies were failing daily all over the States. Then she had a flash of intuition: perhaps he had a $1000 insurance with the company and that was where his wedding present to them was to have come from. She accused him of this and he denied it, but admitted it under pressure. "If a ship spins," he said, "who is to know what happened?" There can be little doubt that Lancaster had had in mind to kill himself flying and at the same time provide a windfall for Chubbie. "East is where my life lies," he had written, "everything I hold dear is there. If it's gone from me I will end this life."

The conversation turned again to Lancaster's flight to Mexico. Much of his account dealt with the actual flying and the difficulties they had overcome, and the interest Chubbie showed infuriated Clarke. "You're trying to win her back through her interest in flying," he accused. "You can't blame me", said Lancaster, "for trying to win her back any way I can." Chubbie warned them she would not stand hearing them quarrel over her again, and they all went back to the living-room. Now if she wanted to escape she could.

Chubbie and Haden sat together on the couch, and Lancaster, sitting opposite them in a chair, told them of the offer made by Gentry's father to buy an amphibian for operation in the Caribbean. Then they discussed Latin-American Airways. The company owed Lancaster a substantial sum in salary and expenses but he saw little hope of getting it. "I'll go and see Huston in the morning," he said.

Clarke remained tense and antagonistic, and Chubbie asked Lancaster if he would let them talk alone. "All right," said Lancaster. He whistled for the dog, and they heard him go out and start the Lincoln. "He'll try to get you back," said Clarke sullenly. "I know what he's up to. I shall never feel secure until we're married. I talked to Huston about it and he said we could probably get married legally here now, before Kay gets her final decree, provided we stay out of California." But Chubbie refused. "We've promised Bill we'll wait at least a month," she said. "In any case we've got to wait until you're cured." Any marriage until then could be in name only.

The situation was far worse than either of them had expected. Chubbie was suffering tortures of self-reproach for her treatment of Bill, while Clarke's attitude was one of unrelieved gloom. His obsession that he would lose Chubbie if he didn't marry her at once was growing. And although his financial situation was desperate, the idea of co-operating with Lancaster on the amphibian project did not appeal to him. "There's no place for Bill here," he said, "he just won't fit into our future. That West Indies stunt won't work anyway." But he admitted that he didn't know what else to do. They were still sitting on the couch talking over their situation when Lancaster returned. Meanwhile Lancaster, driving round the deserted streets in the Lincoln—it was now past midnight—must have felt that the situation had become intolerable for him. After about twenty minutes he returned to the house and announced that he would be leaving at once. "I shall stay in a hotel tonight," he said. "Tomorrow I'll fly back to St Louis."

While Clarke affected complete indifference, Chubbie urged him to stay. Embarrassing as his return was, she could not bring herself to send him finally away. "All right," he said, "I'll stay tonight. But I shall leave in the morning." He picked up the pile of letters again and went upstairs to the sleeping-porch, leaving Chubbie and Haden alone in the living-room. They talked for the next fifteen minutes, but they could not shake off their depression. Eventually Haden said he would go to bed.

"I want you to promise me to lock your door," he asked.

"I never lock my door—I like it open, for fresh air."

"Nevertheless I want you to promise. I don't want that son of a bitch coming in to try to talk you out of our marriage."

Chubbie agreed to lock her door. They kissed, and Haden went upstairs to the porch. Chubbie went round turning the lights off, and then she went up to her room. As she crossed the landing she could see into the porch: Bill was sitting on the end of his bed with his letters spread out on the cover, and Haden too was sitting on his bed. She went in and took the clock to set the alarm. "Yes," said Lancaster, "I want to get up early, I've got a lot of things to do." As she left them she said, "Good night, chaps," but Lancaster didn't answer, and she called again, "Good night, Bill," giving him a smile. He looked up and said good night. Clarke, observing all this, stared at her critically.

As she wound her alarm clock she noticed that the time was a quarter to one. She locked her door as Haden had asked, put a packet of cigarettes by her bedside, and settled down to read a detective-story magazine. The story she chose was a long one and she read for nearly an hour. At first she heard the others moving about, and for much of the time she could hear them talking. Then she switched off the light and fell asleep.

She was awakened by a loud banging on her door. Someone was calling to her to get up. She rose and opened the door. It was Bill.

"A terrible thing has happened," he said. "Haden has shot himself."

CHAPTER X

"*Did you do this?*"

CHUBBIE didn't believe it. "That's ridiculous," she said, "there's no gun in the house."

"Yes, there is. I brought one back for Huston."

She ran across the landing and into the sleeping-porch. Haden was lying in bed writhing and groaning, his face covered in blood. She spoke to him, then ran to the bathroom for a face-cloth. As she wiped the blood from his forehead she told Lancaster to call a doctor, and he went downstairs and picked up the phone. When the operator answered he asked her to send a doctor immediately, giving the address. Then he went back upstairs. Chubbie was still bathing Haden's head, rinsing the face-cloth out in a bowl.

"Haden, old man," said Lancaster, "speak to me." But the twitching, convulsive movements continued, and he groaned repeatedly. Lancaster went across to the table, on which lay Haden's typewriter. "Look," he said to Chubbie. "Haden left these notes." He handed them to her. One was addressed to him, the other to her. "Bill," she read, "I can't make the grade. Tell Chubbie of our talk. My advice is, never leave her again." And the second note read: "Chubbie, the economic situation is such I can't go through with it. Comfort mother in her sorrow. You have Bill. He is the whitest man I know."

"We'd better destroy them," said Lancaster.

"We can't do that."

"There'll be a scandal if that note to you is made public."

Chubbie decided to keep it. It would be unwise to destroy it. Meanwhile the urgent need was to get a doctor for Haden. She was trying to think of the name of his own doctor, but couldn't remember it. Ernest Huston, their attorney, would surely know of a doctor; and she went downstairs and rang him. He promised to call a doctor and an ambulance and to come himself when he had done so.

A few minutes later Chubbie remembered the name of Haden's doctor —Carleton Deederer. The time by then was nearly three o'clock. "Haden has shot himself," she told him. "He's bleeding terribly. Please come at once." Deederer had never visited Clarke at Chubbie's home, and she gave him the address.

She put the phone down and went back upstairs. A moment later the doorbell rang and Lancaster went down and admitted two ambulance men, employees of the W.I. Philbrick Funeral Home. They went upstairs together. Ditsler, the ambulance driver, began to examine Clarke.

"Do you think he'll talk again?" asked Lancaster.

"I doubt it."

"I don't want him moved yet," said Chubbie. "There's a doctor on the way. It might be dangerous to move him." Lancaster supported her, and the ambulance men agreed that they could not move a patient without competent authority. Still no doctor arrived, and the ambulance men became impatient. Ditsler went downstairs and telephoned his office.

"Will you call the police?" asked Chubbie.

"The office already have," said Ditsler.

The next arrival, at three-fifteen, was Ernest Huston. Chubbie was in the living-room with Ditsler when he arrived, and Lancaster, who was upstairs, came out on to the landing. Lancaster showed him the notes and suggested tearing them up. "No," said Huston, "they're important." Chubbie asked Huston and the ambulance driver not to mention the notes because of the scandal they might cause, and she hid the note addressed to her in the telephone desk drawer. "I wish," said Lancaster, "that Haden would talk, so he could tell us why he did it."

Still no doctor arrived, and Chubbie called Dr Deederer's number again to find out what time he had left. She was amazed to hear him answer the phone. He had been out once, failed to find the house, and gone home to get more detailed directions. He knew his way now and was about to leave.

Half an hour after Ditsler's call to his office, the assistant manager of the Philbrick Home, a man named Yeargin, arrived. It was nearly an hour since Lancaster's first call to the operator, and all that time Haden Clarke had lain unconscious on the bed in the sleeping-porch. Apart from Chubbie's ministrations with a face-cloth, nothing had been done for him. Yeargin now gave the ambulance men authority to move him, and Lancaster, mistaking Yeargin for a doctor, raised no objection. As the two men carried Clarke with difficulty down the stairs, Chubbie's protests that a doctor was on the way floated up to them.

"Where are you taking him?"

"The Jackson Memorial Hospital."

Dr Deederer arrived just as the ambulance was moving off. He picked up Lancaster and Chubbie and drove to the hospital. Before they left, Lancaster had a quiet word with Huston, who stayed behind at the house. "If it should be necessary," he asked, "will you act for us?" Huston said he would.

Dr Deederer was as vague about the site of the hospital as he had been about the house, and several times they had to stop and ask the way. When they finally got there they were taken to the ward where Clarke lay. Also present in the ward were a nurse and two police emergency officers. One of the policemen came forward and introduced himself. "I'm Earl Hudson," he announced. "I know all about you and Chubbie, Charlie told me."[1] His manner was friendly, and although they had never met him they had often heard Haden and Peggy Brown talk about him; he was married to Peggy Brown's sister.

The hospital staff now took over, and the visitors were bundled out. Dr Deederer remained in the ward, and Earl Hudson and another police officer named Fitzhugh Lee took Chubbie and Lancaster to a police car and drove them back to the house, where Hudson began a preliminary examination of the scene of the tragedy. The gun lay in the centre of the blood-stained bed and Hudson's first act was to take possession of it. "One ·32 pistol," he called out to his companion.

"It's not a ·32," said Lancaster, "it's a ·38 Colt."

"No," persisted Hudson, "it's a ·32."

The argument continued until Lancaster picked up the box in which the pistol had been sold to him, which still lay on the table next to the typewriter, and showed Hudson the calibre marking on the label. Hudson and Lee then searched for the bullet but failed to find it; it was eventually found in Clarke's pillow next morning. From all this it would seem that Hudson and Lee were not perhaps the smartest cops in Miami; but in the investigation which followed Hudson certainly showed admirable persistence. He had heard from the ambulance men about the notes and he asked to see them. Chubbie brought him the note addressed to Lancaster.

"There were two notes, weren't there? Where's the second one?"

"It's personal."

"I want it just the same."

Chubbie went downstairs to the telephone desk drawer and brought the note to him. Satisfied with their inquiries so far, the two policemen left.

Both Lancaster and Chubbie were anxious to get back to the hospital to inquire about Clarke, and Ernest Huston, who had never left the house, offered to drive them in. They were also anxious to let Haden's mother know what had happened, and they asked Huston to make a short detour to the Everglades Hotel, where she was staying.

Huston, curious to know whether the gun he had seen in the bed had been his own, asked Lancaster if it was. Lancaster told him what had happened to the original gun and how he had bought this one to replace it. "Technically it belongs to you," said Lancaster. "Is it all right if I say it's yours?"

---
[1] Some of Haden Clarke's friends knew him as Charlie.

"I'm afraid not."

"Can I say it's the property of Latin-American Airways?"

Huston shook his head. He had already resigned from the company on learning of the illegal activities they had planned. The less he was mixed up in this shooting business the better.

At the Everglades Hotel, Chubbie, Huston, and Deederer went in to see Mrs Clarke. Mrs Clarke had already learnt of the shooting and was dressing to go to the hospital. They came down together to the foyer, while Dr Deederer began to explain the extent of Clarke's injuries. "I don't want to hear them," said Mrs Clarke, distressed. "Is there any chance?" When Deederer said "No," Mrs Clarke said she saw no need for her to go to the hospital, and she went back upstairs while the others rejoined Lancaster.

When they got to the hospital two detectives were waiting for them. "We'd like to question you at the courthouse," they said. Clarke, they learnt, was still unconscious. They were then driven for questioning to the Dade County Courthouse,[1] a huge tiered Christmas cake of a building on 12th Street, twenty-five stories high. Lancaster and Chubbie were separated and not allowed to communicate, and both were asked for their keys. They were going to search the house and the aeroplane.

The man in charge of the interrogation was the State Attorney, N. Vernon Hawthorne, forty-two years old, born in Plant City, Florida, and State Attorney for the past five years. Short, but dapper and well made, with a high forehead from which the hair—still black—had receded, he had a heavy, sonorous voice when he wanted to use it, but his manner now was fatherly and considerate. After being segregated for several hours, and accommodated meanwhile in cells on the nineteenth floor, Lancaster and Chubbie were taken in turn to Hawthorne's office. Seated facing the light, they were confronted by a semi-circle of attorneys who fired questions at them in rapid succession. Confusing as this was, there was no intimidation, and no pressure was brought to bear. Chubbie went over the sequence many times, answering again and again Hawthorne's questions on what the two men had said to each other, and Lancaster underwent a similar examination. Shortly before midday they learnt that their accounts could never be contested by the third party who had shared the events with them. Haden Clarke was dead.

Hawthorne told Lancaster at this point that Ernest Huston wanted to see him, and Lancaster asked Hawthorne's advice as to whether he needed a lawyer. "It's not up to me to advise you," said Hawthorne, "but you're at liberty to talk to Huston if you want to."

"Isn't it your job to protect the innocent as well as prosecute the guilty?" asked Lancaster.

"Yes."

[1] Dade County, of which Miami is a part, is the largest of the Florida counties.

"Then I'm content to leave the investigation in your hands."

The State Attorney had taken possession of all available material at the house and in the Robin, including Lancaster's diaries and letters. These disclosed nearly everything there was to know about the triangle that had developed. Much of Lancaster's interrogation concerned the notes. Examples of Clarke's typing had been seized and their characteristics compared with the typing of the notes. There were discrepancies. On the other hand, there were similarities between examples of Lancaster's own typing, taken from the stories he had written for magazines, and the notes.

Lancaster made one request of Hawthorne: that the disease Haden Clarke had suffered from should not be made public, so as to protect his memory and in consideration of his mother's feelings. To this Hawthorne agreed. But releases were made to the Press covering most other aspects of the case. Hawthorne himself told the Press that Lancaster had failed to explain certain contradictions in his testimony. "He said he was asleep and was awakened by the shot," said Hawthorne, "yet his pillow showed no signs of having been slept on." Hawthorne also said he was investigating a report by Dr Deederer, the attending physician, that no powder burns were found around the bullet wound in Clarke's temple and that bruises were found on the head and right shoulder. The inference to be drawn from the first point was presumably that powder burns were normally present in cases of suicide, when the gun is naturally held close to the head (there were conflicting theories later about this), while the significance of the bruises was that the shooting might have been preceded by a struggle. The accusing finger was thus clearly pointed by inference at Lancaster, who at this stage had no chance to defend himself.

On the same day, April 21st, the day of the shooting, Chubbie was released to attend Clarke's funeral, which was held that evening. She went back to the house under escort to change her clothing and found that the place had been ransacked. There was no autopsy, and Clarke was buried next day. Chubbie was taken straight back to the gaol. No charges were brought, although both she and Lancaster were still held in custody.

Hawthorne publicly expressed confidence in Chubbie's story and said he believed her when she said she didn't know how it happened, and he also admitted that Lancaster gave the impression of telling a frank and straightforward story. All reports described Haden Clarke as Mrs Miller's fiancé, but her name had been linked so often with Lancaster's that most people drew the obvious conclusion about the events following his return. The impression of a sudden infatuation between Mrs Miller and Clarke, interrupted by the return of Lancaster, was strengthened when it was reported on Saturday, April 23rd, that a young woman had called at the State Attorney's office and declared that she had a much better right to call herself the dead man's fiancée than Chubbie: this was Peggy Brown.

That afternoon, after further questioning and after all letters, papers,

Reunion at Nassau after Chubbie's disappearance
Photo Associated Press

A recent photograph of the house in Coral Gables, Miami
Photo Bob East

and diaries found in the house and in the aeroplane had been examined, Chubbie was called to Hawthorne's office and told that both she and Lancaster were to be unconditionally released. "It has been my privilege to see into the depths of a man's soul through his private diary," said Hawthorne, "which was never intended for anyone's eyes but his own, and in all my experience—which has been broad—I have never met a more honourable man than Captain Lancaster. Because of that I'm going to release him."

On her release, Chubbie was introduced in Hawthorne's office to an attorney named James H. Lathero; he had acted in the past for Mrs Clarke, and she had sent him to help Chubbie. Lancaster, she learnt, was to be rearrested on a charge of conspiring to smuggle narcotics, a charge arising from the revelations made available to federal agents following Hawthorne's study of the diary and letters; so she agreed to Lathero's suggestion that he drive her to the Everglades Hotel. Warrants had already been issued for the arrest of Tancrel and Russell, but after further questioning Lancaster satisfied the authorities that he had not been a party to the conspiracy, and he then joined Chubbie at the Everglades Hotel. There for the first time he faced Haden Clarke's mother. "I swear to you", he told her, "that I had nothing to do with Haden's death." But Mrs Clarke, who had been satisfied at first that her son took his own life, had already issued a statement to say that she could no longer accept the suicide theory without reservations, mainly because of her doubts of the authenticity of the signatures on the notes. One had been signed "Haden", the other "H". She was also puzzled, she said, because of her son's known aversion to firearms. But for the moment she accepted Lancaster's assurance.

Hawthorne was severely criticized for letting Lancaster go, but he apparently felt that he had insufficient evidence to press a murder charge. Without some definite charge he could not hold him longer than three days. Whatever his suspicions about the notes he could not break down Lancaster, and his forgery experts were unable to pronounce with conviction that they were not typed and signed by Clarke. But to add to the general mystification, Hawthorne still hinted that a murder charge might be brought. After again recording his confidence in Chubbie's account, he refused to be committed to any further statement about Lancaster, and referred to Clarke's death as "murder or suicide, whichever it may turn out to be". He would sift all the evidence thoroughly, he said, before abandoning a conclusion of murder. A handwriting expert, he added, was still studying the notes. Hawthorne may well have been playing cat and mouse, releasing Lancaster although perhaps believing in his guilt, interested to see what he would do.

On the way back to the house in the Lincoln, Chubbie waited until they were clear of all traffic and buildings and then stopped the car.

"Make sure there's no one in the boot," she told Lancaster. He got out and opened the boot to satisfy her, and then she asked him the question she had been waiting to ask him for nearly three days.

"Bill, did you do this?"

"No—on my honour I didn't."

They went back to the house and began cleaning up the mess left by the investigators. The telegram Haden had received from his wife was screwed up in a ball in the corner of the sleeping-porch; other discarded papers littered the rooms. The threat of further action by the State Attorney lay heavily upon them; late that afternoon Lancaster admitted forging the notes. He had done it, he said, because he feared that in the circumstances Chubbie might suspect him. The notes had been written for her and her alone. That was why he had asked her to destroy them. Chubbie believed him.

"You must tell Hawthorne," she said. "That's the only way you can finally clear yourself." But first they decided to consult James Lathero. His advice surprised and in a way disappointed them. "Say nothing whatsoever about it for the moment," he said, "certainly not before the inquest. Otherwise Hawthorne will be bound to hold you." But it remained on Lancaster's conscience, while Chubbie urged that he would always feel under suspicion until he told the whole truth. When the inquest was indefinitely postponed, Lancaster went with Chubbie to call on Hawthorne. "When I was awakened by the shooting," Lancaster told him, "my first thought was to protect myself and Chubbie. So I wrote the notes and then tried to revive Clarke to get him to sign them. When it was clear that he couldn't, I signed them myself."

In a voluntary statement, recorded at length by the State Attorney's stenographer, Lancaster said that in earlier questioning he had told the absolute truth with the exception of anything he might have said to lead the State Attorney to believe that he was not responsible for writing the notes. "The incidents connected with the writing of the two notes," he said, "are the only incidents which I feel were unworthy, foolish, and cowardly of any part I may have played in the investigation. The fact weighed heavily on my mind from the start." Lancaster then told how he had gone to see Lathero on the day of his release and told him the true story, and how Lathero had reacted. "I further told him," said Lancaster, "that I should not leave Miami without telling Mr Hawthorne the entire truth. Mr Lathero can verify this statement."

Lancaster then described exactly how the notes had come to be written. "When I switched on the light and found Haden Clarke had shot himself," his statement continued, "I suppose I was a little panicky. I had been awakened out of a deep sleep and may have been befuddled. I spoke to Haden, I shook him, and the only noise that came from him was a sort of gurgling noise. His body was twitching violently and his legs moved.

When the full seriousness of the situation sank in, my first thought was: Chubbie will think I am responsible. I did not know how seriously Haden was injured. I thought he might be dying. I sat down at the typewriter and typed the two notes. I typed them as I honestly thought Haden would type such notes. I used expressions he had used to me that night in a talk we had earlier in the evening. I picked up a pencil which was by the side of the typewriter, and I went back to the bed where Haden Clarke was lying. I spoke to him. I begged him to sign the two notes I had written."

At this point, said Lancaster, he called out to Chubbie. Asked how far away her room was, he said about thirty-five feet. "The doors of the sun-porch were open. Her door was shut. There was no reply to my first call, which was from the sun-porch. Uppermost in my mind was the thought of what Chubbie would think. At that time it never occurred to me what other people would think. I then took the pencil and scribbled 'Haden' on one note and the letter 'H' on the other."

Lancaster went on to describe how he aroused Chubbie and telephoned for a doctor. Then he referred again to the notes. "I realized that they would weigh heavily against me were I suspected of taking the life of Haden Clarke. I can only say that I wrote them in the first place with honesty of purpose, as, had Clarke recovered sufficiently to sign them, it would have had the effect of setting Chubbie's mind at ease concerning the wound.

"I scribbled the name 'Haden' and the initial 'H' on impulse. Those notes were intended for one person to see. Through events over which I had no control, the contents of those notes became common property, and I am pleased that I have been able to make this statement, as it is the only thing that I have done that is not strictly honourable in connection with the death of Haden Clarke. I did not kill him. In no way have I willingly been a reason for his death.

"I trust that the statements made in detail in the first instance in the investigation by Mr Hawthorne's office will satisfy his department that I am innocent of the cause of death of Haden Clarke. That is all I have to say."

Hawthorne then asked a series of questions on Lancaster's purchase of the gun, his diary entries referring to the scandal that had reached him, and his doubts about the trustworthiness of Clarke. Did this indicate any malice in his heart towards Clarke? "It did not. If I had come to Miami and found that Haden Clarke had behaved toward Chubbie in a manner that was dastardly, I would have borne malice, but when I arrived at Miami, as I have already said, I found nothing to indicate this." Clarke's behaviour to Lancaster, of course, was another matter, and Lancaster conceded this.

Chubbie meanwhile was going over the whole sequence again in another room, and at the end of the day she was released. Lancaster, however, was held. Hawthorne's overt attitude was that against his inclination he would probably have to place a technical charge of murder against him. Lancaster's confession of forging the notes was released to the Press, and within a few minutes the cameras were clicking. As Chubbie left the courthouse alone she heard the shouts of the newsboys in the street outside. "Captain Lancaster arrested for murder."

CHAPTER XI

Building a Defence

ADVISED by James H. Lathero, "Happy" Lathero, as they knew him, Lancaster issued a statement that night to the Press from his cell. "It came as a great shock to me, the fact that a technical charge of murder has been made against me. I am absolutely innocent—I know the outcome will prove this.

"I have been treated with the utmost fairness by Mr Hawthorne, but there is a certain amount of circumstantial evidence against me.

"At the right and proper time explanation will be made covering this circumstantial evidence. I voluntarily gave Mr Hawthorne an exact account of the notes and he is in possession of all the facts.

"Mrs Miller is a devoted friend and she, at the right and proper time, will tell the truth about the death of Haden Clarke, so far as she knows it."

Chubbie too issued a statement: "I am absolutely confident everything will come out all right. I know the truth will be learnt and Captain Lancaster will be cleared. He is innocent and I know it. My faith in him remains unshaken. It never has wavered in the past, or now, and it never will."

But in spite of these protestations of innocence, the material on the case already issued or leaked from the State Attorney's office had firmly prejudiced the public against Lancaster. His forging of the suicide notes seemed the act of a guilty man. There was the fact—people believed it was a fact—that his bed had not been slept in; and there were the bruises —people believed there had been bruises—on Clarke's body. Clearly Lancaster had killed Clarke. But the fellow had probably deserved it.

Next day, May 3rd, Lancaster was interviewed by the Press in his cell. "Will you plead guilty?" he was asked. This was an indication of the general attitude towards him. "I most certainly shall not," said Lancaster. "I am innocent. I have cabled my father in England for money and I expect to hear from him. . . . I know I can convince twelve reasonable men, if I am indicted, that I am innocent of the boy's death."

But if Lancaster was innocent, the necessary corollary was that Clarke committed suicide; no one else could have killed him. What sort of evidence could be assembled to show that Clarke was in a suicidal frame of mind? The disease he was suffering from might be a factor, but he was under treatment, and if everyone who contracted venereal disease committed suicide the death rate might show a dramatic rise. It was something to build on, but they would have to improve on it.

Chubbie, of course, had been thinking this out for herself ever since the tragedy. At first she had been incredulous; Haden seemed to have everything to live for. He loved her, and she returned his love; why should he kill himself? But her belief in Bill Lancaster, and the revelations about Haden Clarke, forced her to re-assess the situation. "Happy" Lathero, after questioning her in great detail, drew up a list of reasons why Clarke might have killed himself, indeed, not *might* have killed himself, but *did* kill himself. This was the document which he produced, a copy of which, on his instructions, Chubbie delivered personally to Hawthorne later that day under her own signature.

Reasons why Haden Clarke killed himself

1. Remorse at the situation he had created, after his promise to Bill Lancaster.
2. Doubt of himself and of me. Fear that the past five years would prove too strong a bond and I would return to Bill.
3. Financial worries.
4. Doubt of his ability to write the book and make money with his writing. He talked constantly of this; his writings were all returned.
5. Intense sexual life over many years, suddenly discontinuing.
6. The fact that he was very young and I had placed too much burden and responsibility on him.
7. Physical condition.
8. The fact that he was very temperamental and emotional; that he rose to the heights of joy, and sank to the depths of despair.

With this document before them, it was possible that, when Lancaster was indicted before the Dade County Grand Jury on May 9th, the indictment would be refused and Lancaster freed. Because of the continuing desire to protect Clarke and his family, the document was not released to the Press; thus these inferential arguments in Lancaster's favour remained generally unknown. On the other hand, innuendos against Lancaster, which for the moment he had no chance of disproving, were still current, and on May 7th it was reported that Clarke's mother might ask for an autopsy on her son, on the grounds that the report made out by Dr Deederer, the family physician, led her to believe that her son had been beaten before being shot. In fact, although there was mention of a bruise, no such inference was present in Dr Deederer's report. There is no evidence that an autopsy was in fact asked for at this stage, and certainly none was granted.

When Lancaster came before the Grand Jury on May 9th, 1932, their decision was that he must stand for trial. They returned a first-degree murder indictment, for which the penalty was the electric chair. Chubbie's first thought was that they must get a first-class man to defend him, and Lathero promised to do all he could. "There's Jim Carson," he said, "James M. Carson." Carson, he told Chubbie, was one of the top barristers in Miami, and if he would take the case it would give the defence a terrific boost. But he was a busy man. And they would have to convince him first of Lancaster's innocence.

"Let me go and see him."

Lathero arranged an appointment, and she went to see Carson next day. She found him a rather frightening figure at first, a big, rugged, unkempt man with wiry black hair greying in places, close-cropped at the sides but mounting in front, with black, bushy eyebrows, glasses, and a massive, full-lipped, heavily-creased face. Born at Kissimmee forty-five years earlier, he had been practising law for twenty-two years and had maintained a law office in Miami since 1916. For the last seven years he had confined his practice to the conduct of cases referred to him by other attorneys; that was the measure of his status. No client of his in any criminal case had ever stayed a day in gaol after trial. It was an unenviable reputation, one that he would be unlikely to risk lightly. When Chubbie asked him if he would defend Bill Lancaster his answer was decisive. "I wouldn't touch it," he said. "He's as guilty as hell."

"You're wrong there," said Chubbie, "I know you're wrong. But all I'll ask you to do is to go down to the gaol and see Bill and form your own opinion, because I'm quite sure that when you meet him you'll feel as I do that he couldn't have done it; he isn't a coward."

This direct invitation to visit Lancaster and judge for himself appealed to the practical, homespun Jim Carson far more than any long recital of explanations might have done. He went to the gaol to see Lancaster, and Lancaster told him the full story—of his background, of his relationship with Chubbie, of his trip to Mexico, and the sequence of events the night he returned. Carson was impressed by Lancaster's story and the manner in which he told it, and after three days of investigation in company with Lathero he seems to have become convinced of Lancaster's innocence; anyway, he decided to take the case. "But because of those damned notes it's not going to be easy," he told Chubbie. "He's in a very tough spot." So far as the public were concerned, said Carson, they'd found him guilty already. Also he was a foreigner—that wouldn't help. "I'm afraid I'm going to have to make you the scarlet woman," he said. That was the only way to get the sympathy of the jury. It would mean that Chubbie would have to go on the stand and face merciless examination and cross-examination on the most intimate details of her private life. "The question is," asked Carson, "can you take it?"

Chubbie was still very fond of Bill. That their friendship had withstood the traumatic events of the past three weeks was a tribute to the depth of their affection and respect for each other. Believing in him as she did, Chubbie would have done anything to save him from the electric chair. And here in front of her the best lawyer in Miami was telling her that she could help materially to save him.

"Will everything have to come out?"

"Everything."

"And there's no other way of saving him?"

"In my opinion, no."

Chubbie was a long time before she answered. Had she known how the smallest incident from her life was going to be magnified and distorted to make a disparaging picture utterly unlike the real one, she might have answered differently.

"Very well."

Carson looked relieved. The fact that she was being called as a witness by the prosecution and not by the defence would probably help, he said. All she had to do in any case was tell the truth.

Carson's first move was to get an order from the court giving the defence access to the exhibits; the letters, diaries, telegrams, and so on. His second move was to inform the court that the defence would be that Haden Clarke committed suicide, and that this being so it was material to investigate the background of both the defendant and the deceased, so that the probability of suicide or of murder might be shown: such investigations, it was urged, would take time.

In seeking to establish Lancaster's background, Carson wrote on May 12th to his wife in England. After introducing himself, he forecast that Lancaster would go on trial within two months and that the State "will claim that the circumstances show premeditated murder. The defence is that Mr Clarke committed suicide. You can see that the past life of Captain Lancaster and of Mr Clarke in these conditions are to be very material as bearing upon the probabilities of the action of each of them under a given set of circumstances. If there are any similar incidents in Captain Lancaster's life, his conduct then would be material now."

This, surely, was a remarkable introduction. What could it mean, unless it meant that Carson was sounding Kiki Lancaster on her willingness to lay bare the facts of some attachment of hers during their life together which Lancaster had condoned and overlooked? Would not the existence of such an attachment accord with much in the known behaviour and attitude of both parties? And could Carson possibly have arrived at such a line of questioning without prompting from Lancaster? "The Captain thinks that you would be willing to help him in the case in any way that you honourably can," the letter went on. "His first suggestion is that you give out no interviews or statements to the Press with regard to him. The second suggestion is that if you could appear at the trial without knowledge of your intention upon the part of the prosecution, and give evidence in his favour, based upon his character as you know it, and upon his past life as you have observed it, it ought to have a tremendous effect on his behalf."

Lancaster's attitude throughout was that he wanted to keep his wife out of it, so the melodramatic idea of calling Kiki to give evidence for the defence, and keeping her attendance secret, must have been Carson's. But unless she had been willing to go on the stand and make some personal revelation of Lancaster's extreme forbearance in "a similar incident", it is doubtful whether her presence would have served any purpose. "I have not spoken to anyone about Captain Lancaster's case, nor has anyone from the Press, as far as I am aware, discovered that I and my two children are in London," wrote Kiki. "In fact I have thought that it would be for his benefit if no one at Miami were to know of my existence." She had gone to the trouble of taking counsel's opinion in London on the reported facts of the case, and she sent Carson a copy. It cannot be traced today, but it cannot have agreed with Carson's views on a personal appearance in Miami. "After reading it I should be glad if you would let me know in what way any evidence I could give would serve my husband's interest," she concluded. "I am entirely dependent upon my earnings for the support of myself and my two children, and have not a penny wherewith to pay for a voyage across the Atlantic, and for my children's maintenance whilst I was away, or for my own maintenance in Miami whilst awaiting a trial that might be postponed or last some considerable time."

It is probable that Carson, on reflection, agreed with the view she expressed. He dropped the suggestion of her attending the trial, but remained in friendly correspondence with her. The financial consideration alone may have been enough to dissuade him. Lancaster had no money, attempts to raise money for his defence were only partially successful, and Carson had advised him to take out an insolvency petition. It seemed extremely unlikely that defending counsel would receive any payment for their services.

The necessity of investigating the mental and emotional background of both Bill Lancaster and Haden Clarke remained, and Carson set about the task of finding witnesses who could testify on these matters. With Lancaster it would not be difficult: he had many friends willing to come forward, and in any case the court itself could make its own assessment. But with Clarke it was difficult to know what line to take and where to begin. Since funds were limited Carson was anxious not to spend more money than was necessary on this quest, and he decided to consult a competent psychiatrist under whose guidance they would investigate only those aspects of Haden Clarke's life that were material to the case. As it happened he knew of such a psychiatrist, a Dr Percy L. Dodge, who had been a witness—for the other side—in a recent personal injury suit in which Carson had been concerned; his ability and knowledge had greatly impressed Carson. On investigation he found that Dodge had been a practising physician specializing in nervous and mental diseases for twenty-five years. Currently in charge of nervous diseases at the Jackson Memorial Hospital, where Clarke died, his qualifications were unimpeachable, and Carson consulted him. He quickly realized that he was dealing with a man who on account of the nature of his work had seen very many cases of suicide, experience which had given him a wide specialist knowledge altogether outside his normal psychiatric field.

In cases of shooting by pistol, said Dodge, there were usually very definite physical indications of how the shot was fired. If the muzzle of a pistol was held directly and tightly against the scalp, there could be no external powder burns; but the gases generated by the explosion had to find some place to escape, and the result usually was that the scalp was torn loose from the skull and ballooned, and the powder stains were found between the scalp and the skull instead of on the outside of the head. On the other hand, if the pistol was held against the skull by any person other than the one who was shot, there would be enough flinching even in sleep to allow some escape of gas and powder on the outside of the skin. So if ballooning and powder burns were found between the scalp and the skull, the indications of suicide were practically conclusive; no other person could or would hold the muzzle of a gun tightly enough against the scalp to produce such results. This ran directly counter to the opinion leaked by the State Attorney's office just after the shooting.

A study of the report of the county physician, who had signed Haden Clarke's death certificate, and reference to the newspaper statements of Dr Deederer, did not suggest that any scientific study of this kind had been made. It was a serious omission that ought to be remedied by an autopsy. On the other hand, such an autopsy might produce dangerous evidence against Lancaster. After consideration, Carson decided that his correct course was to put the proposition directly to Lancaster, explaining that an autopsy would be likely to show how the fatal shot was fired. Lancaster's reaction was immediate: he insisted that an autopsy be applied for.

Carson would have preferred, for reasons of strategy, to delay such an application until shortly before the trial, when the news of disinterment would create a greater impact. But his inquiries suggested that Clarke's body might not have been embalmed. Because of the danger that an unembalmed body would not be long preserved he called a motion for disinterment and autopsy at the earliest possible date.

On May 23rd Judge Henry Fulton Atkinson, the circuit judge named for the trial, granted the motion and appointed a medical commission of three. The State Attorney was to name one member, the defence another, and Judge Atkinson the third. Both prosecution and defence would have the right to have other physicians present, and Dr Deederer, representing Clarke's family, was also given the right to attend. Carson named Dr Dodge, and also asked two other physicians, Dr Walter C. Jones Jr., chief of staff at the Jackson Memorial Hospital, and Dr Joseph S. Stewart, an assistant in surgery, to be present. Dr Donald F. Gowe was appointed by Hawthorne and Dr M. H. Tallman was the nominee of the court. The autopsy was fixed for the morning of May 31st, and the commission's report was eagerly awaited by Carson.

In a tiny cell ten feet by eight on the twenty-second floor of the Dade County Justice Building, Bill Lancaster waited for a total of fourteen weeks for the trial that was to free him or send him to the electric chair. During all that time he was allowed no exercise, but he kept as fit as he reasonably could by pacing round his cell. Chubbie was not allowed to see him, but she took a packed lunch to him every day, leaving it with the lift-man on the ground floor. Lancaster sent Chubbie a message asking her to walk to the corner of the street beneath his cell window at the same time each day, so that he could see her and feel that he still had some contact with the outside world, and for some weeks she kept a daily rendezvous, waving to the window where she knew he would be watching. Carson, however, got to hear of it and told Chubbie to keep right away; if she were seen signalling to Lancaster the prosecution might allege some collusion between them. But she still continued to take his lunch to the lift-man each day.

What was the effect of this prolonged solitary confinement on Bill Lancaster? What was his attitude to a world which clearly sought to condemn him? An insight is given by two letters that he wrote during this time, one to his wife and the other to his eldest daughter, Pat. The letter to his daughter is perhaps the more remarkable, written as it was to a ten-year-old child whom he had not seen for five years, setting out the conditions of his daily life, assuring her of his innocence, and providing her, perhaps, with a document to revere and cherish should the verdict go against him.

June 21*st*, 1932
MIAMI,
FLORIDA,
U.S.A.

MY DEAREST PAT,

For you, darling, I am writing a book. It may take a long time, but if time permits it will be completed. There are many reasons why one writes a book. Of course a strong reason is for the monetary gain, if the book should turn out successfully in the eyes of the world. But this is not the only incentive. I want you to understand a little of the thoughts and actions of "Old Bill" during the five years that have passed since you waved goodbye to a small aeroplane on the aerodrome at Croydon.

At the present time my small kingdom consists of a room ten feet by eight in a gaol. Not a nice place, in spite of it being on the twenty-second floor of the Town Hall, and commanding a view of the sea, and the beach, and the boats. The gaolers are not inhuman people, and treat me very well. Fortunately some friends still remain, and I have my food brought to me from the outside world. I have books to read, and a radio which I can turn on and imagine I am far away. Sometimes when certain strains of old songs or operatic music come from the loud-speaker I lean back and conjure up memories of those days that have gone before. India, Australia, New York, and England.

Of course some people will have condemned me already, and will have said that I am lost to the world, at least the world as I would have you know it. A world of brightness, of ambitions, of love. But this is not so, because they put me in this gaol without real cause. They accused me of something that I did not do. And the newspapers carried stories of the circumstances as they would like them to be (to sell their papers), not as they really were.

Soon an opportunity will be given me to tell the true story, and to produce the evidence which will support the story. Then things will be much better, because I shall be released from the gaol, and everyone will say that I was treated badly. It will be then that I shall start writing the book I have spoken about.

Your Mother, dear sweet person that she is, wrote a letter to the lawyer who is helping me with my case, and she told him of two ways to put forward a defence. She did not know the true story, but had just read warped reports printed in the newspapers. Still it was kind of her to obtain the opinion of some learned lawyer in England.

Your Mother, Pat, is one of the nicest mothers in the whole world for a little girl to have, and I hope you will always love her very much, and be sweet to her, helping and loving her so that she too will love you so much.

You see darling, Old Bill knows. He has wandered all over the world, and met many many people. But never has he met anyone nicer than your Mother. Always think of this, and try to do things which will make your Mother happy, and glad that she has you for her little girl. When Nina Ann grows as big as you are now, you must tell her too.

Some day you may meet me again, flying an aeroplane back to the same field that I flew away from. I have tried very hard to make this possible during the last five years, but somehow the days, months, and years have come and gone, and still I have no aeroplane in which to fly back. I wonder if you would be very excited and joyful if this did happen.

I think of you often, and wonder how tall you have grown, and what you are doing, and if you are becoming a clever girl. London, where you are, is the nicest town in all the world. America is not really a nice place to live in. American people are so insincere and crude. Of course not all of them. I have some American friends who are just as nice as anyone in England.

At the present time I have two lawyers, who are very nice men, and very clever. They are working hard to show everyone, that is all who think me guilty of wrong, that I have not been wrong, and should be released from gaol, with an expression from the proper tribunal that it was a shame to have ever put me in here. One is named James Carson, and the other James Lathero. The two James I call them. James number one is Mr. Carson. He is the senior counsel, and is a very learned man, somewhat like Stephen Coleridge, of whom you have doubtless heard your mother speak.[1] James number two is much younger. He comes to see me every day and he runs around all over the place seeing people who can tell him anything about incidents bearing on my case.

When one is in such a fix as Old Bill is in, it takes a lot of money to straighten things out. In America distances are so great, and for people to be brought to Miami to give testimony it costs a great deal to pay travelling expenses.

Perhaps I had better tell you a little of the true story which will be told in a little while for all the world to know. You see they said I shot a man and killed him. But this man shot himself, because he did not want to live any more. He was not a nice man at all. He had no money, and he was a failure. He drank to excess, and he used a dope which had undermined his constitution. Well, he went from bad to worse, and finally he decided he had nothing more to live for, so he took his own life.

Now he was my friend, so I did not want everyone to know what kind of a man he was. But now I am afraid everything will come out, as there are other people who knew all about this, and they insist on telling, as they think they should do this for my sake.

Then the doctors had to confer over the case, and exhume this man, so as to be able to express an opinion as to what caused his death. They were very clever doctors, and I had to pay a lot of money for their services. But they talked and talked, and examined everything, and finally agreed (all of them), that this man took his own life.

All this is not a very nice thing to talk about, and you will have to ask your Mother to explain it all to you. She has probably been very worried about it all. For remember darling, if you ever do wrong, or are accused publicly of doing wrong, it hurts people who are your relations, or friends, as in my case now. But when the truth is made known, and it is shown that you really did not do wrong, in a measure things are put right.

When you write, address your letter to the Army & Navy Club, New York City. Kiss Nina Ann and Mother for me. And remember my

---

[1] Kiki Lancaster was a niece by her first marriage of the Hon. Stephen Coleridge, son of the late Lord Coleridge, a former Lord Chief Justice of England.

thoughts are of you darling. By the grace of God, and the love of your Mother, you will grow up to be like her and never be in a situation such as I now find myself in.

Goodbye darling until my next letter.

BILL

Events were to show that the findings of the medical commission fell short of being conclusive and that the issue was not so clear-cut as Lancaster apparently believed or perhaps had been led to believe by his counsel. No doubt they argued that it might be fatal to his morale not to be reassuring on this point. Again, evidence Carson was amassing on the temperament of Haden Clarke would be challenged by the prosecution. But while the letter may well have been written with an eye to posterity, it was hardly intended to be used to influence anyone at the trial, otherwise the reference to the insincerity and crudeness of some Americans would surely have been omitted. The letter lapses at times into sentimentality, but in substance it is not a document that would have given much encouragement to the prosecution. Three weeks later a letter written to his wife shows only a small deterioration in his mental state after nearly twelve weeks in gaol. Allowing for a natural revulsion from the high-pressure publicity methods to which Englishmen were not then accustomed, it strikes a note of calm confidence.

MIAMI GAOL
July 14th, 1932

Your letter of July 4th reached me this afternoon. It is one of the few things that are worth while that have come to me for such an age.

When Haden Clarke shot himself he placed me in a ghastly position, which I made even worse by trying to get him to sign notes which I had typed—self-preservation instincts caused me to do this. I did no wrong in the matter.

Trial is now set for August 2nd. The authorities have been unfair, but NOT as unfair as have the Miami newspapers. It is going to be an ordeal, but I am fortified by the knowledge that I am innocent of the charge.

Unless there is unfairness, which is not unlikely, the courts here are rotten, I shall be cleared in an honourable way. James Carson, my chief lawyer, is a learned man, a "gentleman".

I have been terribly handicapped by lack of money. In America "justice" is a matter of dollars and cents. Have been 3 months in gaol the *whole* time in a cell 10 feet by 8 feet. They are setting the court in the typical American manner (for a gloating public), wired so that everything can immediately be given out. The various newspaper syndicates sending special representatives etc. etc.

You can depend on my keeping the chin up! No white feathers

Building a Defence 127

around. Just annoyance. I suffer greatly at the thought of such harm as may be done to you and the babes through all this.

Will write again before the trial. Appreciated photos sent by Pat. Kiss the babes for me.

B

Again it is a letter clearly meant for the eyes of the addressee alone.

The trial was due to begin in just over a fortnight—on August 2nd, 1932. As Lancaster was evidently aware, the world Press was getting ready to report it in detail.

CHAPTER XII

The Evidence is Circumstantial

MORE than two hours before the Circuit Court was due to open on the morning of August 2nd, 1932, scores of people were milling about in the lobby outside the courtroom on the sixth floor of the Dade County Courthouse and crowds more were outside at street level clamouring to get in. The lobby and corridors were jammed so tightly that court bailiffs had difficulty in moving people to allow the entry of jurymen and witnesses to the courtroom; these alone made a sizeable crowd. There were over a hundred prospective jurymen and about forty witnesses. Women, young and old, in sleeveless cotton dresses, some with children, predominated in the crowd outside, but there was a liberal sprinkling of shirt-sleeved men. Judge Atkinson had ordered that the public were not to be admitted until a jury had been selected.

Shortly before nine-thirty, prosecuting and defending counsel took their seats and the Press table to the extreme right of the judge's dais began to fill up. The defence table was right-hand centre—facing the judge and to his left—and the prosecution table was facing the judge to his right. On the extreme left of the judge was the jury box, facing inwards like the Press table opposite. Lancaster would thus be seated on the side nearest the jury. Pale after exactly three months in gaol, he had entered with his defence counsel and was at once asked to pose for photographers. Dressed in a light-brown suit, grey shirt, and tan tie, he looked relaxed and actually laughed as he stepped forward for pictures to be taken. Standing to the right of the judge's dais, he was caught for a moment in the folds of the big American flag as it rippled behind him in the breeze admitted by the open courtroom windows. He asked the Press men to send a message to his father: "Don't worry, everything is all right—Bill."

Chubbie stared straight in front of her and did not smile when the photographers asked her to pose for them. Her lips were tightly compressed and she was tense and nervous. Diminutive as she was, she made a striking figure in white silk dress, white hat, and white shoes with yellow insteps. The reporters of the time thought it worth while to add that she was wearing flesh-coloured stockings.

Lancaster sat between his two defending counsel, the bespectacled Carson on his right and Lathero on his left. At the prosecution desk, Hawthorne was conferring with Deputy State Attorney Henry M. Jones and special assistant H. O. Enwall. Then Dr Beverly L. Clarke, brother of the dead man and head of a chemical research laboratory in New York, entered the courtroom and took a seat at the prosecution table. His appearance alongside the State forces was the first shock of the trial.

The next surprise came in an unexpected plea by the defence for a postponement. Dr P. L. Dodge, the medical expert on whom Carson was particularly relying to testify that the wound in Clarke's head indicated suicide, was suffering from heart trouble and would not be able to attend until September, and Carson was reluctant to start the trial without him. In support of his motion he went into full details on Dr Dodge's career, stressing that because of his work he had seen many cases of suicide. Dodge, he said, would testify that the findings of the autopsy were entirely consistent with his personal conviction that Clarke committed suicide. In addition Dr Dodge would testify that he had made a special study of the effects of a drug known as marijuana to which the defence expected to prove that Clarke was addicted; further, he had studied Clarke's mental and emotional background and it was such as to render suicide "eminently probable". Dodge's testimony, urged Carson, was not merely cumulative to the other medical evidence available but widely material: no other expert was in possession of the facts to which Dodge could testify.

There is little doubt that Carson was dismayed at the absence of Dr Dodge and genuinely hoped for a postponement; but he must have known that with forty other witnesses called and prepared to attend, the presence of this one witness, whose basic testimony was available to the court in the form of the report of the medical commission of which he had been chairman, was unlikely to be judged indispensable. The motion was denied by Judge Atkinson, and the selection of a jury was begun. When the ventremen had been whittled down, Carson questioned them closely on their attitude towards foreigners, and whether the fact that Lancaster was a British subject would affect their judgment. He also sought assurance that they would not be prejudiced by revelations of moral laxity. The jury was eventually sworn in shortly after the lunch recess. Before a packed courtroom Hawthorne then began the indictment.

Hawthorne characterized the tragedy as one containing all the varied elements of human interest. Behind the tragedy was the undying love of Bill Lancaster for Chubbie, which was exploded when he received the news that his beloved had been taken from him by his best friend. Hawthorne traced the history of Lancaster's love for Chubbie and referred briefly to the agreement with Latin-American Airways. "Prior to leaving

Miami for the west," he said, "Lancaster became so 'sold' on Haden Clarke that he regarded him as the one individual he could trust to keep Chubbie for him during his absence. Clarke was assigned to care for and to assist in writing the book. That assignment was accepted by Clarke.

"A few weeks after Lancaster left Miami he began to hear rumours and reports that Chubbie was falling in love with Clarke and that they were having wild drinking parties. . . . Lancaster kept a diary daily in which he jotted down his business and love affairs. He recorded his very heart throbs. . . . Finally he heard definitely of the love affair and paced the floor saying 'I'll get rid of him.' "

It was on March 29th that Lancaster learnt of the alleged infatuation and alienation of affection at home. The testimony would show that Lancaster had threatened Clarke's life on that day and again on April 6th. "What he had heard as gossip he learnt in St Louis was based on truth. It was then that he bought a pistol and a box of cartridges. On the last night out from Miami he broke open the box of cartridges in a hotel room and loaded the pistol."

Hawthorne then referred to Lancaster's hurried return to Miami, the quarrel at the dinner-table, and Lancaster's threat, as he called it, to leave. "He was prevailed upon to remain. They retired about midnight. About 3 A.M. on April 21st E. H. Huston, a Miami attorney and treasurer of Latin-American Airways, was called and told that Clarke had shot himself."

The State, concluded Hawthorne, would show that Lancaster had repeatedly asked whether Clarke would be able to talk again. He admitted forging the "suicide" notes. The pistol found in the room was the one Lancaster had bought in St Louis. The State would attempt to prove by its testimony that Lancaster asked Huston to admit ownership of the pistol. No fingerprints were found on the pistol; it had been wiped clean. Thus Hawthorne would show not only premeditation but subsequent fears of discovery and deliberate attempts to mislead.

Carson began by saying that, although there were some details in the prosecution's opening statement which the defence thought it could demonstrate were absolutely untrue, he would agree that the picture to be presented would carry almost every possible element of human and dramatic interest. Right at the outset he made a point of accepting that his client was in a highly precarious position, beset by circumstances sufficient to arouse the gravest suspicion. "Let me start by saying that there shall be no denial that the so-called 'suicide notes' were forged by Captain Lancaster. It will be stated and proven, I think, to you that they were written after Haden Clarke had destroyed his own life by shooting himself in the head with a pistol; and that they were written perhaps with a view in the Captain's mind of preventing the ghost of this dead man coming between him and Chubbie, whose devotion Mr Hawthorne has told you he so ardently desired."

The State's case, said Carson, was one of circumstantial evidence; in such cases the circumstances depended almost entirely for their efficacy upon the point of view from which one looked at them. The investigation by the State was bound to have been made from the standpoint of the prosecution, who quite properly were trying to prove guilt and get a conviction. But if any circumstance was consistent with the innocence of the defendant, it was the court's duty, in accordance with the law of the land, to adopt that construction, since every defendant was presumed to be innocent until he had been proved guilty beyond reasonable doubt.

Thus Carson endeavoured to rid the minds of the twelve jurymen of the preconceptions and prejudices from which he felt they must inevitably be suffering, at the same time conceding that, looked at from one side only, the case against Lancaster was strong. He then moved on to the story of Lancaster's life, his association with Mrs Keith-Miller, their arrival in America, their settlement in Miami, and their introduction to Haden Clarke. After speaking of Clarke's brilliant mind, interesting and vivid imagination, and charming personality, Carson added that he thought the evidence would show that he was also emotionally unstable, almost unbalanced, probably neurotic, and certainly erotic in his disposition.

Carson went over the details of Lancaster's flight west and referred to his business associates, the men on whom the State relied to buttress their case. When they came to the witness stand he would ask them not only what their permanent residence was, but also their temporary residence. This was a reference to Tancrel and Russell, both of whom were in custody.

Carson said they would not deny that when Lancaster decided to return to Miami he had it in mind to straighten out the situation between Haden and Chubbie. He accepted that there had been tension on Lancaster's return, and that Clarke had reacted angrily when Lancaster told him he had acted the part of a cad. Nevertheless the testimony would show that agreement was reached that night that the wedding should be postponed for a month.

Carson now came to Lancaster's movements after the shooting. "He leant up towards the foot of his bed and turned on the light, and over there in the other bed he saw Haden Clarke in his death struggle on his back with blood on the pillow and on the bed. He shouted to Chubbie; she didn't hear him. Then he must have thought of the circumstances; he must have thought of himself; he must have thought of the danger of the situation so far as it affected him, not in the mind of the public nor in the eyes of the court, but of the danger of the situation in so far as it affected him in the eyes of Chubbie; because then he did the most colossally foolish thing that it was possible for a man under those circumstances to do—

then he forged two suicide notes, trying to make it appear to Chubbie's satisfaction that Haden had committed suicide. Except for those two notes, when you have heard the history of this case, I am sure you will all agree that there would be no indictment here. The only possible explanation is that he lost his head and he did fool things, as other innocent men who foresaw themselves accused of crime and were innocent have done before him."

After drawing attention to the fact that there had been no coroner's inquest, although the law of Florida required that where a man was believed to have come to his death by the criminal agency of another there should be such an inquest, Carson mentioned Lancaster's visit to Lathero and his voluntary confession to Hawthorne of forging the notes. He then came to the question of the autopsy. "All this defendant had to do if he had been guilty was to let the body stay where it was, but he made the motion and Mr Lathero and I signed it, and Judge Atkinson granted it. A medical commission of three was appointed." Its brief had been to examine the body with a view to determining the physical signs or indications pointing to murder or suicide. Whether Dr Dodge was able to attend or not, the defence expected to be able to establish suicide by the medical testimony, chiefly because the absence of powder burns showed that the gun had been held tightly against the scalp when fired.

Finally Carson outlined the evidence he would bring on the life and temperament of Haden Clarke. The defence would show that he was drinking heavily, that he was smoking marijuana, and that he had discussed suicide by shooting in the head in considerable detail. His physical condition too was bad. "We ask you, in listening to the evidence," said Carson, "not only to see whether it fits the picture of guilt, but in measuring any circumstance, to decide for yourself whether the circumstance is consistent with that presumption of innocence which the law affords the defendant."

When Carson had finished his opening statement, the court was recessed for the day.

At nine-thirty next morning, Wednesday, August 3rd, the prosecution began the presentation of its case. The first witness for the State was Ernest H. Huston, the Coral Gables attorney. After describing how he was called to the house on the night of the tragedy, he was questioned by Hawthorne on what happened when he arrived. He had met Lancaster on the first-floor landing. "My God, it's terrible," Lancaster had said. He had gone into the sleeping-porch, where Clarke lay on the bed unconscious. Lancaster had shown him two notes said to have been left by Clarke and he had read them. They had gone downstairs, where Mrs Miller had said she feared a scandal if the notes were made public. Lancaster had wanted to tear them up, but he had pointed out their importance. He then described the position of the beds and the gun, which had been under the body, partly concealed.

"Was anything said about the gun to you by Lancaster?"

"On the way to the Everglades Hotel I asked Lancaster if it was my gun and he said no."

"What prompted that question?"

"I was curious. I thought it was my gun as I had lent him one prior to his trip west."

"Did he make any suggestion about the gun involved in the shooting?"

Huston hesitated. "May I ask a question?" Permission was given, and he continued: "I presume that any questions between myself and Lancaster as my client—he was in the position of being my client at that time —have been waived?"

"We waive nothing," said Carson. It was a welcome opportunity to demonstrate that the defence wanted everything brought out into the open. Huston then told of Lancaster's attempts to prevaricate over ownership of the gun.

"Were either you or Latin-American Airways indebted to Lancaster?" asked Hawthorne.

"I was not. I don't know about the company."

Hawthorne retired to his desk and Carson, coming forward to cross-examine, produced as an exhibit a photograph of Lancaster's bed taken by the police on the morning after the shooting. "Is that a fair picture?" he asked.

"No. When I first saw the pillow it was mussed." Here the first vital point for the defence was made.

Carson next interpolated a question about Clarke, the first brush-stroke in the picture he hoped to build up of Clarke's frame of mind. "Was Haden Clarke ever your client in a divorce proceeding?"

"Clarke was never my client. We discussed it about two weeks prior to Lancaster's return."

"Did Lancaster say he wished Clarke could speak *so he could tell why he did it*?" Carson carefully emphasized the final clause.

"He did."

Charles P. Ditsler, the ambulance driver, was Hawthorne's second witness. He described the objections that were made to the removal of the body, and how Clarke was finally carried down the stairs on the authority of assistant-manager Yeargin about forty minutes after he first arrived. Hawthorne then asked a question to which he almost certainly expected a firm negative answer.

"Did Haden Clarke's body strike the walls or banisters while being carried to the ambulance?"

"I'm not sure."

This was the answer Carson needed to explain the bruise found on

Clarke's body, and he did not cross-examine. The latter part of Ditsler's testimony was then corroborated by Yeargin, who was followed to the stand by policeman Earl Hudson. Hudson described how he was called to the Jackson Memorial Hospital soon after 3 A.M. on April 21st because of an attempted suicide. Lancaster and Mrs Keith-Miller, he said, arrived shortly afterwards. Lancaster asked several times if Clarke would recover consciousness long enough to talk. With another emergency man he went to the house at Coral Gables and examined the bedroom. Asked whose gun it was, Lancaster said it belonged to Latin-American Airways. He had heard of the notes at the hospital and when he got to the house he had taken possession of them.

"Did Lancaster say he hoped Clarke would talk so he could tell how it happened?" asked Carson in cross-examination.

"Yes."

The addition of that final phrase again made all the difference, and Carson was taking every chance of underlining it. The coincidence of Earl Hudson's connection with Haden Clarke was also worth establishing: Hudson agreed that he had known the dead man as "Charlie" Clarke and that Peggy Brown was his wife's sister. He also agreed that he found a number of letters from Peggy Brown addressed to Clarke in the Keith-Miller home.

"Did you ask Lancaster if he knew of any reason why Clarke should want to kill himself?"

"Yes."

"What was his reply?"

"He said Clarke had contracted a disease which preyed heavily on his mind."

After her release from gaol Chubbie had gone back for a few days to the house on S.W. 21st Terrace. But when sightseers began peering through the windows she decided it was time to move. In any case Carson and Lathero didn't like her staying there alone, and eventually she moved into the Everglades Hotel. For the past three months she had managed to keep out of the public eye. But the promise to Carson, she knew, would one day have to be redeemed. The moment came on the morning of Wednesday, August 3rd, when she was the fifth witness to be called to the stand. She was called as a court witness, Hawthorne explaining to the jury that he believed she would give prejudiced testimony. Since he himself had questioned her for many hours and finished up by expressing confidence in her story, it is hard to see this manœuvre as other than an attempt to discredit her evidence in the eyes of the jury. However, the move did allow him to reserve to himself the privilege of direct cross-examination.

In order to raise money to meet the expense of getting key witnesses to the trial, Chubbie had agreed, at Carson's instigation, to give an interview to a features agency. The result was a lurid piece of sensational journalism and at first she had flatly refused to sign it. Carson, however, pointed out that it was an essential part of his plan for a successful defence, first to get money, second to help excite sympathy for Lancaster. The story was released on the morning Chubbie was due to appear on the witness stand, so as to make the maximum impact, the release apparently not being regarded as contempt of court. The document did give her an opportunity to reassert her faith in Lancaster's innocence, but it brought home to her the full extent of the sacrifice she was making and the ordeal she was about to face. When the moment came for her to be called to the stand she was shaking with nerves.

As Hawthorne stepped forward to question her, Chubbie was blinded by a volley of photographers' flash-bulbs but even so was aware of a curious, corporate gape directed at her from all round the courtroom. Then some of the faces swam into focus. A few paces to her right, raised slightly above her, was Judge Atkinson. Aged seventy-one, white-haired and benign, he had a reputation for broad humanitarianism, and as Chubbie glanced towards him she felt the quiet encouragement of his presence. Hawthorne and his supporting counsel had their table about twelve feet in front of her to the right; Carson, Lathero, and Bill were the same distance away and slightly to the left. Bill looked pale, but incredibly calm.

After establishing that she had known Lancaster for about five years and Clarke for just over three months, confirming the make-up of the household at 2321 S.W. 21st Terrace, and fixing the date of Lancaster's departure for Mexico as March 6th, Hawthorne came swiftly to the point.

"Mrs Miller, were you engaged to Lancaster?"

"You can't be engaged to a person already married. But I intended to marry him."

"Did he understand that?"

"Yes." The understanding had been reached, she said, about five years earlier. She had changed her mind when she met Haden Clarke.

Because of her nervousness her voice was barely audible, and under the pressure of Hawthorne's questions her lips trembled. Several times he had to ask her to speak up so that judge and jury could hear her answers.

"Did Lancaster suspect anything wrong in Miami before he arrived at St Louis?"

"I believe he did, because Gentry Shelton telegraphed to say that some scandal had reached Bill."

Prompted by Hawthorne, Chubbie described how Lancaster had telephoned her from some mid-continental city and told her that her voice sounded cold. He had pressed her to say if anything was wrong between them and she had begged him not to question her further, telling him that letters from both her and Clarke were awaiting him in St Louis. Her letter, she said, had been handwritten, of three or four pages, while Haden's had been shorter and typewritten. Later they had each written a second letter. Of all these letters, only a carbon copy of one, and brief extracts from another, could now be traced.

"Did you anticipate trouble when Lancaster received the letters?"

"Not trouble, although I knew he would be upset."

"Did he intimate that he was upset by telephone or letter?"

"Yes."

Satisfied that the premeditation he hoped to prove was now firmly fixed in the mind of the court, Hawthorne moved to Lancaster's return to Miami. Lancaster had telephoned from St Louis to say he was coming if she wanted him, and she had told him that of course she wanted him. He had seemed depressed on arrival, but his attitude to both her and Clarke had been cordial. Hawthorne hoped to call evidence to contradict this picture of a harmonious meeting, but now he moved quickly through the conversation as they drove home in the car. Lancaster had asked that the marriage be delayed for a month and she had agreed. Chubbie described Clarke's hasty temper at dinner and Lancaster's apparent composure. They had gone to bed at a quarter to one.

"What was Lancaster's attitude then?"

"I said good night to him and he didn't answer so I called 'good night' again. I didn't want him to think I was putting him out of my life altogether."

At noon the court recessed for lunch, and at two o'clock Chubbie was back on the witness stand. On the night of the shooting, she told Hawthorne, she was awakened by Lancaster hammering on her door.

"Why was it locked?"

Chubbie told of Clarke's request. She had not heard the shot, nor had she asked Lancaster for an explanation of the shooting. Lancaster had said that Haden shot himself, and that was all. She then went through the events that had followed. It was a straightforward story and Hawthorne could find no fault in it.

"Mrs Keith-Miller, do you know who killed Haden Clarke?"

"I am convinced he killed himself."

Hawthorne reminded her that she had assigned, in his office, a number of reasons why Clarke might commit suicide. "He had a nervous, violent temper," she said, under further questioning. "I have frequently seen him in a rage of temper with his mother." He had got drunk often, though not in the presence of his mother.

"Why did he have these frequent fits of anger in the presence of his mother?"

"Because she nagged him. She was always talking about what she had done for him, what he had cost her, and what an ungrateful son he was."

If Hawthorne disbelieved her he could always call Clarke's mother in rebuttal, and this at a later stage he hoped to do. He then came to Chubbie's statement that Clarke had often discussed suicide. Chubbie confirmed this, and said it had happened in the presence of others. Hawthorne intended to call witnesses in dispute of this point as well. But Chubbie now related how she and Clarke had once talked of a suicide pact. "I was frightfully wretched over what I had done to Bill," she said, "and I told Haden that I wished we could end it and both go out together." Haden, she added, had been afraid that Bill might recoup her affections. But the two men had gone to bed that night on friendly terms.

"Didn't you say in my office that you were uneasy until you heard laughter?"

"I had no fear of violence but it was most certainly a relief to know that they were getting along all right."

Moving to Chubbie's long association with Lancaster, Hawthorne reminded her that on May 2nd she had made a narrative statement in his office in which she had stated that Haden Clarke was not aggressive, that she never saw him lose his temper unless he was drunk, and that he did not get drunk often. Now, perhaps out of loyalty to Lancaster, she was telling a different story.

"I certainly did not say that Haden seldom got drunk. If I did, I was trying to shield his memory."

"Are you not equally anxious to protect Lancaster?"

Hawthorne had reached the apex of his examination. He had drawn the inference he wanted—that the untruths Chubbie had been prepared to commit to shield Clarke's memory might well be eclipsed by the lies she might tell to save Lancaster. "In trying to save Lancaster," he went on, "did you not say that you would issue a statement to the newspapers that you killed Clarke yourself if Lancaster was held?"

"It sounds dramatic, but I did say that."

"Was that statement made for the purpose of helping Lancaster out of his difficulties?"

"Yes."

Finally Hawthorne introduced as a State exhibit the slip of paper Chubbie had delivered to his office on May 2nd after Lancaster's arrest, giving the reasons why she was convinced Haden Clarke had killed himself. He had done all he could to discredit it. But Carson began his cross-examination by dealing with it straight away. It was important to show that it was valid and spontaneous, and he went through it with Chubbie point by point, showing that each item would bear close scrutiny and that the document as a whole added up to a powerful reinforcement of the view that Clarke took his own life. He also dealt with Hawthorne's suggestion that Chubbie would do anything, say anything, to save Lancaster's life. Relying on the impression he felt she would make as a frank and honest witness, he made her admit to having done all she could to help Lancaster, undergoing the most microscopic probing of her private life for his sake. This, he felt, argued more for her confidence in Lancaster's innocence than any collusion in his guilt. Then he turned to her Reason No. 5.

"How long was it after Lancaster left for Miami before your relations with Clarke became more friendly?"

"About two weeks."

Carson made her relate the full circumstances. "After the night you spent on the porch," he asked, "did your relations continue?"

"Yes."

"How long was it after your first relations with Clarke before he first talked of marrying you?"

"Immediately afterwards Haden asked me if I'd marry him."

Clarke had written at once to his wife to inquire about his divorce, and his wife had later telephoned to say that she had remarried and that he was free to marry when he wanted to. Chubbie had insisted first on seeing that the divorce papers were in order, and three days later, on April 19th, the day before Lancaster's return, a telegram arrived from Clarke's wife to say that it would be illegal for him to marry until she had got her final decree, which would not be until January 1933. The telephone story of her remarriage, it seemed, had been a misunderstanding.

"What effect did the receipt of this telegram have on Clarke?"

"He flew into a rage and called her all kinds of names. He said: 'Where am I going to get a hundred dollars to start divorce proceedings in Miami?'"

"But he tried to object when Bill wanted the wedding postponed for a month?"

"Yes."

Carson felt that Clarke's neurotic, totally unreasonable state of mind must now be clear to the jury. Chubbie had been on the witness stand for three and a half hours, and the court recessed for the day.

CHAPTER XIII

The Prosecution rests its Case

"YESTERDAY when court recessed," began Carson next morning, with Chubbie back on the stand, "you were telling us about a telegram received by Haden Clarke from his wife Kay in San Francisco a day or so before he was shot. Had you seen that telegram?"

"Yes, Haden showed it to me."

"What became of it?"

Chubbie said she had left it on the living-room table, where it had remained until the night of the tragedy. The next time she saw it was when she and Lancaster were released from custody nearly three days later. She had found it screwed up in a ball on the floor.

"Who had been in charge of the house?"

"The police."

Carson was seeking to establish that the police, who had had sole and unlimited access to the Keith-Miller home while Lancaster and Chubbie were held in custody, and who had ransacked the place for documents and papers, had shown rank carelessness or worse in their treatment of some of these papers. Was it, perhaps, such a coincidence that the telegram, screwed up in a ball and discarded, should prove to be a message the receipt of which must have an important bearing on Clarke's state of mind, and therefore on Lancaster's possible innocence? Then there were the missing letters, which Lancaster said he had brought back from St Louis in a folder. The prosecution would contend that they contained material calculated to incite Lancaster and that Lancaster had therefore destroyed them after the shooting; but didn't the evidence of the screwed-up telegram point to a conclusion that the police had lost or mislaid them, inadvertently or otherwise? By the juxtaposition of his questions Carson was planting this idea in the court's mind.

Chubbie then went through the entire story of the night of the tragedy again, just as she had done with Hawthorne, but if anything in still more detail. Carson was determined to show that they were omitting nothing.

At length they reached the point where Chubbie had asked Lancaster for a few minutes alone with Clarke. Lancaster had gone out for about half an hour, and she and Clarke had talked over the situation. Haden had said that Bill would try to get her back. She couldn't remember all that was said, but Haden had asserted that he didn't know where to turn or what to do. They had both agreed that matters were worse. Haden had then spoken of his divorce plans, explaining that they could probably be married in any state other than California and be legally married as long as they stayed out of California. But she had refused.

"Was there any further discussion about postponing the marriage because of Haden's physical condition?"

"Yes. There was to be no marriage until he was cured."

Lancaster had then returned, and after a discussion Chubbie had persuaded him to stay the night. He had gone upstairs to the sleeping-porch, and she and Haden had been left downstairs for ten or fifteen minutes. "We talked again of the awful situation," said Chubbie. "Then I made a fool suggestion about suicide."

In her examination by Hawthorne Chubbie had mentioned this conversation, but had appeared to place it earlier in time. Her evidence now caused a murmur to go round the court.

"We were lying on the *longue* with my head against Haden's. I said I wished I could put an end to it all. Haden answered that he felt the same way."

Last of all had come Haden's request to lock her door. Then they had gone to bed. Again Chubbie described every move in detail. Afterwards she had read, she said, for a long time. She didn't know how long.

"Could you hear voices?"

"Yes."

"Were they angry?"

"I heard them laugh. About that time I finished my book and went to sleep."

"What happened next?"

"Bill was banging on the door, telling me to get up."

"Then?"

"I ran to Haden and asked him to speak to me. Then I went out and got my facewasher."

"Is that what they call a wash-rag in Kissimmee or Plant City?" Carson came from Kissimmee, Hawthorne from Plant City. Carson was relaxing the tension, humanizing the bare recital of facts, slowing the evidence down, letting it sink in.

"I believe so."

Carson went on to trace her and Lancaster's movements in calling a doctor and in reading and discussing the notes. Then he asked what Clarke was doing.

"He was still moaning and groaning and his feet were striking against the iron end-rail of the bed. So Bill took the pillow from his own bed and placed it under Haden's feet to keep them from doing this. The ambulance man, who had arrived meanwhile, said not to do that as it would make the blood rush to his head." Here was the explanation of how Lancaster's pillow, mussed at first, had afterwards come to appear as though it had not been slept on.

Laboriously Chubbie followed Carson's prompting through the sequence of events that had followed, up to her arrest and ultimate release. She had been under questioning for six hours twenty minutes when she was finally allowed to leave the stand. Hawthorne, however, reserved to himself the right to cross-examine her directly on her evidence given to Carson, and it was a right he intended, at the appropriate moment, to exercise. For the present, though, he excused her, subject to recall. Carson also reserved the right to recall her, and her place was taken by Dr Carleton Deederer.

Deederer, questioned by Jones, told of the telephone-call he had received from Chubbie. "Doctor," she had said, "Haden has shot himself. Can you come right away?" She had given him the address. When he eventually arrived Clarke had been removed to hospital and he had driven there with Lancaster and Mrs Keith-Miller. A temporary bandage had been applied to Clarke's head at the hospital but it was saturated with blood. He had removed it and noted that the right side of the head was bleeding severely. The bullet had entered the head half-way between the right eye and the hole in the right ear and nearly three inches above the hole in the ear. The exit point was above the left ear but higher, near the top of the head. He had treated Clarke, but at eleven-twenty that morning, April 21st, the patient had died. Deederer then identified photographs of Clarke taken after his death showing the position of the entrance and exit of the bullet.

"Witness with you," said Jones to Carson.

"No questions." Deederer's evidence, Carson would submit, was exactly consistent with a self-inflicted wound, the gun held by the right hand, firing into the head, the bullet coming out on the left side high above the ear. Hawthorne would contend otherwise but would deal with this in detail later; for the moment he was establishing the cause of death. His next witness was J. O. Barker, the man in charge of the police identification bureau in Miami. Barker said he had examined the pistol for fingerprints and had actually found some on the barrel, but they had been smudged.

Hawthorne then began reading to the court the detailed statement made voluntarily by Lancaster on May 2nd. When this was concluded he turned the clock back to the events leading up to the shooting, and especially to the threats alleged by the prosecution to have been made by Lancaster. Here his first witness was J. F. Russell. Russell described how he had first met Lancaster at Miami airport in February. He had met him again in the following month in Texas, where Lancaster, he said, tried to borrow $25 from him to send to Chubbie. "He was very much worried," said Russell, "over her financial destitution and his failure to hear from her." Hawthorne introduced into evidence a letter written to Russell by his wife. This, alleged Hawthorne, was one of the letters that Russell had shown Lancaster in Los Angeles, and Lancaster's reaction to seeing it then was crucial to Hawthorne's case. (The letter was badly mutilated, and the defence would contest that this was in fact the original letter.) "I told him that he had lost out with her," said Russell in evidence, "and that since we left I had heard from my wife in Miami that Clarke had the inside track. Bill asked if I thought Haden had double-crossed him. I said I thought he had. Bill turned on his heel and muttered: 'I'll get rid of him.'"

When the turn came for cross-examination next morning Carson decided to deal with what had passed between Russell and Lancaster in Los Angeles when he had Lancaster on the stand. For the moment he was content merely to question the credibility of Russell as a witness, and he began by making Russell admit that he was at present serving a six-months' sentence for smuggling aliens and dope, following other sentences for similar offences. Russell's attitude throughout was evasive and hostile, which suited Carson's purpose well.

"Did you write a letter to Lancaster from Phoenix?"

"I have reason to believe I did."

Carson handed Russell the letter for identification. It was one of the letters Russell had written to indicate the spot in the Arizona desert where Lancaster was to disembark the Chinamen to be smuggled from Mexico.

"Is that it?"

Russell studied it at quite inordinate length while the court waited, their impatience mounting. "I only asked if you wrote it," said Carson at length.

"I can't tell unless I read it." This retort brought such a gust of laughter that the bailiffs had to call for order.

"When Lancaster left you standing on the ground at the Burbank Airport, did you think it was a dirty trick if there were federal men waiting at the other airport?"

Hawthorne interrupted to question whether the witness's feelings were admissible, and a spirited argument developed between the two attorneys, Carson holding that Russell's attitude towards Lancaster was highly relevant to an evaluation of his evidence. Eventually Judge Atkinson allowed Russell to answer. "I hold no feelings against Lancaster. There was no federal officer waiting at the other airport."

"They found you, didn't they?"

"No."

"They didn't?"

"No. I gave myself up at El Paso."

Whatever the truth of this, Carson had done enough to discredit Russell as a witness, to expose him as a habitual crook, and to suggest a motive for perjury, the motive of malice and revenge. But Hawthorne was not finished with Russell's evidence yet, and as soon as Russell was excused from the stand he introduced into evidence the whole of Lancaster's diary from January to April 1932 and all the letters that had passed between Lancaster on the one hand and Chubbie and Haden on the other while Lancaster was away (except those that were missing). Before he began the reading of the diary and letters he explained that it was necessary to connect Russell's testimony with the diary entries: for instance, when Russell showed Lancaster the letters from his—Russell's—wife, Lancaster's diary comment had been "Mental agony. Hell." What Lancaster had written, coupled with Russell's evidence of threats, was the foundation of the prosecution's case.

The reading of the diary and letters occupied the remainder of Friday, August 5th, right to the end of the afternoon session. Tedious as such a reading might seem, the material was of such absorbing interest that the courtroom listened attentively throughout, and as Hawthorne continued the reading he must surely have wondered whether the jury would react as he intended. Even Lancaster himself, who hung his head shamefacedly when Hawthorne began, must have felt the impulses of sympathy that were generated towards him throughout the court, and he soon straightened visibly and began to assist his counsel in checking the original of the diary against the copy from which Hawthorne was reading.

Next morning, Saturday, August 6th, Hawthorne produced his second State witness on the question of the Lancaster threats—Mark G. Tancrel, president of Latin-American Airways. Tancrel, like Russell, was escorted from his cell high up in the courthouse, where he was being held in custody on a charge of impersonating a naval officer. It was now that they learnt that Tancrel was of mixed British and French blood and that he was born in Mauritius. He was, he said, a licensed captain in the merchant marine. Answering questions on the formation of Latin-American Airways, he described the planned division of profits and said that part of Lancaster's responsibility was to bring two planes into the company. But he had brought only one, and even that had been in such poor mechanical condition that half of it had had to be replaced before they reached their destination. Hawthorne then asked him about a conversation he overheard at El Paso.

"Lancaster and myself were at the Houston Hotel," said Tancrel. "Going to our room I found Lancaster there with a stranger, who was introduced to me as Imce or Ince. I then went to bed and was reading while Lancaster discussed Mrs Keith-Miller and Clarke with Ince. He said: 'I don't think Haden Clarke has double-crossed me, but if he has, well, I've seen a lot of dead men and one more won't make any difference.' "

"After Lancaster went on with Russell to California, did you see him later?"

"I saw Lancaster alone in Nogales, early one morning. Russell had wired me to hold Lancaster by all means. And shortly afterwards a telegram came from Lancaster, saying he would arrive. Then, while McKinley and I were in bed, Lancaster walked in. He said: 'Tancrel, I'm tendering my resignation to you. From now on you can paddle your own canoe. I'm sick of it.' And then later, during the discussion that followed, Haden Clarke's name was mentioned and Lancaster said: 'Russell showed me a letter in Los Angeles and told me all about it. I'm going back east to get rid of that lousy bastard!' "

In cross-examination Carson concentrated on exposing Tancrel as a proved liar who in the smallest matters could not stick to the truth, whose ethical standards were non-existent, whose memory was faulty, whose attitude towards Lancaster was malicious, and who had had every opportunity to concert his testimony with Russell. He established that they were in the same section of the same gaol. "Did you tell your escort after your arrest on May 22nd that 'If you put me in a cell with Lancaster I'll kill him. I'm back here now and I'm going to do everything possible to see that Lancaster burns'?" Carson would be calling evidence to this effect.

"No, I did not."

J. O. Barker, head of the identification bureau of the Miami police department, was then recalled by the prosecution to answer questions on the science of fingerprinting. He reiterated that no fingerprints had been identifiable on the gun used, suggesting that someone had wiped it clean. No evidence had so far been presented to suggest that Lancaster had done this. Carson, in cross-examining, concentrated for the moment on showing the state of the gun when it came into Barker's hands. He had his own ideas on who had wiped it clean.

"Was there any blood on the pistol when you received it?"

"No."

"Could blood have been wiped off without wiping fingerprints from the gun?"

"No."

Barker was excused from the stand, and K. B. Bess, an embalmer employed at the W. H. Combs Funeral Home, where the body of Haden Clarke had been prepared for burial, was Hawthorne's next witness. Hawthorne questioned him about the state of the wound and what it tended to show. Bess said that he found no powder burns, although he made a careful search.

"Do you know of any alleged suicides where the bullet entered on some part of the body not covered, where there were no powder burns?"

Carson was on his feet before the witness could answer. "The witness is not qualified as an expert to answer the question." But his plea was rejected by Judge Atkinson, and the witness was allowed to answer.

"There usually are powder burns showing."

This ran directly counter to the interpretation placed on the medical evidence by the defence, but it wasn't quite good enough for Hawthorne, who had reached the climax of the prosecution case. The witness was being too cautious, anxious no doubt not to commit himself. It would leave an element of doubt. Somehow he would have to persuade Bess to a more categoric pronouncement than this. His object clearly was to leave a firm impression in the court's mind that the evidence of the embalmer ruled out suicide. He tried again.

"Do you recall, in all your experience as an embalmer, any case where you were unable to find powder burns on uncovered portions of bodies of alleged suicides?"

"None that I can remember."

Hawthorne was satisfied, and he handed the witness over to Carson for cross-examination. Carson asked Bess if there was any evidence of disease found by him in his examination of Clarke's body, and Bess replied that there was. After answering a number of questions on the various methods of embalming, the witness stood down. Carson had indicated that he doubted Bess's credentials when it came to expressing an opinion on indications of suicide, and he was content to leave it at that for the moment.

Earl Hudson, the police emergency officer, was then recalled to the stand by Hawthorne. Hudson testified that three people, Mrs Keith-Miller, Lancaster, and Fitzhugh Lee, were present when he found the gun. Huston might also have been nearby.

"Was there any blood on the grip of the pistol?" asked Hawthorne.

"Yes, there was."

"How did you take the gun from the bed?"

"I dropped my handkerchief over it and slipped the pistol into its box, which I found on the table at the foot of Clarke's bed. Later I gave the gun to Barker, fingerprint man at police headquarters."

Carson cross-examined with the object of showing that Hudson's evidence was biased because of his sister-in-law's relationship with Clarke and hopelessly confused over what he did with the gun. He referred first to parties that his sister-in-law had attended at the Keith-Miller home, and drew the inference that drink for these parties might have come from stocks seized by Hudson in police raids. Hudson denied it. Carson then pointed to the gun. "You say you didn't put that gun in your pocket?"

K

"Yes, I did—after placing it in its box."

The box, too, was an exhibit, clearly visible to the jury. "Then you shoved the box in your pocket?"

"Yes."

The size of the box made this statement manifestly ridiculous, and Carson allowed the jury to draw their own conclusions. The handling of the pistol was a point to which he would return.

The newspapers that Saturday morning had announced that several well-known aviators were coming to the trial to give evidence on Lancaster's behalf. Among those listed were Clyde Pangbourne, the round-the-world flyer, Clarence Chamberlin, who had flown the Atlantic with Charles Levine a month after Lindbergh, Rex Gilmartin, commander of the aviation post of the American Legion, New York, and Lieutenant "Bing" Boyer, famous U.S. Army pilot. All, it was stated, would arrive in Miami by air on Monday. The story was run again in the Sunday papers, but the headline news of the trial was that the prosecution planned to recall Mrs Keith-Miller to the stand next day. "State Attorney N. Vernon Hawthorne . . . it is believed . . . will go over point by point the story she told in the six hours and twenty minutes she spent on the stand last Wednesday and Thursday. Hawthorne is confident he can shake the testimony she gave at that time," wrote Francis P. Malone of the *Miami Daily News*. Such a forecast would surely be regarded as contempt of court in Britain; but it proved to be an accurate reading of Hawthorne's intention.

Interest in the trial had mounted steadily in the previous week, and the expectation that Chubbie was to face a gruelling cross-examination by Hawthorne brought hundreds of people to the courtroom on Monday morning. Prospective spectators began to gather on the sixth floor of the courthouse at six o'clock, and once again huge crowds were unable to get in. The leak to the Press proved to be an inspired one, and promptly at nine-thirty Chubbie was recalled to the stand. Hawthorne was out to find inconsistencies in her evidence and discrepancies between one set of answers and another over a period, but Chubbie's replies to his opening questions were confident and consistent. However, Hawthorne had worked out a circuitous but closely reasoned line of questioning about the "suicide" notes and Chubbie's reaction to them which he hoped would embarrass her, and he embarked on it now. He reminded her of their discussion of the notes on the day she was released from gaol, and asked whether she had believed they were authentic. Chubbie confessed to having been puzzled.

"Then you knew Lancaster wrote the notes?"

"No."

"Were you shown fourteen discrepancies existing in the notes?"

"Yes."

"Did you not say that Lancaster didn't and couldn't have written them?"

"No."

"Did you say the language made you know Lancaster didn't type those notes?"

"Yes."

"Didn't you assert that Lancaster's code of honour wouldn't have permitted him to write those notes?"

"I did state that."

"Then the first time you knew of the forgery was when you asked Captain Lancaster directly at the house after your release?"

"Yes."

Hawthorne had reached his point. "If you had asked him if he had killed Haden Clarke and had received the answer yes, would that have surprised you more than the admission of forgery?"

"Most decidedly."

"Although you had stated to me previously that you were as positive that Lancaster had not written the notes as you were that he had not killed Haden Clarke?"

The trap had been beautifully laid, and Chubbie could find no answer to this final taunt. She remained silent, and Hawthorne changed to another tack. Again he began quietly, but again he knew exactly where the line of questioning was taking him.

"Do you still love Haden Clarke?"

"No."

"Do you love Lancaster?"

"No."

"When did your affection die for Lancaster?"

"About two years ago."

"Did it die a natural death?"

"Yes. I am still intensely fond of him."

"Was there anything Lancaster did to cause a natural death of your love for him?"

"No."

"Then did you deliberately betray him in every letter, telegram, and telephone message to him?" Hawthorne's voice rose to a crescendo. "Weren't you a traitor to him during all that time when he was sending you every dollar he could beg, borrow, or steal, when he was sending you even single-dollar bills in his letters?"

Carson interrupted to object to the use of the word "steal", and Hawthorne said he was merely quoting from Lancaster's diary. Carson had warned Chubbie of what she would have to face, but for the moment she could find no answer. Hawthorne, aware that Carson's objection had reduced the cumulative effect of his attack on Chubbie, put the question again.

"Weren't you a deliberate traitor to Lancaster in all those letters, in all those telegrams, all those times you said 'all my love to you'?"

Chubbie had had time to recover. "You don't understand the feeling that exists between Captain Lancaster and myself. We have been through hardships and misfortunes. We were pals, not ordinary friends. We trusted each other."

"I understand your feeling, Mrs Keith-Miller, but I am trying to bring it before the men of this jury," said Hawthorne heavily. The depth of their friendship was vital to his case. He began another circuitous line of questioning which Chubbie followed as best she could.

"So you no longer love the memory of Haden Clarke?"

"No. I have been completely disillusioned."

"By what?"

"Proofs."

"Are you referring to his illness?"

"Yes, and other things. I can't tell you all the reasons."

"What do you mean, Mrs Keith-Miller?"

"I believed in, trusted, Haden Clarke, and he lied to me."

"Did he lie about his love for you?"

"No, I don't think so."

"What then?"

"He lied to me about his age, his university degree, he told me he had never had that malady before, he lied about things he had done."

Hawthorne now underlined the point he had been trying to make. "Then the principal thing that killed your love for Haden Clarke was because he was a liar?"

"Yes."

But Lancaster, whom she now defended so tenaciously, was also a liar, or so Hawthorne intended to show. "You say you don't love Lancaster, but are fond of him. Do you know he pleaded guilty of a crime for which he was not guilty to save you?"

"He always tried to save me, to help me."

"At all costs?"

"Yes."

"You don't love him even though you have said you would die for him?"

"No."

"You'd lie for him?"

Chubbie saw this one coming. "No—because you would know." The tables were neatly turned, and Judge Atkinson had to rap for order. Hawthorne, however, refused to be put off. His endeavour was to show that Lancaster in his way was no more noble a character than Clarke had been, and that Chubbie's revulsion from Clarke and loyalty to Lancaster were explained by other impulses.

"One of the principal things you admire in Lancaster is his code of honour?"

"Yes. He is one of the finest men I ever knew."

"He'd steal for you, wouldn't he?"

"He doesn't steal." Chubbie's anger was immediate.

"Didn't he steal a chicken for you?"

"No," said Chubbie, "it was a duck."

At this the whole courtroom shook with laughter, and the tension Hawthorne was trying to build up was broken beyond recovery. The bailiffs were some time restoring order, and Hawthorne may have been stung into his next question by the reaction of the court. More probably, though, he took advantage of a moment when he thought everyone might be off their guard.

"Do you know Lancaster has a wife?"

"Yes, but —" Chubbie wanted to say that he hadn't been living with her when she met him, but Hawthorne cut in.

"From whom he is not divorced?"

"Yes, but —"

"And two little girls?"

"Yes."

Carson's objection to this line of questioning came surprisingly late and although it was sustained Chubbie had answered and the damage had been done. The image of the honourable Lancaster, man of integrity, was thus seriously tarnished. Hawthorne followed up his advantage. "If Lancaster committed perjury to save you from the penalties of a fine for driving after you'd been drinking, did that increase your admiration for him?"

This time Carson's objection was immediate, the judge sustained it, and Chubbie did not have to answer. But Hawthorne hadn't finished yet. After a series of questions designed to show that Lancaster, because of his polo-playing, broncho-busting and boxing exploits, was a man of action and perhaps of physical insensibility, and that Clarke must surely have been afraid of him and feared his return, he said, "You said earlier that you intended to marry Lancaster; that you believed it inevitable?"

"Yes, I always felt that when Bill was free from his wife in England I would marry him."

"But you weren't in love with him?"

"Being in love and just loving a person are two different things. I was not thrilled or infatuated with Lancaster, just terribly fond of him."

"Were you infatuated with Clarke?"

"Yes."

"Now you do not even love his memory?"

"No." Chubbie broke down as she said it, and the tears welled in her eyes and then flowed. "Unfortunately no." Having brought her down at last, Hawthorne surrendered her to Carson.

Carson did not involve himself or the defence in the labyrinthine arguments traced by Hawthorne. He stuck to the main lines of the defence argument. First there was the dead man's temperament. His rages, said Chubbie, were frequent and indiscriminate and were directed at his mother, at Peggy Brown, even at Chubbie's dog. She agreed that Peggy Brown had often brought quite considerable quantities of liquor to the house. Then, as a reminder to the jury of their conscientious behaviour towards Lancaster's wife and children, Carson referred to the monies they had made from the Australia flight. Thirty pounds a month had been sent to Mrs Lancaster, said Chubbie, and total sums amounting to one-third of what they made. Hawthorne was unable to shake her on these points, or on her earlier revelation of a last, impulsive discussion of suicide after Lancaster had gone upstairs on the night of the shooting. Chubbie, however, was in tears again when she left the stand.

Letters and documents relevant to the case were still missing, and Carson decided to recall Earl Hudson for further cross-examination. Lancaster and Chubbie, he argued, had had no opportunity to sort, select and destroy papers. Earl Hudson, in reply to his questions, claimed that he turned all letters and papers found in the Keith-Miller home over to J. B. Rowland, the State Attorney's chief investigator, on the morning of the tragedy. He had destroyed nothing. Carson held up the telegram addressed to Haden Clarke from his wife. "This telegram, which was found rolled up in a corner of the sleeping-porch—you didn't do that?"

"No."

"What did you do with it?"

"I gave it to Rowland."

Rowland was to be Hawthorne's next and last witness, so Carson left the matter of the missing documents for the moment and recalled Ernest Huston: he wanted to go over one or two points on the ownership of the gun and its condition after the shooting. Huston agreed that his memory had been refreshed since he was last on the stand and that what Lancaster had said was that, as he had bought the pistol to replace the one lent to him, it was already technically Huston's. This helped to excuse Lancaster's statement that the gun was the property of Latin-American Airways. Huston added that when he lent Lancaster the gun he impressed on him that he valued it and wanted it back, which was another useful point for the defence.

Huston then answered questions on the condition of the pistol: Earl Hudson had taken it from the bed, covered it with his handkerchief, and slipped it in his hip pocket. He had not placed it in a box.

"Was there blood on the gun?"

"It was running with blood."

This was a vital point for the defence, showing that the gun had been wiped clean after Hudson had taken possession of it and before it was examined for fingerprints. Huston left the stand and was replaced by J. B. Rowland, who began by giving a damaging piece of evidence against Lancaster. After identifying copies of the "suicide" notes, he told in answer to Hawthorne's question how he had pointed out to Lancaster back in April several similarities between the typing of the notes and copies made under police supervision by Lancaster. "Why, Mr Rowland," Lancaster had said, "isn't that a coincidence, I can't understand that." He had gone on to suggest that the State Attorney employ handwriting experts from New York, and had even offered to assist in finding them. Hawthorne questioned Rowland about the finding of the bullet in the feathers of Clarke's pillow, and the slug was exhibited to the jury with copies of the notes.

"Hudson testified that he saw a telegram signed Kay Clarke and that he gave it to you," began Carson in cross-examination.

"There were a number of letters and papers turned over to me and I don't remember that telegram."

"After her release Mrs Keith-Miller found it crumpled in a ball in a corner of the porch."

"Then it was not turned over to me."

"Did you see two letters from Chubbie to Bill in St Louis?"

"If I saw them now, I could tell you."

"So could we, they're missing."

"I don't remember them."

"Did you see a letter from Virginia Clarke addressed to Clarke in New Orleans?" This was the first mention of Virginia Clarke, whom Carson would show Clarke had married bigamously some time earlier.

"No. But there was lots of correspondence that I didn't read."

Again Carson was suggesting that the State Attorney's investigators had seized documents favourable to the prosecution and ignored those which might help the defence. Above all he was trying to show that the blame for the missing documents must lie with the prosecution.

At this point the State rested its case, and shortly after three o'clock that afternoon, Monday, August 8th, Lancaster took the witness stand.

CHAPTER XIV

Lancaster on the Stand

CARSON'S first task was to introduce Lancaster to the jury not as a possible murderer, or even a man wrongly accused, but as a human being. He wanted them to know him, as Carson himself had got to know him, and to this end he felt it was relevant to go briefly through the whole of Lancaster's past life. In this way he would establish a pattern of behaviour, and defy any prosecution attempt to point to anything in Lancaster's past that might support a contention of guilt. Thus Lancaster's testimony began with details of his birth in Birmingham, England, in 1898, the move of his family back to London, his schooldays, and his departure for Australia. His war service, his studies at London University, his return to the Royal Air Force, his service in India, and his transfer to the reserve in 1926, were all touched on. Lancaster may have felt that his transfer to the reserve was a point against him, because he actually testified that he had applied for the transfer to make the Australia flight, which appears to have been untrue: his short service commission had expired in 1926. Then in 1927 had come the flight to Australia with Mrs Keith-Miller. Lancaster described his relations with his flying partner as "friendly but business-like", the exception being an occasion during a stop in Persia. The money they made from the flight was divided three ways, he said, between his wife, Mrs Keith-Miller, and himself. In answer to a question by Carson he explained that his wife had private means and was a widow before her marriage to him soon after the War. This put the best possible complexion on his separation from his wife and family; but the reference to private means was misleading as Kiki had lost her war-widow's pension when she married Lancaster.

The effect of Lancaster's autobiographical narrative was to quicken public interest in him and at the same time to lower the dramatic tension, as Carson no doubt intended. The meeting with Kingsford-Smith and the crew of the *Southern Cross*, the invitation to America, the early disappointments, the association with George Putnam, demonstration flights with the Cirrus engine, the crack-up in Trinidad, and the various jobs held with other well-known American firms—many of these incidents touched a chord of memory among the public and jury. This was doubly true when Lancaster answered questions about Chubbie's flight to Havana in 1930 and his own attempts to find her. Eventually the narrative was brought to the point of Lancaster's return from New York on February 7th, 1932, the meeting with Tancrel, the quarrel over funds, and the final departure west. Carson had just completed his prompting of this narrative when the court recessed for the day, and it was useful to leave this sober record of an eventful and robust but far from dishonourable life in the minds of the jury. They saw Lancaster for a moment in the round, and the impression would remain.

Next morning Carson selected incidents from Lancaster's narrative and questioned him more closely on them. But before he did so, and perhaps provoked by criticism of his slow start of the previous day, he asked the ultimate question. "Captain Lancaster, did you kill Haden Clarke?" Lancaster replied in a flat, dispassionate tone, but the effect was good. "No, I did not." Carson then settled back into his ponderous exploration of Lancaster's life.

"You told yesterday of intimate relations with Mrs Keith-Miller in Persia on your flight to Australia. When again did you have intimate relations?"

"In Sydney, Australia."

"When did you first find yourself in love with Mrs Keith-Miller?"

"Mrs Keith-Miller and I suffered many dangerous trials on the trip to Australia. I grew to admire her character. We suffered many things together. I am sure I was intensely in love with her on our arrival."

"Was it physical passion or unselfish love?"

"Both." Their partnership had endured through prosperity and adversity. His love for Chubbie had increased over the years.

"When did you first meet Haden Clarke?"

Lancaster consulted his diary. "February 9th, 1932." Lancaster told of his discussion with Clarke on finance and on how Chubbie's book was to be written. Clarke was then living in an apartment in Coral Gables, and Lancaster had proposed that he move in right away. He had shared Lancaster's room—the sleeping-porch.

"You roomed together from the first day?"

"Yes."

"Did any other person share a room with Clarke except yourself?"

"Yes, women."

"How many times?"

"Well, on at least three occasions."

"After Clarke moved in, did he do any writing?"

"Very little. I blame myself for that, somewhat, because he always wanted to accompany me on walks, when I took the ship up, and whatever else I did, and I let him." It seemed a fair-minded reply.

"Would Clarke fly into rages?"

"Yes."

"What would he do?"

"Oh, just shout a bit." The lack of undue emphasis must again have been noticed. Asked if he could recall some of the occasions, Lancaster mentioned an outburst in Huston's office, also the incident when a creditor had taken the tyres off Clarke's car and put them on his own.

"Was there drinking at the house?"

"Yes."

"By whom?"

"Oh, all of us, and any guests we might have." Carson had to drag it out of Lancaster that Haden and Chubbie had done a good deal more drinking than he had. He agreed that he had known Peggy Brown, and that she had brought flasks of drink to the house.

"Did she tell you Clarke and herself were engaged to be married?"

"I don't think she used that expression, but she loved the fellow. I remember once she said: 'When Haden and I are married. . . .'"

"Do you know if she had a husband in the offing?"

"He wasn't mentioned. I don't believe so." Carson would later show that she was in fact married. He asked some questions to introduce Gentry Shelton and how he came into the team, then took Lancaster through his involvement with Tancrel and the Latin-American Airways project. The contract had been signed, said Lancaster, the day before he met Clarke.

"Did Clarke outline to you his qualifications for ghost-writing Mrs Keith-Miller's life?"

Lancaster repeated the claims made by Clarke. Their relations had subsequently become close, and he had told Clarke much of the story of his life with Chubbie.

"On the day before your flight westward did you tell him additional details of that life?"

"I had a confidential talk with him on the sun-porch that morning." Clarke had promised to take care of Chubbie for him. "Bill," he had said, "I will care for her in such a way as to make you remember my friendship for ever." It was the first time he had discussed his private life with Clarke; the talk had lasted about half an hour. Carson thus established beyond all doubt that Clarke was fully aware of the nature of the relationship he was disturbing.

Lancaster then answered questions on his suspicions of Tancrel and his efforts to check up on him. "I was still doubtful," he said, "but as I had accepted money—over two hundred dollars—I felt I should go through with the deal. If I had had two hundred dollars at the time I would have returned the money." He had had no suspicions of Russell, except that Tancrel had said that he didn't trust Russell. "He didn't have a uniform," quipped Carson, but Lancaster's reaction amounted almost to a rebuke. "Russell never posed as anything," he said. "At one time he showed me his honourable discharge from the army. He was a private." This spontaneous defence of Russell, one of his chief accusers, again seemed indicative of a sense of fair play.

Carson now asked about the final arrangements for the trip to Mexico. Clarke, Peggy Brown, Chubbie, Tancrel, Gentry, and himself had gone to the airport together. At the airport Tancrel had given him $25 to give to Chubbie. Tancrel was to pay him $100 a week, but Lancaster knew the company was short of money, and Tancrel promised to give him what he could and to make up all his back pay when the company funds were replenished. Having established Tancrel's indebtedness to Lancaster, and the reasonableness of Lancaster's behaviour, Carson switched to an earlier take-off.

"Captain Lancaster, who saw you off on the start of your Australian flight?"

"Many people, my wife among them."

"What is your wife's religion?"

Hawthorne objected at once on the grounds that the question was irrelevant, and Judge Atkinson sustained the objection. But Carson had not asked the question without careful preparation, and he argued his case. "The State first introduced Mrs Lancaster into the testimony," he said. "Under those conditions the defence is entitled to pursue a similar line of questioning." Judge Atkinson then changed his mind and ordered Lancaster to answer.

"She is a Roman Catholic."

In all the circumstances it was an important point to make, and Hawthorne's objection, and the argument that followed, only served to underline the answer in the jury's mind. Carson now moved patiently through the events of the flight to Nogales.

"When and where did you discover the true purposes of the expedition?"

"I doubted Tancrel's story of the expedition's purpose from the start, but wanted to make sure. This I couldn't do without going. At El Paso, Tancrel said Russell had talked to him about Chinamen. Back in Miami, Tancrel had insisted that all flying would be done in Mexico, never crossing the border into the United States, but in El Paso he suggested that the company could ford Chinamen across the border."

"And what did you say?"

"I told him I would have nothing to do with anything illegal."

Tancrel had brought the subject up again frequently in a roundabout way, and a definite proposal was made for the first time when they reached Nogales. One of Russell's letters giving details of the secret landing ground where Lancaster was to disembark the aliens—the letter already shown to Russell by Carson under cross-examination—was exhibited to Lancaster and identified.

"When was dope first mentioned?"

"While in El Paso." Lancaster related the proposal in detail. He had told Tancrel he would have nothing to do with it. The proposal was put to him again later, but he had refused to discuss it. He told them he was going back to Miami.

"Why did you take Russell to Los Angeles?"

"Russell told me he could obtain money in Los Angeles and give me funds for the return flight to Miami."

"Russell planned to leave Tancrel and McKinley at Nogales?"

"Yes."

Much play was made by Hawthorne later with what he castigated as the excessive detail into which Carson had gone over Lancaster's early history and the flight with Latin-American Airways. Hawthorne drew the inference that the defence case must indeed be poor if they needed to confuse the issue with such a wealth of background. But Carson's handling of the examination seems purposeful and logical. Not many men on trial for murder, perhaps, could afford to have their past life held up to the mirror of such an examination; biographical details are often withheld until after a trial. And the more Carson probed the Latin-American Airways project and the people connected with it, the more Lancaster stood out as a decent and law-abiding human being against a background of tempters and crooks. Not one statement of Lancaster's on the business background of the trip had been challenged or indeed would be challenged by the prosecution. Everything he said in evidence, or anyway the substance of it, was confirmed by his letters or by the entries in his diary. The one point at issue was the threats he was alleged to have made; and Carson was coming to them. But first, so as to inconvenience them as little as possible, the friends of Lancaster who had travelled to Miami to testify as to his character were called to the stand.

Carson's belief in character witnesses was also ridiculed later by Hawthorne, and in introducing them Carson was certainly laying himself open to the accusation that he was trying to shore up a crumbling case. No doubt he felt that Lancaster's fame and reputation were worth-while assets and that some at least of the lustre of famous friends would rub off in court. Frank Upton, Rex Gilmartin, Irving Boyer, Clyde Pangbourne, and the Australian Keith Bon, who had travelled specially from Europe, all declared Lancaster to be, to the best of their knowledge, of high reputation as a peaceful, law-abiding citizen. It seemed innocuous stuff, but Hawthorne thought it worth while to cross-examine, his endeavour being to show that all these men knew Lancaster as an aviator rather than personally. Then Lancaster returned to the witness stand and Carson continued his questioning on Lancaster's trip to Los Angeles with Russell.

When Carson came to the point of the alleged threats, Lancaster denied them absolutely. The conversation had taken place, he said, when Russell was unsuccessfully trying to persuade him to fly a plane for alien and narcotic smuggling purposes. Carson referred to two passages from Lancaster's diary for April 2nd, which quoted from one of Mrs Russell's letters, and he asked Lancaster what discussion followed.

"Russell showed the letter to me to encourage my embarking on an expedition with illegal cargo. He said: 'It's no good going back to Miami now. Clarke has taken your place. What you need is some quick money, about five thousand dollars, and then you can go back and get rid of him.' " Lancaster was thus attributing to Russell the very phrase of which Russell was accusing him.

"What else did you say?"

"I told Russell I didn't believe his statement. I told him I knew Chubbie and trusted her." (In a letter to Chubbie from Tucson Lancaster had written: "Mrs Russell wrote Russell, but I told Russell: 'You don't know Chubbie. To hell with what you may say or think.' " And the diary entry written in Los Angeles adds confirmation. "Russell finishes himself as far as I am concerned—because he talks about Chub in a nasty manner." So it seems that Lancaster's account of the conversation may well have been the true one.)

"When was the next time you saw Russell?"

Lancaster told the story of the odd-looking man who Russell said was going to buy stock in Latin-American Airways in return for being taught to fly; of how he, Lancaster, was to be on exhibition with the plane while Russell brought prospective buyers of stock to the field. "I asked him", said Lancaster, "how he expected me to teach all these prospective purchasers and how they were to be given employment with the company, and he replied, 'Oh, by that time we will have left town.' " None of this was ever denied or rebutted by the prosecution, though Hawthorne contended that it was irrelevant to the charge.

"Did you ask Russell for money to send to Mrs Keith-Miller?"

"Yes."

"Did you get any?"

"None."

Lancaster described how he had left Russell behind because of the inquiries by the federal agent. Mrs Stewart, his passenger, had agreed. After flying to Tucson they had been met by Mrs Stewart's husband and driven to Nogales, where he had been reunited with Shelton. He had seen Tancrel next morning.

"Was anyone with you?"

"Yes, I took Stewart with me as I wanted a witness."

Lancaster was thus claiming that for this final interview with Tancrel, when threats were again alleged to have been made, he had a witness.

Curiously enough, neither prosecution nor defence seems to have known of this in time to subpoena Stewart. A witness had also been present during the first series of threats alleged by Tancrel: the ex-RAF pilot Joe Ince at El Paso. Frantic efforts were being made by the defence to find Ince, efforts that were ultimately successful, so it could be that similar attempts were being made to find Stewart; but no record of these attempts survives.

"What did you tell Tancrel?"

"I told him I was through, and he was a fool, and that Russell was a crook." Leaving Tancrel in Nogales, he had returned with Shelton to Tucson.

Lancaster then testified that he had called Chubbie on April 11th from Tucson and told her he had left Russell and Tancrel and resigned from Latin-American Airways. From the sound of her voice he had feared that something was wrong. He had decided to go to St Louis primarily to enable Shelton to visit his parents; awaiting him at the Shelton home were the four letters. "All four were very beautiful and sincere," said Lancaster. They told him that Clarke and Chubbie had fallen in love and planned to marry. Clarke's letters, he said, gave him the impression that Clarke had kept his word but had fallen in love. After a few days in St Louis he had borrowed $100 from Shelton's father, bought a gun to replace the one lent him by Huston, and started east in the plane. He had spent the first night out at Nashville, where he had loaded the gun. Carson did not question him further on this for the moment, allowing the narrative of events to flow unimpeded. Next day he had flown to Miami, where he was met by Mrs Keith-Miller and Clarke. After he had related what passed between them on the drive home, the court recessed for the day.

"Did you ever tell Tancrel and Russell that you were going back to Miami and get that lousy bastard?"

"No. The entire testimony of Tancrel and Russell was a tissue of lies."

This forthright denunciation of the evidence of the threats made a noticeable impression on the court next morning, when Carson resumed his examination. Another point Carson wanted to return to was the loading of the gun. "Yesterday you testified that you loaded the gun at Nashville. Why?"

"I don't know exactly. Mr Huston's gun was loaded when he gave it to me and I wanted to return it in the same manner."

It seemed a convincing answer, not least because of the initial hesitation. It didn't come too pat. Lancaster then repeated the story of the quarrel at dinner. Afterwards Clarke had calmed down. Later Chubbie had promised to delay the marriage four weeks or until Clarke got his divorce.

"Did Clarke say anything?"

"Yes. Clarke came in and said: 'Chubbie, he's trying to talk you out of this.' I went to the other room then and didn't hear the remainder of the conversation."

"Did you say anything about going back to St Louis in the morning?"

"Yes, I planned to leave at dawn for St Louis. I told Chubbie I could work out my future there." Chubbie hadn't wanted him to go, but Clarke hadn't seemed to care. "I told Clarke I didn't care what he said or thought, I was interested only in Chubbie's wishes." He had told Clarke he would like to talk to Chubbie alone, and Clarke had said it was up to Chubbie.

"Did you talk to her privately?"

"No, she refused." This differed from Chubbie's account, but it was the kind of conflicting detail that suggested that both, so far as memory allowed, were telling the truth. They differed slightly too on the exact sequence of events, suggesting that they had not put their heads together to concoct a story.

"What then?"

"I said I would talk to her the next day, and then went out to get some cigarettes while they talked. They were on the *chaise longue* when I returned. I talked with them a short time and then went upstairs." He prepared for bed, then went through a number of letters. He was not sure how long it was before the others came up. Chubbie had said good night and then gone to bed.

"Then what did you talk about?"

Lancaster hesitated. "I refrained from telling Mr Hawthorne much of our conversation when I was first arrested," he said. "I did this to protect Clarke's name and to keep his mother from knowing about the malady from which he suffered. I do not want to tell of that conversation now and I will not unless it is absolutely necessary."

"On my shoulders rests the responsibility for your defence," said Carson. "Please answer my questions."

"Haden talked of his illness. He was almost in tears. He expressed great remorse and regret over what had happened between him and Chubbie. Previously we had discussed the beginning of their intimacy."

"Was there any discussion then regarding the permanence of Clarke's and Chubbie's love for each other?"

"Yes, he was very frank. He said, 'I have had many affairs in my life, but this time I am absolutely in love. I shall do everything in my power to make her happy. Now I have something to work for.' I was impressed with his sincerity."

"Was the question of his age discussed?"

"Yes. He said 'I'm sorry, but I'm not thirty-one.' He said he was either twenty-six or twenty-seven, I can't remember which, and he asked if I thought it would make any difference to Chubbie."

"Did you discuss any other of his false claims?"

"Only about the book. He said he didn't know whether he would be able to put it over. I remember the phrase he used. He said he didn't know if he could 'make the grade'. He also told me that he didn't have his degree."

"Was there any discussion of his claims to previous experience?"

"No. It was a very short discussion."

"Did he say anything about his writings being accepted?"

"Yes. He said the depression started everybody writing. He remarked how terribly hard it was to get money, and he showed me the telegram from his wife, remarking it would cost him from fifty to a hundred dollars to get a divorce in Miami and that he didn't know how to raise the money."

"Was anything said of the month's delay?"

"Yes, I told him to talk to Chubbie in the morning, that he must tell her what he had told me tonight, and that if she loved him she would overlook his mis-statements."

"Was there any other subject discussed?"

"Yes. I remember switching the subject. He appeared so frank and honest and so very sorry at what had happened that I tried to get his mind off it by telling him of the trip. I remember telling one incident at which he laughed, about Tancrel's statement in El Paso. I said: 'Can you imagine a United States Navy captain carrying a paperhanger's union card and claiming to have hung thousands of square miles of wallpaper?'"

"Was Clarke's mother discussed?"

"Yes. He acted rather as if he treated me as a father-confessor. He talked of how he might have done more for her than he had and how sorry he was."

"Was there anything else said?"

"I was lying back on my bed yawning, half asleep, and I said 'Let's talk it over in the morning with Chubbie.' I can remember his last words: 'You're the whitest man I ever met.' Then I turned off the light. It was brilliant moonlight that night."

"Were you tired?"

"Darned tired."

"How was the trip?"

"Bad trip."

The next thing that happened was that he was awakened by a noise. When he first came to, his impression was that a window had fallen. He had called out, "What's that, Haden?"

"What did you hear then?"

"A gurgling sound came from Haden's bed. I turned on the light and looked at Haden's bed. I could see something had happened. It was blood running over his face."

"Did you see the wound?"

"No, not at that time."

"Did you see the pistol?"

"No. I said to him: 'What have you done?' His right arm was bent upwards at the elbow, with the hand turned in towards the body. Then I saw the pistol half under his body."

"When and where did you last see the gun?"

"On the table between our beds. Haden had picked it up and I told him to be careful, it was loaded. We had talked about my buying the gun to replace Huston's, earlier in the evening."

"Where did you first see blood on Clarke?"

Lancaster indicated the location by pointing to his own lower right jaw and under his neck.

"What did you do?"

"I asked him the second time to speak to me. He just moaned. I looked around for a note indicating what had happened. It flashed through my mind that Chubbie might think I'd shot him, prompted by jealousy. I sat down at the typewriter. It took me about five minutes. I then took a pencil and the notes and went to the bed and asked Haden to speak to me again. I asked him to try to sign the notes. Then I shouted 'Chubbie', and got no reply. Then I did something I shouldn't have done. I scribbled 'Haden' on one note and wrote 'H' on the other."

"And then what did you do?"

"I banged Chubbie's door."

After relating Chubbie's reaction to the news, Lancaster said he had gone downstairs and telephoned for a doctor. Going back upstairs, he found Chubbie holding Haden's head up. He suggested she call Haden's doctor as well, which she went downstairs to do.

"How long were you alone in the house?"

"I don't remember. Not very long, I don't believe."

"Who arrived first?"

"The ambulance or Huston arrived at about the same time. I met somebody at the door and took them upstairs. Chubbie was still there. Haden Clarke was moving his head slightly from side to side."

He recounted the incident of the pillow, Chubbie's anxiety not to move Clarke except under specialist supervision, and the final decision to move him. He and Chubbie had followed the ambulance men downstairs, and shortly afterwards Dr Deederer had arrived and they had driven with him to the hospital.

"Who was there at the hospital?"

"A nurse, the doctor, and two policemen. I saw Policeman Hudson first. Although I had never met Hudson I felt I knew him because of the many times he had been discussed by Haden Clarke and Peggy Brown. I called him Earl and he called me Bill. We returned to the house in the police car."

L

"Was anything said about Haden Clarke talking?"

"Yes. I said to Hudson: 'I wish to God he'd talk,' and 'Do you think he'll talk, as he could tell why he did it.' " When they got back to the house the gun was in the centre of the bed. It was picked up by Earl Hudson, who wrapped his handkerchief round it and slipped it into his hip pocket. He had not put it in its box. They had rummaged around for the bullet.

"You then went to the Everglades Hotel?"

"Yes—in Mr Huston's car." Lancaster related the conversation with Huston about the ownership of the pistol.

"Was there any argument over his refusal to say it was his?"

"No."

"Did you see Mrs Clarke at the hotel?"

"No."

"Who did?"

"Dr Deederer."

This was an incomplete picture of what happened at the Everglades Hotel, as would emerge later. Lancaster then related how they had gone on to the courthouse where, after a preliminary questioning, he and Chubbie were separated and put in the county gaol. After waiting for several hours he was questioned by Hawthorne in his office.

"How many times?"

"At least twice."

"Did you ask for a lawyer?"

"No." Lancaster described how after a discussion he had told Hawthorne he was content to leave the investigation in his hands. He had been called to an inquest, but it had been indefinitely postponed.

After the lunch recess Carson questioned Lancaster on the events from the time of his release until his re-arrest, and then, after Lancaster had defended himself on the stand for a total of nine hours ten minutes, Carson intimated that his examination was at an end and the witness was at once taken over by Hawthorne for cross-examination.

CHAPTER XV

Cross-examination

"CAPTAIN Lancaster—the first question asked you this morning was: 'Did you kill Haden Clarke?' Your answer was in the negative. Who did kill him?"

"Haden Clarke committed suicide."

"In your presence?"

"I didn't see him."

"Was it in your presence?"

"I must have been in the room with him."

Hawthorne picked up one of the "suicide" notes and waved it in front of Lancaster. These notes gave him an advantage that he meant to press home. "So Haden Clarke committed suicide?"

"Yes."

"This note on Latin-American Airways stationery." He read it to the court. "Did you write that note?"

"Yes."

"Positive?"

"Yes."

Hawthorne put the note down and picked up the second one. "This note addressed to Chubbie. Is that your work?"

Lancaster's discomfiture was obvious. "Yes."

"Positive?"

"Yes."

"Are you as positive as you were on April 23rd that it *wasn't* yours?"

"Yes."

"Did anyone ask you in my office on that date if you wrote these notes?"

"No."

"Didn't Jones?"

"No."

"Did you afterwards send word to Jones that you were sorry you didn't tell him the truth about the notes when he asked you?"

"I didn't mean that. I meant I was sorry I acted a lie."

"When you were shown these notes in my office and the discrepancies between the typing of Clarke and the typing of the notes, and the similarity between them and your own, what did you say?"

"I believe I said: 'Isn't that a coincidence?'"

"What else did you say?"

"I can't recall."

"About these notes?"

"I suggested getting outside experts to look at them."

"What was your purpose in suggesting that?"

"To put you off the scent."

Hawthorne then asked whether any pressure had been put upon him or inducement offered, whether he had been subjected to any abuse or discourtesy, whether he had been in a similar state of shock during his interrogation to that when he wrote the notes. He needed to show that whatever excuse Lancaster might have for writing the notes under the sudden impulse of an unreasoning fear, no such excuse could be offered for his deceitful conduct under comparatively relaxed conditions two days later. To all these questions Lancaster was obliged to answer no.

Like most leading attorneys, Hawthorne had an actor's awareness of his audience and it could not have escaped him that, in spite of Carson's fears to the contrary, Lancaster had the sympathy of the crowd and therefore perhaps of the jury. It was important that Hawthorne should show that the State was capable of sympathy too, and of conducting the investigation and the trial with fairness and consideration. His next line of questioning was designed to this end. He reminded Lancaster that he had respected his wish that Haden Clarke's memory be protected and his malady kept secret: that had not come out until the trial. He had protected both Lancaster and Mrs Keith-Miller from newspapermen, taking them out through side doors to avoid them. Lancaster was given the opportunity of unburdening himself of any resentment he might feel towards the State Attorney's office, but all that emerged was that he and Chubbie had been treated with humanity. Hawthorne now felt he could look forward to a less hostile atmosphere. "That covered," he said, "let's get back to the gun." He picked it out from the exhibits. "Does that look like it?"

Lancaster agreed that he had purchased the gun for Huston, paying about $30 for it. Storing this information away for the moment, Hawthorne embarked on a line of questioning designed to show that Lancaster was careless over money matters and indeed over the truth. Lancaster conceded that he had given Gentry Shelton senior a cheque for $100, but only on the understanding that it was not to be presented.

"Then he too betrayed your trust, Captain Lancaster, by presenting that cheque?"

Lancaster said that Shelton hadn't presented it, and Hawthorne handed him a slip of paper, asking him to examine it and see if he could identify it. Lancaster glanced at it briefly. "That looks like—it is a photostatic copy of my cheque."

"And on the back is Mr Gentry Shelton senior's endorsement. On the front is marked 'Returned, account closed.'"

Lancaster looked bewildered. "Until this moment I didn't know that cheque had been presented."

"Then he has betrayed your trust?"

"Yes, he has. Very much so."

It was clear from the reaction of the court that they believed Lancaster. But Hawthorne's course was fixed and he persisted.

"Why did you give him the cheque? Why not a memorandum—an I.O.U.?"

"His son asked me to."

"So you gave him the cheque on a bank where you had no account?"

"The account was closed since I have been in this gaol. I didn't close it."

"Then, Captain Lancaster, the bank has betrayed you too?"

The edge of sarcasm in Howthorne's voice was having the opposite effect to that intended. "To my knowledge," said Lancaster, "the account is not closed. But all my cheques and statements are in the State's possession."

Hawthorne disputed this. "I have also been charged," he said, "with having letters Haden Clarke wrote to you in St Louis, but I have never seen them." Carson at once jumped to his feet. "May it please the court," he said, "we have never accused Mr Hawthorne of having these letters, but if he wishes to plead guilty we will accept his plea."

The sympathy generated for Lancaster in the previous hour now burst across the court in a boisterous wave of foot-stamping and applause. Bailiffs called in vain for order. "This is not a vaudeville show," shouted Judge Atkinson, pounding his gavel. Threats to clear the court had no effect for at least a minute. Then Judge Atkinson warned that any further demonstration would certainly result in the court being cleared. The crowd quietened down and Hawthorne resumed his cross-examination.

"Isn't it true that the manner of closing an account is to take all your money out of the bank?"

"Yes, unless they write that they no longer want your account and enclose a cheque for the balance."

"Did they write to you?"

"As far as I know, no. I just have a two or three dollar balance there."

"Didn't you make an affidavit in this court that you were totally without funds?"

Lancaster had been obliged to do this in order to file his bankruptcy petition. "Yes."

"Are you?"

"To the best of my ability I can say I am without funds. Gentry Shelton was indebted to me."

"What amount?"

"One hundred and twenty dollars."

"Have you tried to collect that?"

"Yes. Gentry Shelton told Mr Lathero in a phone conversation that he would send five hundred dollars to pay off that debt and to assist me here."

"Did he send it?"

"No." It is a curious fact, never satisfactorily accounted for, that Gentry Shelton, although presumably subpoenaed to attend the trial, never came. There are several possible explanations. His father, sick of the whole association—as suggested by his presentation of the Lancaster cheque—may have put his foot down. His son was clearly very much dependent on him. On the other hand Shelton may have felt his evidence would not help Lancaster.

"Does Latin-American Airways owe you any money?"

"Yes. Two or three hundred dollars."

"Did you mention that in your affidavit?"

"No. I had no hope of getting it."

A sympathetic murmur from the crowd at the outcome of this line of questioning was quickly silenced by Judge Atkinson. Hawthorne switched back to the gun.

"Didn't you say you didn't know why you loaded the gun at Nashville?"

"Yes."

"Didn't you tell me the reason you loaded it was because you wanted to return it to Huston as he gave it to you?"

"Yes."

"Nashville was the last stop out of Miami, wasn't it?"

"Yes."

"Did you load the gun at night or morning?"

"Night."

"The next night you were in Miami, weren't you?"

"Yes."

Hawthorne went on to underline the apparent inconsistency of Lancaster's paying $30 for a gun when he knew Chubbie was in dire need of funds. Next he emphasized that Lancaster's suspicions had been aroused some time before his return and that his diary had recorded his anxiety. "The reason you were so worried about Chubbie was because you loved her better than anything in the world, wasn't it?"

"Yes."

"You found out before you got home and from the lips of Clarke that he had a serious malady?"

"You're quite right."

"Did the love affair of Clarke and Chubbie still appear quite beautiful to you?"

"Yes."

"The knowledge of the malady didn't affect you?"

"No. They were very much in love and I saw only that."

"Then you learnt of the intimacies between them while you were away, and it still appeared beautiful to you?"

Lancaster was not put off by Hawthorne's sarcasm. "There was a beautiful side to it that I wanted to consider. That was the better side of Clarke's character."

"He proved that in the end by committing suicide, didn't he?"

"Not in the *manner* in which he did, but the *fact* that he did showed he had good intentions." It was a difficult answer to fault.

"Do you still feel that way?"

"I would like to."

"I'm asking you."

"Yes."

"Did you feel relieved when you dropped off to sleep that night?"

"Yes. In my heart I knew that Clarke would never marry Chubbie."

"Why? Because he would commit suicide before morning?"

"No, because he had promised to tell Chubbie in the morning all of the mis-statements he had admitted to me that night, and if he didn't I would."

"But you were going back to St Louis."

It was a sally that misfired. "No, that was earlier in the evening when I planned that." The testimony supported Lancaster.

Hawthorne then moved to the question of Lancaster's apparent stupidity in leaving Clarke alone with Chubbie. Lancaster replied that Clarke's reputation was quite good.

"According to your standards, Captain Lancaster? Hadn't he spent nights there with girls?"

"Two or three times—yes."

"Had anybody else?"

"No."

"But Clarke had—with your knowledge, consent, and approval."

"I didn't consent, but I didn't hold it against him."

"It was beautiful to you."

"No."

"Who was head of that household?"

"Mrs Keith-Miller's name was on the lease."

"Didn't you live with her?"

"I didn't live at her apartment with her in New York."

"But you lived under the same roof in Miami?"

"Yes."

"So it became beautiful in Miami."

"I never described the relationship as beautiful."

Hawthorne's efforts to portray Lancaster as morally decadent had hardly succeeded. All he had done, perhaps, was to help the court to a better understanding of the life he had led. But he had another card to play.

"Did you write an entry in your diary for January 7th?"

"Yes, there is one here."

"Read it."

Lancaster read from his diary. "Fined fifty dollars with a suspended on a complaint filed by driver of Buick. American justice is all wet. The evidence given was insufficient to convict me but, like all matters in American courts, they are subject to the inefficiency of the court officials and police."

"What did you mean when you wrote: 'American justice is all wet'?"

"I had been found guilty of something I hadn't done. I now realize that I should not have written it. I'm sorry you don't like it."

Hawthorne snorted. "Being an American," he said, "I don't like any of it." Lancaster's apology had seemed dignified and sincere, and this appeal to national prejudice brought Carson to his feet to object. Hawthorne withdrew the remark. Whether these excursions of Hawthorne's into the realms of obloquy and innuendo really advanced the prosecution's case seems doubtful. Some may have been impressed by them; others clearly felt that most of his sneers and traducements had recoiled on him. The prosecution's case seemed so powerful in its essentials that it was surprising that Hawthorne should succumb to the temptation to play on the jury's prejudices and susceptibilities. Now he got back on course.

"Did you ever utter threats about Clarke in front of Tancrel and Russell?"

"No."

"Did you ever tell Gentry Shelton that you had seen hundreds die under machine-gun fire and you wouldn't mind seeing another dead man?"

"No."

"Shelton isn't here, is he?" Hawthorne injected a wealth of meaning into this rhetorical question.

"He promised me he'd come down."

Lancaster with some of the famous flyers who testified at his trial. *Left to right*, Lancaster, Irving "Bing" Boyer, Clyde Pangbourne, Rex Gilmartin, and the Australian Keith Bon
Photo U.P.I.

ubbie on the witness stand
Photo U.P.I.

Lancaster with his counsel—Jim Carson (*left*) and "Happy" Lathero—at the opening of the trial
Photo U.P.I.

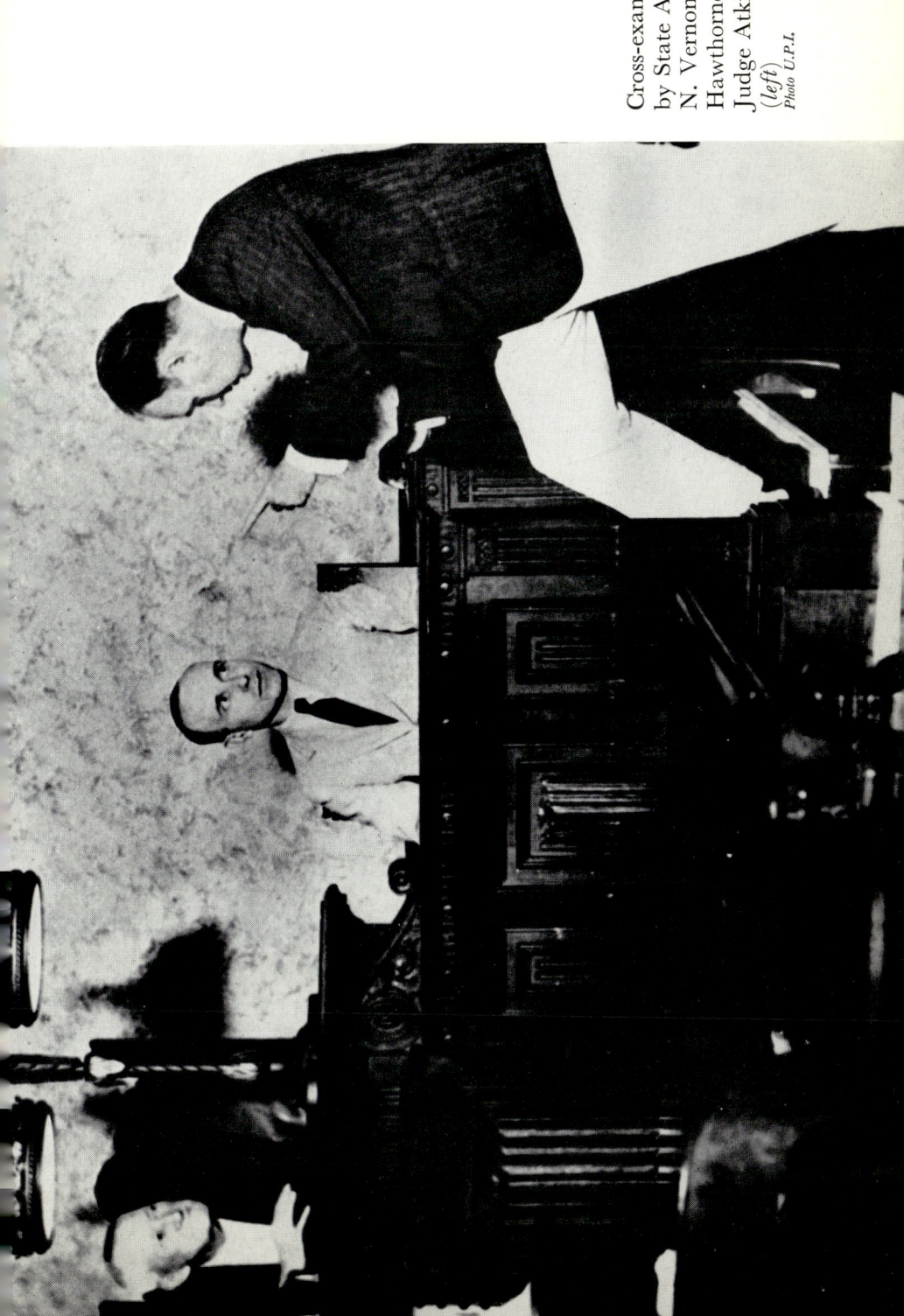

Cross-examination by State Attorney N. Vernon Hawthorne, with Judge Atkinson (*left*)
Photo U.P.I.

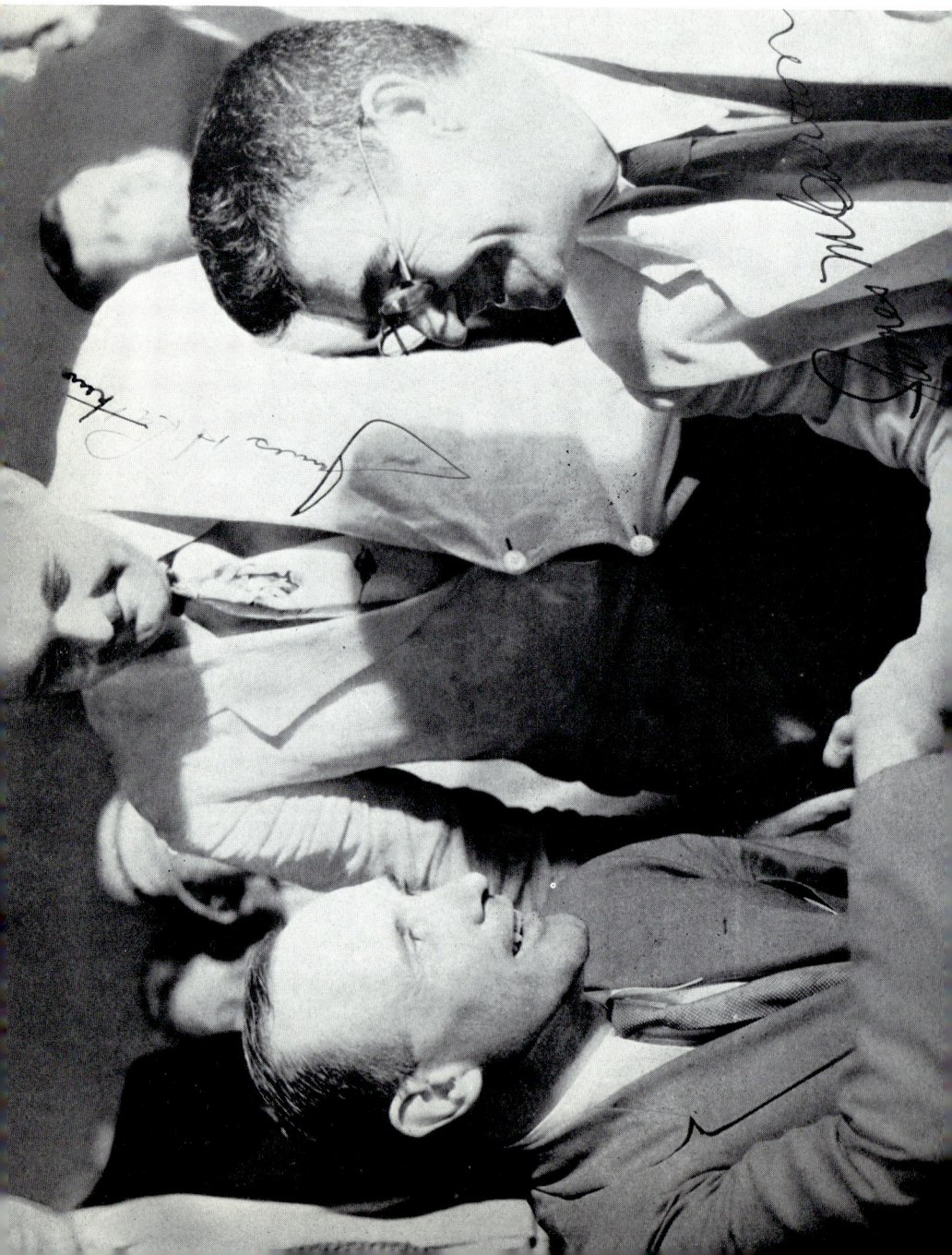

Acquittal
Photo U.P.I.

"He promised *me* he would too." Again Hawthorne managed to convey that the defence, for reasons of its own, was hiding Shelton.

"If Russell testified that he showed you in Los Angeles letters from his wife containing news of Clarke and Chubbie, was that true?"

"Yes, true."

"If he told you he would meet you at the Burbank Airport, was that true?"

"Yes, true."

"Then your statement that Russell's testimony was a tissue of lies relates only to what he testified you told him about Haden Clarke?"

"No."

"What then? You previously said all was a tissue of lies."

"Yes. I should like to point out the untrue things in his testimony."

"Go ahead."

"You produced letters which Russell said he showed me, untrue. He said I made threats against Haden Clarke, untrue. He said he had been for gasoline for the flight to Los Angeles, untrue. If you will have the reporter read Russell's testimony I can point out other lies."

This wasn't bad at short notice from a man being cross-examined for his life, and Hawthorne declined the invitation. "Just state what you remember, Captain."

"The only thing I told him about Haden Clarke in Los Angeles was: 'Oh, don't worry about that, I trust Chubbie.'"

"Did you tell Gentry Shelton you would see Haden Clarke dead before he would marry Chubbie?"

"I did not. That night I drank the pint of Scotch I might have uttered threats." Since no evidence of any threats made in St Louis had been brought, this was a surprising admission.

"What leads you to believe you might have?"

"Because I can remember people telling me not to worry. I said 'If Haden Clarke hurts Chubbie, he'll have to answer to me.'"

"Would you consider his behaviour as harming her?"

"I would, but when I arrived here I overlooked it."

"You went to bed with an entirely different picture as a result of that confidential talk with Haden Clarke, didn't you?"

"Yes."

"And Haden Clarke went to bed laughing?"

Lancaster took the question at its face value. "Yes, he laughed at the story of Tancrel's paper-hanging exploits."

"And his last words were?"

"'Bill, you're the whitest man I know.'"

"And he also said: 'Bill, you can have Chubbie'?"

"I have never said that."

"But did he say that?"

"No."

"And in the stress and strain you wrote the notes before calling for a doctor?"

"Yes."

As Hawthorne proceeded to question Lancaster about the wound and the gun, Lancaster was plainly tiring. But there was no escape; the afternoon session still had some distance to run.

"You saw many persons die in the War?"

"Yes, quite a few."

"Did you ever remember a person living with a similar wound in the head? Live or talk again?"

"Yes, I have."

"You tried to talk with Clarke?"

"Yes, but all he would do was to moan."

"How long did it take you to type the notes?"

"Five minutes."

"Why two notes?"

"I can't tell you." Lancaster could have found perfectly plausible reasons for typing two notes, but he was mentally exhausted.

"You were under a terrible strain?"

"I was shocked."

"You would describe your condition as panicky?"

"Yes, that would be correct."

"Why did you write a note to yourself?"

"I don't know."

"Why did you write a note to Chubbie?"

Lancaster had explained his reason for writing a note to Chubbie at the time of his first admission of forgery nearly three and a half months earlier, and repeated it many times since. Plausible or not, it was the most essential prop in his defence. But in his utter fatigue he had forgotten it. "I don't know."

"Why did you sign one Haden and the other H?"

"I don't know."

"You referred to yourself several times before Haden as the best friend he and Chubbie had?"

"Yes."

"And you gave Haden Clarke no reason to doubt that?"

"None."

"Who went to bed first?"

"We were lying on the beds together."

"You were not over three feet from the muzzle of the gun when it exploded?"

"Not more than three and a half feet."

"It was before 2 A.M.?"

"It was, perhaps."

"Would you consider Haden Clarke a man of calm or flighty nature?"

"He was a man who would act on impulse."

"And you left your gun in his plain view and where he could easily reach it?"

"I never thought of it."

"Did you write the notes hurriedly?"

"Yes."

"Did you make any other attempts?"

"No."

"How long had it been since you had used the typewriter?"

"About six weeks."

"How long was it from the time the shot was fired until you had completed the notes and called Mrs Keith-Miller?"

"Not more than eight minutes."

Hawthorne sought to show that this was an optimistic estimate, and he went over the sequence of events as previously related by Lancaster in minute detail. "All this," he concluded, "before calling for a doctor. And you say it only took you eight minutes?"

"It took less time than it does to tell about it."

"Would you mind rewriting the notes on the typewriter now?"

"Certainly not."

The typewriter was moved from the exhibits and placed on the court reporter's desk, with the two notes beside it. Also placed with the notes was the pencil Lancaster had used to sign them. Lancaster left the stand and walked across and sat at the desk. A sheet of paper was handed to him, and he inserted it in the typewriter. The clerk of the court set his watch. Lancaster had typed only a few words when, seeing Carson signalling to him, he stopped.

"Am I being timed?"

Hawthorne showed his impatience. "This is not a contest, Captain Lancaster, it is just an exhibition."

"Then you want it to be a fair exhibition?"

"Yes, I do."

Lancaster put the sheet of paper back in the typewriter and began again, and the clerk of the court reset his watch. When Lancaster had finished Hawthorne asked the clerk of the court for the time.

"Two and a half minutes."

Lancaster had not seemed to hurry, and the typing of the notes was much the same as in the originals. He had proved that his estimate of a lapse of eight minutes between the shooting and the time he called

Chubbie, so far from being an underestimate, erred on the side of exaggeration.

"You attempted to put into the notes the exact words Clarke used in the conversation that night?"

"I don't know if I made any special effort to do so." In Lancaster's long statement of May 2nd he claimed to have done this. Now he had forgotten. In his present state of mental exhaustion this was perhaps understandable.

"You told Mr Carson this morning that Clarke had said he was 'not making the grade'. Were you trying to use those words or did they come to you spontaneously?"

"I must have been. I came to the typewriter, thought for a second, and then typed the notes."

"You wrote the notes in the same manner and touch as you wrote them here?"

"Not much difference. I am under a strain here, but I was probably under a greater strain that night."

Next morning, after ordering that the jury be taken from the court, Judge Atkinson formally warned spectators that he would tolerate no further expression of approval or disapproval for one side or the other, and he asked the State and defence lawyers if they would care to supplement his remarks. Carson availed himself of this invitation and asked the crowd to refrain from further demonstration so as not to prejudice Lancaster's chances of a fair trial; but Hawthorne said he did not wish to speak. He was, perhaps, chastened by his experience of the previous day; anyway he surprised the court by announcing that he would not cross-examine Lancaster further for the present. The jury returned to the courtroom, and one or two questions arising from Hawthorne's cross-examination were put by Carson.

It was important, if the jury were to follow an argument about the shooting that Carson intended to develop, that the position of the two beds in the sleeping-porch was fixed exactly in their mind, and Carson's first question was directed towards this end. "The beds were closely against the wall and table," answered Lancaster. Photographs taken after the shooting were shown to him, and he pointed out several changes in positioning of the beds compared with the time of the tragedy. These had come about, he told the court, because one of the ambulance men had pushed Clarke's bed out from the wall in order to get round and lift Clarke from that side.

Carson moved on to his next point, the background to Lancaster's relationship with Gentry Shelton and the cheque Lancaster had given to Shelton's father. Lancaster said that when he received the money from the Uptons it had been divided on a fifty-fifty basis, with much of it going

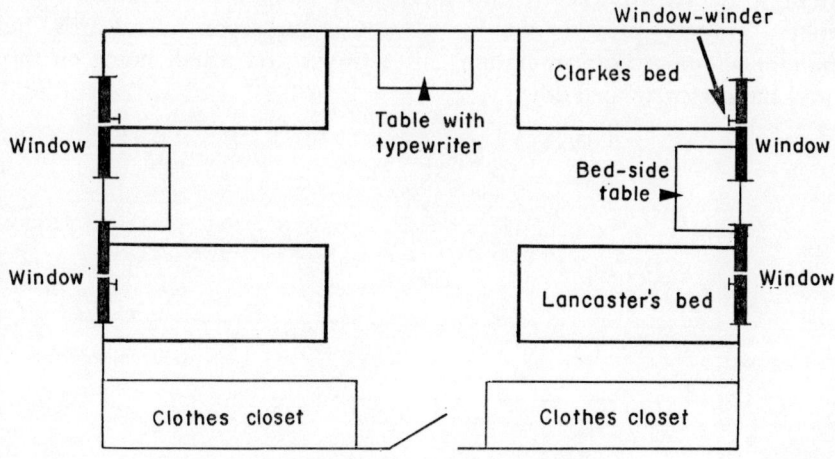

Layout of the sleeping-porch

to pay Gentry's hotel bill and for repairs to the ship, which was Gentry's. "I make no claim on Gentry," he added. "We were friends. What one had, both had."

"When you gave that cheque to Shelton senior on April 18th it was with the understanding it was not to be deposited by him?"

"Clearly."

"Examine the photostat copy and tell me the date the cheque was presented for deposit."

"May 16th."

"So that Gentry Shelton senior did keep his promise until after you had been indicted for murder?"

It was a logical submission, suggesting that events were entirely consistent with the story told by Lancaster. The attitude of Shelton senior had apparently changed after the indictment, no doubt influencing his son. The Shelton cheque attack had ricocheted.

"Did Clarke ever discuss suicide with you?" asked Carson.

"No."

"Do you know of him ever discussing suicide with anyone?"

"I learnt after his death that he had."

"But until the time of his death?"

"No."

Once again Lancaster's answers sounded untutored and truthful. And Carson was making an important point: Lancaster had had no reason to suppose there was any danger in leaving the gun so accessible. Further attempts by Hawthorne to find fault with Lancaster's testimony over money matters proved equally abortive, and soon afterwards he abandoned the cross-examination. After twelve and a half hours on the stand Lancaster stepped down.

CHAPTER XVI

Of Haden Clarke and the Medical Evidence

IN developing the case for the defence, Carson would rely principally on evidence he would bring of Haden Clarke's mental state and debauched physical condition, together with an interpretation of the medical evidence wholly favourable to Lancaster which he would support by putting on the stand the men who had formed the medical commission—with the exception of the absent Dr Dodge—plus a well-known criminologist who had offered his services. In addition he would keep pounding away at the unreliability of the State's witnesses. In pursuit of this latter point he called a deputy marshal named J. P. Moe, who agreed that he had admitted Tancrel to the Dade County gaol on transfer from another gaol to give evidence at the Lancaster trial.

"What did Tancrel say on the way to the cells?"

"I asked him how he'd like to be put in the same cell with Lancaster, and he said: 'Don't do that, I'd have to kill him.'"

"Anything else?"

"Yes. He said: 'I'll do all I can to see that Lancaster burns.'"

This piece of evidence from a United States deputy marshal, hearsay or not, was calculated to make a profound impression on the court. Carson had already suggested the presence of malice where Russell was concerned; Moe's evidence pointed to a similar conclusion with Tancrel.

It was now Carson's unpleasant task to embark on the character assassination of Haden Clarke, and his next witness was one Dick Lavender, a young man who had roomed with Clarke early that year in New Orleans. The two men had spent most of their time drinking; Clarke, said Lavender, had also smoked marijuana cigarettes frequently. His physical condition had been bad, and he took no precaution to protect others. "'Somebody gave it to me,'" Lavender quoted Clarke as saying, "'and I don't care if I give it to somebody else.'" Money that Lavender had received from the Veterans' Bureau had been stolen by Clarke.

"Did he discuss with you the proper method of committing suicide?" asked Carson.

"He said the best method was to shoot oneself in the head, as death came instantly and promptly."

Hawthorne took much the same line in cross-examining Lavender as Carson had done with Tancrel and Russell: he was out to discredit him. Lavender was out of work, he got most of his money from the Veterans' Bureau, and he drank heavily. Hawthorne asked him if Clarke had seemed happy when he left New Orleans early in February—on his way to Miami and the meeting with Chubbie and Lancaster—and Lavender agreed that he had. He conceded that he hadn't had to hold him down to keep him from committing suicide. No one else had been present when Clarke delivered his thesis on suicide, and he hadn't paid much attention to it.

"Did he say he would ever commit suicide?"

"He said if he ever got in a jam he would."

"Was Clarke cheerful or blue at the time of your last conversation with him?" This had been at the Keith-Miller house, where Lavender had paid a call on Clarke before Lancaster's departure for Mexico.

"Cheerful."

"Did he have a cowardly nature?"

"Apparently not." Hawthorne moved quickly on to his next question, but the significance of this reply was not lost on the court. The witness believed that Clarke had committed suicide. The cross-examination was not going well for Hawthorne.

"Did you ever see him blue?"

"He was the last day he was in New Orleans. He was blue because his story had been returned."

Mrs Alan Troupe, a restaurant proprietor, said Clarke had confided in her his love for Mrs Keith-Miller. She had given him a meal and the money for his car-fare home on numerous occasions, she said, and he was always in a depressed state. Hawthorne planned to bring evidence in rebuttal of this, but he did not cross-examine. Carson then called Dick Richardson, a writer, the man who had visited the Keith-Miller home to see Clarke and who had talked at length about his play *Rasputin*. Richardson testified that he had known Clarke for about a year. He too had frequently helped Clarke financially. He agreed that Clarke was a heavy drinker.

"Did you ever hear him discuss suicide?"

"Yes, at the home of Mrs Keith-Miller three weeks before his death."

"Who was present?"

"Mrs Keith-Miller, Clarke, and myself."

"How did the conversation start?"

"I had written a play, *Rasputin*, and remarked how difficult it was to kill him."

"Did Clarke explain an easy and sure method?"

"Yes, he said the best way was to shoot oneself above and a little behind the right ear." Shooting oneself in the temple, according to Clarke, often resulted only in blindness.

Carson next introduced into evidence the report of the medical commission that had performed the autopsy on Clarke after permission had been given for the body to be exhumed. Hawthorne protested against it on the grounds that it was not evidence that ought to be put before a jury, but Judge Atkinson overruled him and the report was read to the court by Lathero. This took up the early part of the afternoon. The report was clinically factual and avoided any expression of opinion on whether or not the wound was self-inflicted; but Carson intended to call the members of the commission individually to give evidence and answer questions next day.

Four love-letters written to Haden Clarke by women other than his wife were then read to the court. One was from Peggy Brown, the other three from Virginia Clarke, the girl he had married bigamously. Evidence was brought that they had lived together in an apartment in Coral Gables in 1931; the apartment manager, who had ejected them for non-payment of rent, testified that he had seen a marriage certificate in the apartment. One of the letters from Virginia Clarke averred that there could be no happiness for them together until Clarke learnt to depend on himself. Earl Hudson, recalled by the defence, then admitted under pressure that his reference to "Miss Peggy Brown", his wife's sister-in-law, had been inaccurate; she was in fact a married woman. With this Carson felt that his task of showing Clarke's mental instability and the tangled complexities of his love life was complete.

Carson's difficulty with the medical evidence was that the members of the commission, while standing absolutely by their findings, were reluctant to extend these findings into the realms of theory, logic, and conjecture. They were not and did not pretend to be criminologists. This was why he had seen the attendance of Dr Dodge, a man of special experience in this field as well as being a member of the commission, as of such vital importance to his case. Dr Dodge was still unable to attend, but Carson was about to produce on the stand a man of vast experience and expertise in criminal cases who was prepared to stake his reputation that the medical evidence and exhibits, which he had studied minutely, were an absolute indication of suicide. Hawthorne's reply would be to develop an attack on that reputation and to rely on the evidence already given by the embalmer, K. B. Bess. First on the stand in this session, however, was Dr M. H. Tallman, the court's representative on the medical commission.

Carson called him first because of an exhibit he wanted to enter on behalf of the defence.

"Do you have any exhibit?"

"Yes."

Tallman had taken a box with him to the stand, and from it he now produced a blackened object. It was the exhumed skull of Haden Clarke. As a concerted gasp went round the crowded courtroom, and at least one woman spectator hurried out, Lancaster leant forward in his chair. So far from recoiling from the exhibit he showed intense interest in it. With it Tallman displayed a slide of tissue, taken within one inch of the wound entrance, which the defence also wanted to offer in evidence. Tallman said that the tissue appeared to contain powder grains but that this would have to be determined by a chemist.

Before questioning the medical commission on their findings Carson proceeded to prepare the ground so that those findings when they came would argue a certain conclusion. For this purpose he now excused Tallman and called his expert witness, Dr Albert H. Hamilton, who described himself as a chemical and ballistics expert, and a criminologist of forty-seven years' experience. Carson began by asking him if there was any definite way to determine if a death was suicide or homicide. In some cases, replied Hamilton, it was simple: in others it was impossible. "For example, when the pistol has been held a very short distance from the skull." In this situation the same indications might be present no matter who fired the gun. Within certain limitations the distance a gun was held from a body when a shot was fired into it could be determined. The degree of contact could be determined too. Hamilton explained the degrees of contact and described how the powder marks would be found on the membranes within the skull when the contact was "sealed", as he called it. His exposition tallied exactly with that put forward by Dr Dodge.

Carson handed Hamilton the exhibits to comment on one by one. Of the gun, Hamilton said that the person who cleaned it had failed to do a good job; a residue of bloody tissue and smokeless powder could still be seen on the front face of the sight, and there were also two human hairs embedded in the sight. He also found a deposit of aluminium powder, which he could not account for. An examination of the exploded shell and the firing pin of the pistol showed that the shell had been fired from the exhibited gun.

"I hand you the skull cap," said Carson. "What are your observations?"

Rotating the skull in his hands, Hamilton pointed out various features, and the skull was then handed to the jury. "By sighting through the entrance hole and exit aperture," said Hamilton, "we can obtain the line of firing." One by one the members of the jury proved this for themselves. Hamilton went on to say that the skull showed numerous fractures on the left and three on the right. The hair, as evidenced from the photographs, was not singed or scorched, showing that the gun was held hard against the head and the head hard against the gun. Another important point for consideration was the relation of the trigger to the head when the gun was fired, as in some positions the hand was unable to exert enough force to pull the trigger. Hamilton produced diagrams to illustrate his theories, and these were offered into evidence. "The bullet," said Hamilton, "was fired across the head and slightly backward. I found it easy in this position to pull the trigger without cocking the gun."

Carson now referred Hamilton to the autopsy report. Hamilton said he had checked every measurement and every statement as far as possible and it was the best report he'd ever seen.

"And did you make a conclusion, Dr Hamilton?"

"Yes, I did. There was but one conclusion, and only one conclusion that could be arrived at from this examination, and that was that this shot was a self-inflicted, close, hard-contact shot at the instant the gun was hard against head and head hard against gun."

"Was it suicide or homicide?"

"Absolutely suicide. There is not a scintilla of evidence to support a theory of homicide or murder."

The evidence of the members of the medical commission would support Hamilton's description of a "sealed contact" wound, and since this medical commission had been appointed by the court, Hawthorne could hardly challenge its findings. What he could do was to urge that when it came to translating these findings into a conclusion it was largely a matter of opinion. If at the same time he could expose Hamilton as a quack and impugn his good faith, he might hope to undermine the whole defence interpretation of the medical evidence.

Hawthorne began by asking Hamilton if he was a handwriting and fingerprint expert, to which he replied in the affirmative. Asked what process he would employ to take a fingerprint, Hamilton explained that there were two methods, one by dusting the print with powder, the other by photography.

"Do you ever use aluminium powder in dusting a print?" asked Hawthorne.

"Not if I can avoid it." It was, he said, too coarse.

"What foreign substance did you find on this gun?"

"Aluminium powder. I can hardly believe anyone would use aluminium powder."

Hawthorne would present another view on this. Meanwhile he moved to Hamilton's evidence on ballistics. Hamilton, it seemed, was an expert on this too. His answers, however, could not be faulted, and Hawthorne moved on to chemistry. Hamilton testified that his microscopic examination of the skull smear showed that it was composed of blood, tissue, and smokeless powder; he was, he said, by profession an analytical chemist. Hawthorne's raised eyebrows conveyed his reaction; he was dealing with a versatile fellow. He then named several accredited experts in the field of criminology, and Hamilton correctly identified them all.

It was important to contest the view that a gun pressed hard against the head was a certain indication of suicide, and Hawthorne continued his cross-examination with this in mind. "If you were asleep," he asked, "and subconsciously felt a gun barrel against your head, would you try to push your head out against the gun?"

"I'd say it was impossible."

"If a man is struck or touched while lying in bed, isn't his tendency to rise?"

"No, dodge away." This agreed with Dr Dodge's submission that flinching was the likely reaction.

"You claim it would be impossible to hold the head of a man lying down asleep and kill him by shooting him with a pistol and produce similar exhibits as at this trial?"

"Impossible."

"How did you acquire the title of doctor?"

"Lawyers started that. I am not a doctor."

At this point Carson intervened. "Do you find any evidence at all from the exhibit to support any theory other than suicide?"

"I found nothing to support anything but suicide. I say this not as an opinion but actual knowledge."

The court then recessed for the jury to be taken to the scene of the shooting.

Next morning, Saturday, August 13th, the end of the second week of the trial, Judge Atkinson allowed Lancaster to take the witness stand and make a statement. "The position of Haden Clarke's bed at the house yesterday," he said, "was not the same as on the night of the tragedy. I remember distinctly that the window-winder came through the rails of the head of the bed so that the windows might be closed by the person in bed. Yesterday the bed was a considerable distance from the wall." In addition the beds had been pushed closer together.

"Do you remember if the windows were open the night of the tragedy?" asked Judge Atkinson.

Lancaster said it had been a very hot night and all the windows were open. The porch had been bathed in brilliant moonlight. He had turned the lights off himself, at which point Clarke had been lying back on his bed, wide awake. Nothing had been said after the lights were turned off.

"Did your visit to the house yesterday remind you of anything?" asked Carson.

"Yes. There have been several previous references to the four letters

I received in St Louis, two from Haden and two from Mrs Keith-Miller. I recall now that I saw one on the table after the shot was fired."

"Did you make any use of the letter that night?"

"Yes. I attempted to copy the name 'Haden' from it. It was a single-page letter. Previously, in my testimony, I said I scribbled Haden on the note. That is not a correct description. A more accurate one would be that it was a deliberate attempted forgery."

Hawthorne immediately indicated his intention to cross-examine. "Why was the letter out that night?"

"I took the letter out to show Haden and I wanted him to read it. Included in it was a statement by Haden that Chubbie was more important than either of us. I wanted him to read that but he refused. The letter was there when I left for the hospital, and must have been there when Policeman Hudson began his search of the house."

"There has been considerable testimony about the four letters. Which one was this?"

"A single-spaced typewritten letter, signed in ink."

"Did you attempt to copy the signature hurriedly?"

"Yes." The letter was on the floor at the base of the table when he last saw it. Excusing this amendment to his evidence he reminded Hawthorne that Judge Atkinson had said he could correct his testimony at any time.

"How did Haden sign his letters?"

"Sometimes he would type Haden on the letters and other times he would sign."

Hawthorne produced a bundle of letters. "I hand you State exhibit letters from Haden Clarke to yourself, and ask you to state to the jury how they are signed."

Lancaster glanced through them. "They are signed on the typewriter."

"There is no writing on them?"

"None."

If Hawthorne could break down this piece of additional testimony, belief in the whole of Lancaster's evidence might be shaken. "How many letters from Haden Clarke do you remember were signed?"

"Two. The ones I received in St Louis were signed in ink. Green ink."

If Lancaster was making it up, the addition of the corroborative detail of green ink was a master-stroke.

Carson next presented the evidence of the various members of the medical commission, beginning with Dr Donald F. Gowe, the member appointed by the State Attorney. After outlining his medical experience, Gowe explained the autopsy report to the jury. The work, he said, had been hampered by the condition of the body, but a bullet wound had been found in the head. Five radiating fractures had been discovered, mostly caused by escaping gases inside the head.

"From that, can you say how close the gun was held to the head?"

"I feel sure the gun was held closely against the head."

"Can you express an opinion as to whether the wound was self-inflicted?"

"I could say in probability, not certainty."

At this point Hawthorne objected to both the question and answer, the objection was sustained, and Carson's next question was stillborn. Why should Hawthorne have assumed that Dr Gowe's answer would be unfavourable to the prosecution? And why didn't Judge Atkinson allow Carson to continue? Surely the opinion of the State Attorney's own nominee would have been of value to the court?

Gowe was followed by Dr Walter C. Jones, chief of staff of the Jackson Memorial Hospital and a defence nominee. Jones said he was thoroughly in accord with the autopsy report. He was confident that the gun was fired when held in direct contact with the head.

"Was the wound self-inflicted?" asked Carson.

"I do not feel competent to express an opinion on that."

Hawthorne did not object to Jones answering this question, so clearly he had foreknowledge of what these medical opinions were. From this it seems clear that Gowe, the State Attorney's own nominee on the commission, thought the medical evidence pointed to suicide.

Two more members of the medical commission, Dr Tallman and Dr Stewart, were then called in turn by Carson; both said the fractures were caused by an explosion of gases within the skull and both stated positively that the gun must have been held firmly against the head. There was no cross-examination. Carson then announced that he had completed the case for the defence but reserved the right to reopen it for the purpose of examining one more witness on Monday. He did not disclose who this witness was, but a news story next day revealed that the witness was Joseph Ince, the man who had been present at the hotel in El Paso with Tancrel when Lancaster was alleged to have threatened Clarke's life. Ince had been discovered in Detroit by a news agency.

Meanwhile Hawthorne wanted to have a final thrust at both Lancaster and Hamilton before introducing his own witnesses in rebuttal of certain defence testimony, and Lancaster was called once again to the stand.

"Did you ever have a discussion with Mrs Clarke about the notes?" asked Hawthorne.

"I have no recollection of such a discussion."

"Were the notes not in possession of Policeman Hudson and were they not shown by him to Mrs Clarke at the Everglades Hotel on the first visit?"

"They were standing some distance from me. I believe she was shown the notes by Hudson, as I have a faint recollection of what she said. I think it was: 'It may be Haden's signature and it may not, I haven't got my glasses.' "

"Do you recall if she had the notes read to her because she was unable to see them?"

"I can't say."

"On another occasion, when you had been released, did you not talk with Mrs Clarke?"

"I did."

"Did you attempt to console her?"

"I did."

"Did you ever tell Mrs Clarke that 'Sometimes I think I killed Haden'?"

"I did not. I never made such a remark."

Lancaster stood down for the last time, and Hamilton replaced him. The duologue that followed lasted the rest of the morning and early afternoon, Hawthorne trying every trick he knew to discredit and embarrass Hamilton. His only questions which had any bearing on the trial evidence concerned Hamilton's diagrams and his chemical analysis of the smear, which Hamilton had testified contained blood, brain tissue, and powder residue. Hamilton stood by his diagrams and confirmed his analysis, which Hawthorne would later contest. Eventually Hawthorne released him and the prosecution's rebuttal evidence began.

Ditsler, the ambulance driver, was asked to confirm the time he received the call from the Keith-Miller home; he said it was 2.30 A.M. The prosecution were setting the time of the shooting at before two o'oclock, so there was a gap of half an hour that was not fully explained. But Ditsler admitted under cross-examination that he had not recorded the time until he returned to the Philbrick Home at 4.30 A.M. Fingerprint Officer J. O. Barker was then called to confirm that he had used aluminium powder to raise fingerprints on the gun. Photographs of other prints taken by this method were displayed. "I offer this testimony," said Hawthorne, "in rebuttal to the testimony of the witness Hamilton, who said photographs could not be made of fingerprints raised by aluminium." Carson objected—this wasn't what Hamilton had said at all, he had simply described it as an imperfect method—but Judge Atkinson overruled him and the rebuttal testimony was entered. Hawthorne then moved that the entire evidence given by Hamilton be excluded from the record, but in this he was himself overruled. This concluded the second week of the trial.

On Monday the defence case would be reopened long enough to allow Ince to take the stand, and Hawthorne would deal in rebuttal with the picture the defence had built up of Haden Clarke's behaviour and character. The Sunday papers reported that one of the most important rebuttal witnesses would be Mrs Ida Clarke, who would take the stand to defend her son's memory. Final arguments by defence and prosecution, it was forecast, would follow her testimony.

Joseph Ince, the first witness on the stand on Monday morning, August 15th, told the court that he had been a flying officer in the Royal Flying Corps and Royal Air Force during the War. He had fought with Lancaster in the same squadron in 1918. He couldn't remember the exact date, but he agreed that he had met Lancaster in El Paso and that a conversation had taken place in a hotel room there with Lancaster and Tancrel.

"Relate the conversation as far as you remember it," asked Carson.

"Lancaster said Clarke was in Miami with Mrs Keith-Miller. He impressed me as being rather glad of this." This impression accords with the tenor of Lancaster's diary and letters at that time. Ince went on to say that Lancaster was very worried about money and that as he was so low in funds he pawned a pistol, which was of no use to him. He never showed any resentment towards Clarke or evinced any doubt of him.

"You fought in the War with him?" asked Hawthorne, cross-examining.

"Yes."

"You are now a good friend of his?"

"Yes."

What war-time comrade would not come along to put in a good word for a friend? That was the inference of Hawthorne's questions. Carson then came back to ask one question—a question of considerable significance, because it fixed the date of the conversation at El Paso precisely.

"You spent but one night in Lancaster's hotel room?"

"Yes." This, from Lancaster's diary, was Saturday, March 19th.

Hawthorne then presented his rebuttal evidence on the temperament of Haden Clarke. Latimer Virrick, who said he had played bridge with Clarke twice weekly on average, denied that he had ever seen him in a depressed state. He was playing bridge at the Keith-Miller home the night Lancaster telephoned from California, when Chubbie handed the call to Haden Clarke. After putting down the receiver, Clarke had seemed upset. "I think there'll be trouble, damn it," he had said, according to Virrick. "He's coming back." The story was confirmed by another man who had been in the same bridge party, Paul Prufert. He recorded Clarke as saying: "There'll be trouble—that son of a bitch is coming back here." He too denied ever having seen Clarke depressed or downhearted.

Four more witnesses were called by Hawthorne on this subject, and all testified that they had never seen Clarke depressed. Completing the picture for Hawthorne, a mechanic from the Viking Airport testified that

Lancaster, on his arrival on April 20th, had not shaken hands with Clarke and that his attitude towards him had not appeared friendly.

Which side was the court to believe? The rebuttal evidence seemed credible enough—yet the forecast that testimony from Clarke's mother would form part of it was not fulfilled. Hawthorne's excuse was that her distraught condition had prompted him not to call her. Thus Chubbie's evidence on Clarke's temperament, and the rages he got into with his mother, remained unchallenged, as did Lancaster's denial that he had ever said "Sometimes I think I did kill Haden."

Hawthorne's final move was to call evidence to dispute Hamilton's chemical analysis of the smear made at the autopsy and of the substance remaining on the gun barrel after cleaning: a doctor, a chemist, and finally the county physician, all testified that, at a special examination the previous day, the "two human hairs" that Hamilton had detected on the gun-sight had turned out to be cotton fibres, while they had been unable to determine the substance of the smear.

"Was anything established at your examination yesterday in conflict with what was determined at the autopsy?" Carson asked.

"No."

"Did you find powder burns?"

"Yes."

"On the outside of the wound?"

"No."

"In the wound?"

"Yes."

In a few seconds Carson had re-established the basic defence position on the medical evidence; and shortly afterwards he called E. B. Leatherman, clerk of the circuit court, and asked him a significant question, one calculated to discount the evidence called in dispute of Hamilton's analysis of the gun-sight and the smear.

"Was there any defence representation in your office yesterday when the exhibits were considered by the witnesses who have this morning testified for the State?"

"No, sir."

Three men would address the jury on behalf of the prosecution: Hawthorne, Jones, and Enwall. One man alone, Jim Carson, would carry the burden for the defence: this was at the instance of James Lathero, Carson's assistant on the case, who believed the development of all the defence arguments by one man, that man being Jim Carson, would be Lancaster's best chance of acquittal. Soon after eleven-thirty on that Monday morning, and continuing into the afternoon, Henry M. Jones began for the State.

Jones asked the jury to consider the three people who were in the

Keith-Miller house at the time of the shooting. One was dead, while a second, the defendant, was the most interested person of all in the outcome of the trial and his testimony would therefore be coloured by the natural law of self-preservation. The third witness was the other corner of the triangle. The man whom she professed to love more than any other lay dying, the man at her side was her devoted lover of many years. At that point, and even before that, when the defendant wrote the notes, the defence of suicide was concocted. Yet that defence was about the weakest the jury could ever have seen. It didn't stand up on its own merits, hence the notes.

The reasons advanced for Clarke's suicide were flimsy in the extreme. If every man who drank to excess, who ran after a woman, was short of money, or had a violent temper committed suicide, it would be a grand funeral. Haden Clarke had a place to eat and sleep and a woman who loved him. "Why," said Jones, "that fellow was on top of the world!" As to his talking about suicide, Clarke was said to have impressed upon a defence witness the danger of shooting oneself in the temple because of the risk of failure: yet this was where he had been shot. "That testimony," said Jones, "is a monument to the danger of overbuilding a defence." How could they suppose Clarke committed suicide when he was cock of the walk at that house? So great was his influence over Mrs Keith-Miller that he had been able to keep Lancaster from talking to her. "That's the man the defence tells you was conscience-stricken, depressed, and killed himself."

In murder, motive was all-important, and no man who ever lived had greater motive than Lancaster. "Sex, if you please, was the motive. You have but to scratch the veneer of civilization to get down to the animal that is in all of us. The greater a man's love for a woman the greater his motive for killing a rival." And bursting forth from Lancaster's diary was his undying love for the woman he was about to lose. Jones ridiculed Lancaster's story that he knew on the night of the shooting that Clarke would never marry Mrs Keith-Miller. Clarke, he repeated, was cock of the walk. He had made Mrs Keith-Miller lock her door. She had chosen him, "chosen him," he stressed, pointing to Lancaster, "in *his* face, and written him so in St Louis." As for Clarke being a coward, he had written to Lancaster that "if you do lose your head, I can do nothing but meet you half-way." That sentence forever belied any insinuation that Clarke was a coward. He had stood his ground, at the airport and at the house. "I wish we could know more truth," continued Jones, "about that supper that night, but the only person who is likely to tell the truth about the supper-table scene is dead.

"When Haden lay sleeping that night this man like a coward sent a bullet through his head. It was the most dastardly and ignominious murder ever committed." Lancaster had bought the pistol in St Louis to kill the man who stood between him and the woman he loved. "Oh, he told you from the witness stand that he had to return Huston's pistol to him, but Huston, as treasurer of Latin-American Airways, owed him two hundred and fifty dollars. So honourable was this defendant that he would give a worthless cheque to restore that pistol to the man who owed him two hundred and fifty dollars."

The earmark of guilt was an overmade defence. First the notes, then the multiplicity of reasons why Clarke killed himself. Then came Hamilton, the expert. "When you get out there in the jury room, lie down on the floor and see if you can shoot yourself through the head where this man did." A man didn't lie down to shoot himself, especially in the position that this man was supposed to have done. It was more reasonable to think that the defendant did it.

"The man of all men in this world who would leave a note is Haden Clarke, a writer, a man who expressed himself daily on the typewriter. And there was the typewriter at the foot of his bed. Certainly he would have left a note to the woman he loved—certainly he would have left a note to his old mother. And this man knew that the first thing that would be asked was 'Did he leave a note?' So this man, in the darkness and stillness of the night, laboriously forged the notes while that man lay dying.

"He didn't call a doctor, he didn't call the woman in the house. Was there anything more cold-blooded and calculated than that? What would you do if you were awakened in the middle of the night to find your roommate shot and dying? Sit down and forge his name to some notes you wrote, or would you call a doctor?"

The truth about the four letters the defendant received in St Louis, continued Jones, came out the last time the defendant was on the stand. He would have the jury believe that the State had wilfully destroyed them. But the State wanted those letters. "He's the man who carried that pistol he says he loaded without reason at Nashville. There were no fingerprints found on that gun. A very significant sign. Isn't that answered by the fact that a man usually overdoes a thing when he tries to hide it?

"He is a supreme actor, shrewd beyond degree. Cold, calculating. Why did he say, when asked about the forged notes, 'Get more experts!'? That's the man who tells you of his honour."

Jones's speech was a competent enough restatement of the prosecution case, but it evaded or ignored nearly all the defence submissions against that case. Lies may well have been told to blacken Clarke's character, but to picture him as a man on top of the world was surely a distortion. It was all very well to call Chubbie a liar, but such an accusation needed making good, and Jones either did not or could not do so. Even Hawthorne, way back in May, had admitted to believing her story. Clarke merely posed as a writer; there is no evidence that he was a man who expressed himself daily on the typewriter, rather the reverse. Lancaster cashed a cheque with Shelton to get back to Miami; only a part of it was spent on the pistol. So far from Huston owing Lancaster $250, Huston confirmed in court that he personally owed Lancaster nothing. Lancaster had given a reason for loading the pistol, though Jones chose to ignore it. Evidence on the wiping of the gun barrel presented by the defence was similarly ignored. Nearly all these points might have been put forward as suspicious or cumulative circumstances but to cite them as proven facts wholly favourable to the State was misleading.

One facet of the case that Jones turned his back on was the evidence of Tancrel and Russell; he virtually abandoned them as of any value to the prosecution. But, prompted perhaps by Hawthorne, H. O. Enwall, who succeeded Jones, did what he could to rehabilitate them. Their testimony, he insisted, was still binding on the court. Enwall also urged the court to beware of being swayed by the eloquence of defence counsel, and reminded the jury of Lancaster's unguarded diary comment on American justice. But these were no more than the curtain-raisers to the verbal battle about to be waged between the main actors left in the drama, Jim Carson and Vernon Hawthorne. On that same Monday afternoon, Carson began his argument.

CHAPTER XVII

The Final Speeches

"WHEN I was a boy attending Osceola High School in my home town of Kissimmee," Carson began, "I learnt a declamation." It consisted of part of a speech about the great soldier Robert E. Lee. " 'Just as the oak stripped of its foliage by the wintry blast, then and then only stands forth in solemn and mighty grandeur against the wintry sky, so Robert Lee, stripped of every rank that man could give him, towered above the earth and those around him. . . .'

"If you will permit the paraphrase, William Newton Lancaster, four thousand miles from his home, facing an American jury upon a charge of murder in the first degree; having gone through periods of financial distress, deprivation, and almost starvation; and having for many months paced the narrow confines of his lonely cell, deserted by many, but not by all of his friends, stands forth above those who have surrounded him in such pure sweetness, strength, unselfishness, and sheer nobility of character, that we can only begin to appreciate it when we see it shine like a brilliant diamond against the sordid background of this trial."

Lancaster, Carson reminded the jury, was charged with murder in the first degree, not with adultery, or passing dud cheques, or stealing chickens, rabbits, or ducks. These matters had been dragged in by the prosecution for the obvious purpose of prejudicing the jury. And since the evidence was entirely circumstantial, it must exclude beyond a reasonable doubt every other hypothesis except the guilt of the defendant to warrant a conviction. There might be damaging circumstances, but if one started out believing the accused to be innocent, one had to study his explanation of those circumstances.

Referring to the warning they had been given that he would try to sway their emotions, Carson repudiated any such purpose. Nevertheless it was not possible to weigh the evidence without discussing things that might appeal to the emotions. If the facts made such an appeal, that was not his fault but was inherent in the nature of the case.

Carson said that he could not altogether acquit the prosecution of suppressing evidence which might establish his client's innocence; on the other hand, the defence had made no attempt to minimize the gravity of the circumstances through which Lancaster was under suspicion. The five circumstances were, first, the tremendous, unselfish, and undying love of the defendant for the woman in the case; that they had not at any time denied. Second were the so-called threats made to Tancrel and Russell. Third was the purchase of the pistol in St Louis; they had not denied this, but Carson submitted that they had explained it fully. Fourth was the forgery of the notes, which had been admitted and explained. The fifth circumstance the prosecution relied on was that Lancaster had asked whether Haden Clarke would speak again. Those five circumstances, standing alone, might create a suspicion of guilt, though they wouldn't prove it. "But the psychology of this case," said Carson, "is based upon the danger of stressing isolated circumstances without painting in the whole background." The perfect illustration of this danger was the Lancaster diary, where the State was only interested in stressing five or six passages which showed Lancaster's mental anguish.

The State argued that Lancaster had the perfect motive, and Carson would not dispute it. But this tremendous stress on motive boiled down to the proposition that if Lancaster didn't kill Clarke then he should have done.

The clues put forward by the State, said Carson, had crumbled. First there was the witness Ernest Huston. Lancaster had asked Huston if he could say it was Huston's gun; but later Huston had agreed that what Lancaster had really said was: "This is the gun I bought to replace the one you loaned me, and therefore it is technically yours." And Huston confirmed Lancaster's story about the lending of the gun in every detail. Huston said in his direct examination that Lancaster had asked whether Clarke would talk again. Under cross-examination he quoted Lancaster as saying: "My God, I hope he can talk, so he can tell us why he did it." Shown a photograph of the scene of the tragedy, he had said "It is not a fair picture because when I first saw the pillow it was mussed." And finally, Huston's evidence was important on how Earl Hudson picked up the pistol, which explained what happened to the fingerprints. All these clues, vital to the prosecution case, were gone.

Next came the policeman Earl Hudson. Hudson said Lancaster kept asking if Clarke would talk again. Could Hudson's memory of Lancaster's exact words be relied upon? Carson argued that by Hudson's own evidence it could not. Hudson had said he met Lancaster and Mrs Keith-Miller in the emergency room at the hospital; all the other testimony was that when they arrived with Dr Deederer, Clarke had been moved to the ward. That might seem a small thing, but in fact it was a matter of the highest and gravest importance, because it showed the danger of bringing in a verdict on circumstantial evidence based on the testimony of a man with a faulty memory, or perhaps with a motive.

Carson moved on to the telegram. "You have either got to find that Earl Hudson was lying or that Johnny Rowland was lying." Hudson was the policeman who took charge of the house; the second policeman who accompanied Hudson had for some reason never been brought into court to corroborate Hudson's evidence. Hudson agreed that he found the telegram and said he handed it to Rowland. Rowland on the witness stand said he had never seen it. After Lancaster and Mrs Keith-Miller had been in gaol three days, they went back to the house and found the telegram crumpled up in a corner of the porch. That crumpled-up telegram was now in evidence. It might be merely a matter of coincidence that the papers that were destroyed were the papers that were most valuable to the defendant. But the issue lay between Hudson and Rowland, not with the defence.

Hudson had called his sister-in-law "Miss Peggy Brown", but when pressed had admitted that she had a husband. Carson interpreted this as a deliberate and wilful attempt to mislead the court. With Earl Hudson's testimony out of the case, there was no case at all.

The next witness was Mrs J. M. Keith-Miller. Hawthorne, knowing that the tale she would tell wouldn't help his case, would never have put her on the stand at all if he could possibly have avoided it. The story she told had withstood attack from every angle. Every detail in so far as it was capable of corroboration had been corroborated by indisputable testimony. Jones had implied that the story was too well rehearsed, but the court should remember that Hawthorne and Jones had taken her over and over every detail of it months ago. "I didn't have to ask her anything about it," said Carson, "they drilled her until she knew it. She started by telling the truth, and she kept on telling the truth, and don't you know that if they had found her telling any falsehood in those three days of continuous testimony they would have trotted in one of those statements that they so carefully preserved?"

Then there was the statement given by Captain Lancaster on May 2nd, which had been read to the court; voluntarily Lancaster had gone to tell Hawthorne the truth about the notes. That statement was part of the prosecution's case, yet it corroborated in every detail the story that Lancaster told now, and the story told by Mrs Keith-Miller.

"Now we come to the big boy, Mr J. F. Russell." Lancaster said that Russell told him of the scandal about Clarke and Mrs Keith-Miller to induce him to run Chinamen and dope across the border, and that of course had been Russell's motive. Lancaster, in a letter to Chubbie of March 27th, had warned that both Russell and Tancrel might be expected to be vindictive. That brought Carson to Tancrel, the officer in the United States Navy, Mr, Captain, Admiral and General, Ambassador Tancrel, the man who had papered his own home thousands of times. It was upon the testimony of such men that the case had been brought into the courtroom and presented for serious consideration.

Bess, said Carson, had undertaken to testify to two facts: first, that there were no powder marks on the outside of Haden Clarke's head, and second, that he had embalmed the body. Bess had also expressed the view that he could not remember having seen the body of a person who had committed suicide lacking powder marks on the outside. But the gruesome photographs taken at the time of the autopsy, alleged Carson, showed that no embalming fluid had been put in or around the body. As for Bess finding no powder marks, Dr Thomas, the county physician, had testified that he examined the wound after death and that he found powder stains inside the wound; he had made a written report of this fact and passed it to the grand jury at the time of the indictment. Thomas was under the pay of the county and one of his duties was to perform autopsies as directed by the State Attorney; yet he had not been ordered to perform an autopsy in this case. "The State Attorney in presenting his evidence to this jury did not, as part of the State's case in chief, put Doctor Thomas on the witness stand. Did the State know that if they did put on the county physician, who had examined the wound after death, who was upon the payroll of this county, and who had discovered powder marks on the inside of the wound, then the last final clue would be gone?

"We have already missed somebody's letters from that house out yonder. Now we miss from this witness stand the testimony of the county physician, known to be in documentary form in the hands of some at least of those connected with the prosecution side of this case, and available to them, and it is a proper matter to go before this jury. We know the medical man who made the examination for the specific purpose of serving justice, and you find that he does not go upon the stand as a part of the case in chief, and that instead this undertaker goes on the stand and undertakes to tell this jury just how people commit suicide, and what the after-effects and the physical results of it are."

Carson was reaching the climax of his attempt to destroy the prosecution case; but more than that, he was about to attain an eloquence that marked him as an advocate of rare ability. "Trials of lawsuits," he continued, "are not mere contests of wit. Trials of lawsuits are more than games between opposing lawyers. If I conceived that the trial of lawsuits were mere trickery, mere strategy, mere tactics, then I would hunt myself another job. Bear in mind that the purpose of courts, the purpose of trials, is to arrive at and determine, so far as it be humanly possible, the facts in cases where there is a controversy or dispute as to the facts. If a trial is not conducted with that as the final and the ultimate goal, then the courts are not worth preservation.

"You have heard a lot in this case about your duty to society. Let me tell you about society. Just so far as society falls short of assuring to you your inalienable rights, just so far as society fails in its duty of protecting the individual citizen in his rights, just that far has society fallen short of being worth preserving. Men are not made for laws; laws are made for men. Government in the abstract may be something before which we can stand in reverence and awe, but the history of the world has written in blood on many thousands of pages that unless that strength, unless that power, unless that sovereignty, unless that majesty comes up from the individual citizen, then your government is bound to fall.

"You may as well understand now that you owe to society no higher duty than to see that the innocent are protected, than to see that men wearing your uniforms and bearing your commissions in their pockets should give to all even, equal, exact justice before the law."

Captain Lancaster, cool, calm, courteous, and collected, had answered all the questions put to him. He had been scrupulously fair not only to his questioner but also to the memory of Haden Clarke. Hawthorne had undertaken to cross-examine Lancaster, kept it up for an hour or two, and then stopped; he had had enough. Then the final denouement had been the reconstruction of the typing of the notes. "The purpose of that carefully staged scene was to show you that Lancaster could not have written the notes in five minutes. But he sat there and picked the words out in two minutes and thirty seconds as timed by the clerk of this court. Having failed in that final dramatic coup, there was no further cross-examination."

Carson next referred to United States Deputy Marshal J. P. Moe, who had quoted Tancrel as saying that he was going to do his part to see that Lancaster burned. The defence's theory of vindictiveness was thus fully corroborated.

Jones's argument on the question of suicide had proved too much: he had somehow managed to prove that nobody ever took his own life because no motive was adequate for it. The same argument could be used to show that nobody ever committed murder. This was the kind of false and specious reasoning with which Jones had sought to ridicule the defence case. It was impossible to say with certainty what prompted a person to commit suicide; but the State itself had introduced a document listing eight reasons—not necessarily exhaustive—and these were the reasons the defence sought to establish.

There had been no wanton attempt to attack Clarke's character, but it would have been criminal weakness to shrink from the task of probing his deeds and motives. Evidence had been brought to show that Clarke's malady was an old case, that he had thought it cured several times, but that he just couldn't stop drinking; that he was a weak and unstable character, was mixed up in many love affairs, and indulged in dope habits. Additional factors were remorse and his failure at his chosen profession. Clarke, perhaps for the first time for years, had had to stay sober and face the truth about himself—"and if we can face ourselves," said Carson, "we can face anybody". The facts as a whole were certainly such as might make a man commit suicide in his despondent moments. As for the character witnesses put forward by the State, the two people who knew Clarke best of all—his mother and his brother—had not testified. If the facts about Clarke produced in evidence by the defence could be disputed by anybody, they could have been disputed by them. But they had not come forward, and the evidence stood in the record.

Carson now moved to what he called the phase of the case which absolutely demonstrated the innocence of the defendant: the fact that Lancaster had signed the motion for disinterment and autopsy of the body and asked for a commission of medical men to be appointed. The court's own doctors had testified that the muzzle of the gun was held tight against the skull and that the entire explosion of gases had taken place inside the skull. The conclusion was irresistible, first from the filing of the motion and second from what was found at the autopsy, that Clarke killed himself.

The report of that medical commission had been on file in the court since June 22nd. But the State had ignored it, preferring to rely upon the medical testimony of Carleton Deederer, who did no more than certify the cause of death, and that of K. B. Bess, an undertaker. The commission doctors were officers of the court, but the prosecution did not call them to give evidence. The defence, however, which from the outset of the trial had sought to exclude nothing, had called them all.

Carson then dealt with Jones's theory of the shooting. All the testimony was that Clarke was lying on his back and that the bullet went into the right side of his head and penetrated into the pillow. Clarke had not said back of the right ear at all; he had said above and slightly behind. If he had shot across the bed the bullet might have hit Lancaster, but he was not trying to kill Lancaster, he was trying to kill himself. All the evidence was that he was lying on his back and turned his head so that the bullet would not hit the whitest man he had ever met.

Jones had also testified that a man would not lie down to commit suicide. No evidence had been brought to support this. The defence, said Carson, only had to produce one case of such a shooting and the theory was exploded. Carson proceeded to produce two, one two years earlier and another only a week before the Lancaster trial started, both in Miami. Yet, fired by the prosecutor's zeal to convict, the State was arguing that men don't shoot themselves lying down.

As for Hamilton, Carson contended that his findings and reputation had been proof against all the State's attacks. Two other doctors had been present when Hamilton made his analysis of the substance found on the pistol, but neither of them had been put on the stand to testify as to what they found on that occasion. All the testimony about cotton fibres related to an examination made two days later, when no one representing the defendant had been present.

The Final Speeches

Carson asked members of the jury what they thought they might do, sleeping in the same room with a man they had earlier quarrelled with and waking up to find the man had shot himself but had not left a note. This was not the first case where a man had done foolish things in an effort to escape from a difficult situation. But the true explanation of the forged notes was surely that they were meant only for Mrs Keith-Miller; that interpretation was substantiated by Lancaster's asking both her and Huston to destroy them. As for premeditation, the fact that the notes were not written until after Clarke was shot proved that the thing was not premeditated.

Lancaster had been asked why he loaded the gun at Nashville, and his answer had been that he supposed because Huston had given it to him that way. That was a perfectly natural explanation. When Huston was asked why he loaded the gun he had pointed out that it wouldn't have been much use to Lancaster for protection unloaded. The same reason stood for Lancaster.

Finally Carson reminded the jury once again that if one started out assuming guilt, every circumstance looked guilty, whereas if one started out assuming innocence, circumstances fell into their proper place unless there *was* guilt. And he gave one final illustration. Although he preferred to believe that the mistakes Hawthorne had made in the case had been involuntary, a cynic might argue differently. Suppose one started out with the assumption that Hawthorne had seen a chance to prosecute in a case that carried with it world-wide publicity. Suppose, when asked for circumstances on which one based that charge, one was to call attention to the quick burial; the failure to hold a coroner's inquest, which the law made it the State's duty to hold; the fact that the other officers who visited the scene of the shooting were never placed on the stand; the fact that the autopsy had to be ordered at the motion of the defendant, and that the subsequent report was never examined by the prosecution; and finally the thoroughly unsatisfactory nature of much of the evidence of leading prosecution witnesses, amounting in the case of Tancrel and Russell to something very like perjury, which it was somebody's duty to prosecute. Faced with all that, a cynic might believe the worst.

"Where is the State's case?" concluded Carson. "We have been over it step by step, and it is gone. They have utterly and completely failed."

In his final speech for the prosecution, Hawthorne sought first to disperse the smoke-screen which he charged Carson with laying in an effort to obscure the vital evidence. First there were the reflections cast by Carson on the integrity and honesty of everyone in the courtroom connected with the prosecution case. Carson had taken the list of State witnesses and shown them one by one to be grand rascals and perjurers. It was, Hawthorne said, the usual defence. Then there were the insinuations that the prosecution had suppressed testimony and evidence. Carson had even questioned the probity of the clerk of the court, in whose custody the gun had been when, according to Carson, hair present on it on a Friday had changed into cotton fibres by Sunday. "He tells you to believe what Lancaster says—that he made no threats. There are threats on every page of this diary!" And Hawthorne slammed the diary down on the table in front of the jury. "Carson told you in his opening address that the defence would prove that Clarke committed suicide. He told you Clarke had consulted suicide experts. He told you he would produce witnesses who would tell you exactly where Clarke said he would shoot himself. The State has proved to you that the red-hot bullet from St Louis hit Clarke just where he said it never would."

All the autopsy amounted to, contended Hawthorne, was a little more testimony about the internal explosion—which added up to nothing more than the fact that the victim died of a gunshot wound. A second conclusion of the autopsy was that the gun was held at close range. This too had never been disputed. By no form of human reasoning did this preclude murder, especially when planned across a continent.

The defence had tried to argue that the State hadn't made a case. That was true—the State never made a case. Russell, Lancaster, Haden Clarke, Mrs Keith-Miller, and Tancrel had made the case. The State hadn't selected them, they were Lancaster's chosen companions. "About Russell: you jurors are sworn to use common, everyday sense and make the case tell the truth. Russell says he did talk to Lancaster, and Lancaster's diary confirms it. Russell quotes Lancaster as saying 'I'll get rid of him', and the diary confirms by inference."

Hawthorne returned to the many factors introduced into the case which had nothing whatever to do with the death of Clarke. Why did Carson have to take Lancaster from England to Australia, through school, the world war, and across oceans? What was the purpose of the character witnesses? What had all this to do with Clarke's death? Then there was the dastardly attack on the dead man: such tactics were a blot on American justice. But the whole purpose had been to conceal the weakness of the defence's case.

"There has been talk of missing letters in this case—four of them, two from Haden and two from Chubbie. The last one to see those letters, by his own admission, was Lancaster, yet the State has been accused of having them.

"This diary breathes threats. It also breathes a great love, and that love has aroused your sympathy as it has mine. There is nothing in Lancaster's career to show he is a coward, nothing to show he would allow any man to take from him the woman he loved. He was true to this woman. He would do anything for her. He would die for her, lie for her, he would violate for her the laws of the country within whose borders he was an honoured guest.

"Haden Clarke most certainly was not depressed or had suicidal tendencies. To the victor belongs the spoils—and Haden Clarke was at the top that night, Haden Clarke was in the driver's seat that night at the Keith-Miller home. Haden Clarke had told Chubbie not to speak alone to Lancaster, and she obeyed. Haden Clarke in that fit of rage at the dinner-table showed he was not a coward—and only cowards commit suicide—told Lancaster he was the head man at the house that night. Lancaster, realizing this, said he would leave the house, go to a hotel, and start back to St Louis in the morning. Lancaster foresaw trouble; Haden Clarke expected it.

"At the airport he meets the man who alienated the affections of the woman he loved more than anything in the world and he doesn't speak to him. He doesn't even shake hands. The meeting was not friendly. He, at the house, threatens to commit suicide—he might or might not have meant that threat. It may have been but to sell Chubbie on his love for her. But she tells him she loves Haden Clarke. Clarke forbids Chubbie speaking with Lancaster alone and Lancaster threatens: 'If I don't talk alone with her tonight, I'll talk alone with her in the morning.'

"Chubbie comes into the sleeping-porch and says: 'Good night, chaps', and Bill doesn't speak. Then she told him good night again.

"Don't you see where the poisoned arrow points?

"The gun goes off and he thinks, he says, a window slams. I submit that the report of a ·38-calibre pistol, held less than three feet away from your head, would burst your eardrums.

"At the opening of this case two weeks ago, you were told that every element of human interest known to man would be brought in. But you are sworn to reject those interests not bearing directly on the death of Haden Clarke. Regardless of the sordidness and the morbidness, you are sworn solely to determine if this defendant killed Haden Clarke. You cannot take into account the character of the dead boy, his alleged suicidal tendencies. There are many facts and circumstances surrounding the death of Haden Clarke to indicate that maybe this defendant is entitled to mercy. But mercy and justice are not synonymous.

"You heard Mrs Keith-Miller, a court witness, tell that she had not loved Lancaster for two years; you heard her say she loved Haden Clarke, but not now; you heard her tell exactly the same story as Lancaster did. I suppose that gives you an idea that there has been co-operation there, between Mrs Keith-Miller, Lancaster, and Lancaster's counsel.

"What is sometimes known as the unwritten law doesn't apply in this case to a man living in adultery.

"There is not a single fact or circumstance when the rule of common reason is applied that does not point to the guilt of this defendant. Every page in his diary points to his guilt. His own testimony that he bought a gun while Chubbie was hungry and that he loaded that gun the night before he arrived in Miami points to his guilt. A guilty conscience needs no accuser, and the fact that he wrote those notes when Clarke was dying doesn't sound so good. Lancaster asked Huston if he could say the death gun was his. Over and over again he asked if Clarke would be able to speak again. These things point to his guilt."

Hamilton had said that for a so-called "sealed contact" wound there must be pressure from both directions, head and gun, and that this was a clear indication of suicide. But the testimony showed that Haden Clarke's head was on the pillow when the bullet was fired, and the bullet found in the pillow proved that this was true. The proposition that Haden Clarke, with his head on the pillow, pushed the gun firmly against his head and at the same time pushed his head up against the gun—as Hamilton would have it—simply wasn't reasonable. It couldn't be done without straining every muscle in the body. "Why lie down and then rear up to meet the gun? But if someone else should suddenly, while the victim is asleep, bury a gun in his head, his subconscious mind would make him come up, not dive through the pillow and mattress. . . .

"Finally, let me say this, before this case is put away—that you are a trial jury, not a pardon board. . . . Do not let sympathy or emotions play a part. Decide simply if Haden Clarke committed suicide or if William Newton Lancaster killed him."

The arguments for prosecution and defence had taken over two days by the time Hawthorne finished; the time was eleven-thirty on the morning of Wednesday, August 17th, and the trial had been in progress for over a fortnight. During his final speech, indeed, Hawthorne had confessed that everyone in the courtroom working on the case was exhausted, and this must also have applied to the jury. There was a short recess before Judge Atkinson's charge to the jury, and then they retired to consider their verdict.

CHAPTER XVIII

Consider your Verdict

THE judge's summation in an American court is not the equivalent of the summing-up at the conclusion of a trial in England. Judge Atkinson's address to the jury was brief and dealt mainly with points of law; there was no attempt to evaluate the evidence. Thus when the jury retired they had to rely almost entirely on their personal impressions gained at the trial.

However faithfully evidence is compressed and presented, however impartially the analysis of it is attempted, the impressions of frankness and spontaneity, or of deceit and premeditation, gained by those who hear it at first hand cannot be reproduced with certainty. Thus comparatively minor or peripheral matters may exert an influence on a verdict disproportionate to their apparent significance in print. Even the impact of facts cannot be accurately gauged. But one impression that does emerge from a study of the trial is that Hawthorne, in developing the prosecution case, was content to rely on a chain of apparently damning circumstances to gain the verdict. He did not feel it necessary to follow all these circumstances to their logical conclusion, nor did he feel obliged to deal other than summarily with the defence put up by Carson. Whereas Carson dissected every prosecution point and endeavoured to refute or explain it, the prosecution for the most part treated the defence submissions with contempt and simply restated their case. A well-prepared defence and an attack that takes too much for granted may of course argue nothing more than skill on the one hand and over-confidence on the other; or they may reflect the conscious and unconscious convictions and doubts of the protagonists.

What kind of man was Lancaster, and what sort of impression had he made in court? The answer to the second question seems to be that from the reaction of the court he must have made a very good impression indeed, and Chubbie later confirmed this. "Bill was marvellous," she said afterwards. "One would never have guessed he was on trial for his life." The demeanour of a witness, perhaps unjustly, is often held to be a reliable indication of the veracity of his evidence. It is pertinent that

Carson, whose initial reaction to the circumstantial evidence was the popular one ("He's as guilty as hell"), seems to have become convinced of Lancaster's innocence after meeting and talking to him.

The answer to the first question, although less easy to come by, ought to be apparent from a study of Lancaster's past life. Was Lancaster a man who normally told the truth? Chubbie had found that he was not above a little romancing about himself, and this would be consistent with his earlier tendency to show off. But although he could delude himself and did not always face facts, the overall impression is that he was not fundamentally a dishonest person. Yet he was capable of deception in minor matters, as illustrated by his resource over the procuring of commercial licences in Canada; and he could act a part, as he did that day in the automat in New York. There were some white lies too in his evidence. notably over his discharge from the RAF and the reference to his wife having private means. But it might be idealistic under any circumstances to expect a man to present his past in other than a favourable light.

An interesting indication of Lancaster's basic naïveté is his admission that he loaded the gun at Nashville the night before he took off for Miami. There was no evidence on this point but Lancaster's, nor could there be, but it was a point that the prosecution successfully exploited against him. Yet if Lancaster's story was a concocted one, why play into the prosecution's hands like this? Why not say he loaded the gun when he bought it, or immediately afterwards? That would be a perfectly natural thing to do, and it would have reduced the significance of the loading of the gun considerably. Other indications of a basic naïveté were his admission that he might have uttered threats in St Louis, although none were alleged, his self-confessed "deliberate attempted forgery" of Clarke's signature, and his admitted abruptness to Clarke ("I told Clarke I didn't care what he said or thought")—all suggestive of a man so unaware of his predicament that he was not much concerned at guarding his tongue.

Despite his naïveté, however, he was certainly not unintelligent. He realized from the first that his forgeries would never pass any sort of scrutiny, which explains why he wanted them destroyed after Chubbie had read them. Later, when he realized that his bluff would be called, he was intelligent enough to own up.

Lancaster's outstanding characteristic, perhaps, was fearlessness. But was he reckless enough to make the threats in front of Tancrel and Russell and at the same time subtle enough to plant the phrase about their being vindictive in the letter to Chubbie? Coolness in a crisis was another of his virtues, but did it amount to the prosecution's picture of a man with an icy, calculating, almost inhuman calm? Chubbie had decided from the first that he wasn't a schemer, and she had done most of the thinking for him. Lancaster's particular brand of courage does not predicate a strong imagination, and there was little in his life to suggest that he had the cunning, the ruthlessness, and the artifice to plan and execute such a cold-blooded murder and then act the part so blandly of an innocent man.

Although he was not hot-headed—or, from the evidence available, particularly hot-blooded—Lancaster had an impulsive nature, and murder on impulse might be more in character. But no evidence was brought to support such a theory. The prosecution case was that the murder was planned across a continent. To get the maximum penalty Hawthorne was out to prove premeditation, and he seems not to have appreciated that the principal clue on which he relied, the forging of the notes, was an irreparable flaw in such an hypothesis.

If Lancaster had planned murder in the guise of suicide, would he have greeted Clarke so coolly at the airport in the presence of others? Would he have risked announcing the decision to stay the night in a hotel and leave next morning for St Louis? Would he have talked in terms of giving Clarke a year to make Chubbie happy? Would he have sulked when Chubbie said good night? Wasn't his whole behaviour that evening consistent with a man under severe strain but innocent of any conscious intent to murder? The thought itself, though, may well have occurred to him, as it occurs to most men confronted with a similar breach of trust, though they dismiss it. Threats too are uttered in these circumstances without any resolve to carry them out. These natural impulses might be quite sufficient to give Lancaster a guilty conscience and explain the forging of the notes.

To balance his thoughtlessness, Lancaster appears to have been a warm-hearted person with a well-developed sense of fair play. He tried to see the best in people, and he made friends easily, if not always wisely. The friendship that developed between him and Clarke was unmistakably genuine: that much emerges from the correspondence that passed between them. If Lancaster shot Clarke he was not just removing a rival; he was murdering a friend, one for whom, as he seems to have recognized, he had become something of a father-figure.

Years later, Chubbie's answer to the question "Did he do it?" was simply "I don't know". But her instinct was that he couldn't have done, because to have killed Clarke that night in that manner would have been a cowardly act, and Lancaster, as she knew better than anyone, wasn't a coward. The possibility that he acted out of character under pressure, as others have done before him, might be easier to credit, but it was never put forward, the prosecution's endeavour being to show Lancaster as habitually shifty and dishonourable.

There were several other possible points against Lancaster which the prosecution failed to make. During his examination Lancaster said: "We had talked about my buying the gun to replace Huston's, earlier in the evening." No evidence seems to have been brought to support this, and Chubbie's reaction at the time of the shooting was that there wasn't a gun in the house. An explanation may have existed but none was sought. Again, Carson's contention that Lancaster's agreement to an autopsy demonstrated his innocence ignored the dilemma Lancaster was in. To have refused to ask for an autopsy when the idea was put to him by his attorneys would have been to admit his guilt to them. Once before—over the scrutiny of the notes by experts—he had tried to brazen it out. Perhaps he was trying to do so again.

Why did Lancaster cease to write up his diary after reaching St Louis and receiving the letters? Could it have been that his thoughts were too terrible to commit to paper? Why didn't he talk to Clarke's mother at the Everglades Hotel on the night of the shooting? He was there in the lobby, and everyone else went across to speak to her, but Lancaster remained a little way off, close enough to hear something of what was said but not close enough to come face to face with Mrs Clarke. Later he sought her out and assured her of his innocence, but he had had time to strike an attitude by then.

The knowledge that he had forged the notes, of course, could account for his initial avoidance of Ida Clarke. It could also account for his anxious questions as to whether Clarke would speak again. In other respects his conduct and demeanour seem more compatible with innocence than guilt. He seems serenely confident of the outcome throughout. Again and again in court the phrasing of his answers seems relaxed and involuntary. His letter to his daughter, if written by a guilty man, is surely a masterpiece.

The conclusion would appear to be that any plan Lancaster had of shooting Clarke must have been an unconscious one, and that if indeed he shot Clarke at all it was on impulse. The corollary would be that Lancaster, fighting for his life, was able to draw on hitherto unsuspected reserves of deceit and cunning.

So sure were the prosecution that the circumstances alone were enough to convict Lancaster that they did not explore the precise details of the shooting as it must have occurred if he was guilty. Of the two men, Lancaster after his early start from Nashville must have been much the more fatigued. But after his talk with Clarke he must have waited until Clarke was asleep. In brilliant moonlight he can see the gun on the table, and Clarke in the bed three feet from him. Clarke's head is turned towards him. Stealthily he gets out of bed, reaches over to the table and takes the gun from its box. Then he leans over Clarke so as to angle the bullet slightly towards his own bed rather than away from him—the natural angle of the bullet if Clarke were to shoot himself in the position in which he is lying, but for Lancaster a difficult thing to do, besides being a move of extraordinary prescience. He fires the gun, then switches on the light, makes a weak call for Chubbie in case she has heard the shot, and then types the notes. It is a plausible picture; but less plausible surely than the one that can be drawn purporting to show how Clarke killed himself. What corroborative detail, for instance, could be more persuasive than Lancaster's description of how he first saw Clarke after the shooting, with blood running over his face so that the position of the wound was obscured, and with the pistol half under his body so that it couldn't be seen?

Which brings one back to the state of mind of the two men at the time. So far as Clarke is concerned, Chubbie's evidence is informative of his state of mind and consistent with the view that he was heading for a psychological breakdown; Lancaster's story of the talk he had that night with Clarke fills out the picture. The prosecution, of course, alleged that, in that undefined lapse of time before the ambulance men came, they put their heads together. Yet the theory of collusion, like the theory of premeditation, did not fit the notes, which Lancaster wanted to destroy but which Chubbie decided must be kept.

An impartial view of Clarke's temperament came from the girl he had married bigamously: there could be no happiness for them, she had written, until he learnt to rely upon himself. He had become equally dependent on Chubbie.

The prosecution's view that Clarke held the upper hand that night cannot be conceded without reservations. It was common ground to defence and prosecution that Lancaster had secured for himself what he most wanted—time, a month in which to convince Chubbie that Clarke could never make her happy. Why kill Clarke within an hour or two of gaining that advantage? It was Clarke who would be depressed by it. "I knew in my heart that he would never marry Chubbie," said Lancaster. "He told me he had never had that malady before," said Chubbie. Chubbie admitted in court that she no longer even loved Clarke's memory. Clarke was a sensitive enough person to have anticipated this.

One point omitted by Carson in his final speech was that the threats alleged to have been uttered to Tancrel at El Paso in the presence of Ince must have been made not, as the prosecution claimed in the indictment, on March 29th, but on March 19th. No other date will fit. Lancaster was worried at this time at not hearing from Chubbie, but there was no hint in his diary that any scandal had reached him until nine days later, nor indeed does there seem to have been any basis for such scandal at this time. "There are threats on every page of this diary," alleged Hawthorne. But there weren't, and Hawthorne could not point to them. He had to rely on Tancrel and Russell. Hawthorne disputed that Clarke was depressed or suicidal; but neither Clarke's mother nor his brother would go on the stand to testify. "You cannot take into account the character of the dead boy," contended Hawthorne. But he did not say why not. The prosecution lawyers in their final speeches made many statements which misquoted or were contrary to the testimony. And Hawthorne's attitude to the report of the medical commission confirms the impression that it was entirely favourable to the defence.

These, perhaps, were some of the many conflicting arguments that were tossed back and forth in the jury room in the hours that followed. An attempt to take a ballot early on proved abortive and the arguments continued. The jury, it seems, were deeply impressed by the awful cumulative weight of the circumstances, especially the forging of the notes. Yet the step from these misgivings to finding the prisoner guilty of murder was one they found difficult to take. At 4.22, after over four and a half hours of discussion, they returned to the courtroom to ask two questions. First, they wanted Judge Atkinson to elaborate on his instructions to them regarding what constituted a reasonable degree of doubt. Second, they wanted to view the exhibits again.

The fact that the jury had come back to ask these questions must have seemed a hopeful sign to Jim Carson. Whatever they believed the truth to be, they were reluctant to find Lancaster guilty. Judge Atkinson's directions to them on what constituted a reasonable doubt were bound to work in Lancaster's favour, and as for the exhibits, Carson had no intention of allowing those to be viewed again. The legal position was that either side could deny such a request without it being known to the jury which side had done so, and Carson availed himself of this rule. Clearly there was doubt in the jury's mind, and doubt that remained unsatisfied must lead to a verdict of not guilty. That doubt and that verdict must be on the basis of the evidence as a whole, and Carson was not likely to take the risk of some minor academic point connected with the exhibits swaying the jury either way at this late stage. Provided the jury were kept in the same state of knowledge, his client would win.

Carson's reaction proved to be right, and a few minutes later, after four hours forty-eight minutes of deliberation, the jury returned to the courtroom and the foreman stood up to give their verdict.

"Not —"

The second word of the verdict was drowned by a thunderous outburst of cheering and handclapping. Men stamped their feet, women wept and shrieked with delight, one shrill voice cried over and over again "Amen, Amen." The situation got quickly out of control as the crowd, in a spontaneous demonstration of relief, sympathy, and joy, pushed past bailiffs and policemen and surged towards the defence table where Lancaster sat. Then, as some semblance of order was restored, Lancaster shook hands with his counsel, the photographers took their pictures, and eventually he was prevailed upon to make a statement. "I have been convinced all along that my innocence would be established," he said, "and I will always be grateful to Mr Carson and Mr Lathero for their splendid defence of me. My trial has been eminently fair and I have been treated cordially and courteously at all times."

What was the reaction of the State Attorney? Did his last speech to the court lack conviction and thus fail to carry it? Asked for a statement, Hawthorne said, "The performance of my duty to the best of my ability is sufficient compensation. The jury, the only agency provided by law to determine the issue, has rendered its verdict and I accept it, without regret." Those last two words might well be taken to mean that he recognized the justice of the outcome. Carson, for his part, said he had never doubted what the verdict would be.

The reporters turned back to Lancaster. "Do your present plans include Mrs Keith-Miller?"

"Please don't ask me to answer that. I don't know now what my answer would be."

As one of the witnesses, Chubbie had not been allowed in the courtroom during the trial except when she was actually on the stand, and she had not been present when the verdict was announced. Her own selfless part in the procuring of that verdict, and the personal tragedy the whole case involved for her, were forgotten for the moment. She was standing now in the lobby just outside the courtroom and she heard the cheering and understood what it meant. One of the Pressmen spotted her, and she could not avoid him. "I'm delighted," she said. "I knew old Bill would come through."

CHAPTER XIX

The Last Flight

"ARE you going to marry Captain Lancaster?" That was the question that reporters were still firing at Chubbie when she sailed from New York two months later. Apart from pointing out that Lancaster was still married she had refused to answer. Both she and Bill Lancaster had made up their minds to leave America and return to England, and Lancaster, who had already crossed the Atlantic, was preparing to meet Chubbie at the King George V dock in London on October 24th, 1932. In order to avoid reporters he had arranged for her to disembark before the liner actually docked: thus as the ship approached its berth a slim figure in a black hat and fur coat climbed precariously down a swinging rope ladder while a seaman carrying two light bags and a travelling rug followed. A few moments later she was on the dockside, where a familiar figure waited to greet her.

"Bill."

"Chubbie."

Lancaster took the luggage over to a waiting taxi, and they drove away. What could the future hold for them? Aviation remained their abiding interest, but neither had the money to buy an aeroplane or finance a flight. The conflicting quotes and rumours that reached the newspapers faithfully reflected their own confusion of thought. "I must start life all over again," Chubbie was quoted as having said before she left New York. She would stay in London with an aunt. "I don't know what I shall do afterwards until I've seen Bill." Lancaster had told reporters that he planned to rehabilitate himself by making a record long-distance flight in the New Year, but it sounded a vague ambition. First he would look for a job. "My son will stay with me and his mother," announced Lancaster's father. "We hope he will be reconciled to his wife, who is now in London." Another report said that Lancaster had promised his parents not to see Mrs Miller for six months. But this clearly lacked authenticity in the light of an interview Chubbie gave to a newspaper a week after her return. "Bill and I have been wanting to marry for five years," Chubbie was quoted as saying. "Bill's marriage had gone on the rocks before I even met him. Those long five years of waiting to get our lives settled, with things just drifting along, were hard for me. Bill loves me and I love him and always will. As soon as Bill can get his divorce we will marry and do our best to forget whatever mistakes we have made and the terrible price we have had to pay." Lancaster was quoted in the same interview as saying: "I've been waiting to marry Chubbie for the last five years, and I want to get that accomplished just as soon as ever I can." But the publication of this interview brought a statement from the traditional "close friend" of the Lancaster family: "There is not, and never has been, any question of divorce between Captain and Mrs Lancaster." So the basic situation was unchanged.

For Chubbie, the chance to sell her story for serialization to a national daily newspaper—and other similar serializations followed—meant that for a time at least she could pay her way. But for Bill Lancaster, no such offers came. The unspoken opinion in England was that he had probably killed Haden Clarke and been lucky to get away with it; but it was the woman's story that had the appeal. For a time Chubbie lived with her aunt in Hampstead, but soon she moved to a bed-sitting room in Oxford Terrace, off the Edgware Road, so as to be near the ghost-writer who had already begun working on her life story for book publication. Once again, however, Chubbie was to be disappointed in this project: although the ghost-writer's work was serialized it never appeared as a book.

As Chubbie settled down on her own in Oxford Terrace she began to realize, if only subconsciously, that a complete break with her past was what she really needed. Bill Lancaster would always have a special place in that past, she was still very fond of him, and had he been free to marry her she would undoubtedly have done so; but as the months passed and the hopelessness of their situation became more and more apparent, she began to realize how much she was still a prisoner of her past. Loyalty to Bill at the time of the trial and in the weeks that followed had led her to declare a love for him that, perhaps, was now no more than affection and friendship. Yet as he struggled to remake his career, and to find a niche for himself in an aviation world hit by the depression, where his name at once recalled his sensational past, she shrank from doing or saying anything that might hurt him further. Thus for the whole of that winter of 1932–33 she continued to see him fairly frequently, and never at any time did she deny him the one thing he needed—hope.

Once when he called on her in Oxford Terrace he was looking especially cheerful; he had had an interview for a job as a pilot with a small airline operating from Croydon. But his lack of airline experience told against him, and someone else got the job. After this failure he became despondent, and by early 1933 he had become convinced that his only chance of rehabilitation as a flyer, and of living down the stigma of the murder trial, lay in doing something spectacular. His father, now seventy-three, agreed to finance him, and the record he made up his mind to beat was the record from London to South Africa, held at that time by Amy Mollison. Two months earlier, in November 1932, she had flown from England to the Cape in four days, six hours, fifty-four minutes, beating the record, formerly held by her husband, Jim Mollison, by ten and a half hours. The record was still in the public mind because Lady Bailey, the first woman to make the flight (Lady Heath had flown in the reverse direction), had recently failed in an attempt to beat it. She had left Croydon on January 15th, 1933, reached Oran that night, taken off again for the Niger, and disappeared. She had been missing for four days when French air patrols found her 300 miles east of the Niger and 1450 miles from Oran. Lancaster had been approached to fly out to look for her; why not attempt the record himself?

The most suitable aircraft available, it seemed to Lancaster, was of a type he knew well—a later mark of Avro Avian which had been specially built for Kingsford-Smith eighteen months earlier. "Smithy" had left Melbourne in it in September 1931 in an attempt to beat the record from Australia to England, but had been compelled to give up through illness. A long-range single-seater with a Gipsy II engine, the machine had been dubbed by Kingsford-Smith *Southern Cross Minor*, and the letters were still painted in white on the blue fuselage. This was the plane, now re-registered G-ABLK, which Lancaster bought with his father's money at a cost of just over £700. The range of 1600 miles was adequate for the route planned by Lancaster, but the cruising speed of 95 miles an hour was 20 miles slower than Amy Mollison's plane had been, which on the face of it was a serious drawback. Yet if he succeeded under such a handicap the achievement would be all the more meritorious. He could only hope to beat the record by accurate flying and by allowing himself practically no rest.

By the end of March the plane was ready to be collected from the Avro airfield at Woodford in Cheshire—where Lancaster had collected the Avian III five and a half years earlier—and Lancaster's plans were complete. Permits for landing en route and for over-flying various territories, including the Sahara, were requested, and a sum to help defray the expense of a search—about £100—was deposited with the London agent of the Trans-Saharienne Company. Chubbie helped plan the route but otherwise took no part in the preparations. It was entirely a Lancaster affair.

The route they had planned followed closely the route already taken by both Jim and Amy Mollison. The first leg would take Lancaster across France, the Pyrenees and the Mediterranean to Oran in Algeria, a distance of 1100 miles. He intended to take off from Lympne in the early morning and fly this first leg in daylight. Amy Mollison had been able to fly the next leg, the 1400 miles from Oran to Gao on the Niger,

Lancaster before leaving New York to return to England, October 1932
Photo Associated Newspapers

Entries by Bill Lancaster and his parents in the visitors' book at Lympne
Photo R. D. Muir

Lancaster says goodbye to his mother
Photo London Express News and Feature Services

in one hop, but the Avian would barely have the range for this and Lancaster planned a short refuelling stop at Reggan, an oasis outpost on the trans-Saharan motor-track 630 miles south of Oran. The difficulty here was that he would reach Oran after nightfall and would have to fly the leg to Reggan in darkness, as he could not afford to take more than an hour or so's rest. He knew Reggan would be difficult to find at night; if he were to miss it, the vast expanse of the Sahara lay beyond. From Reggan he would continue across the Sahara after another short rest to Gao, then cross Nigeria and the Bight of Biafra direct to Cape Lopez, cutting out Douala. This, he hoped, would save him several hours on Amy Mollison's time. He would still have nearly 2500 miles to go to reach Cape Town, but he would have the African coastline beneath him as a constant check on his position from then on.

In the final few days before his departure Lancaster met Kiki and the children and took them out for a meal. Then on Saturday, April 8th, he visited his solicitor, a man named Isaac, and made a will in which he named Chubbie as the sole beneficiary, his only asset being a small insurance policy on his life. Chubbie had spent every penny she could lay her hands on to help with the expenses of the trial, so this gesture was not as unreasonable as might at first appear. Lancaster's father had taken out a policy on the Avian.

After saying goodbye to Chubbie, Lancaster went by train to Manchester, where he had left the Avian, and flew it down to Heston next morning, Sunday, April 9th, continuing to Lympne in the afternoon. His parents travelled down by train, and they booked in at the Grand Hotel in Folkestone. Lympne was then a popular take-off point for record flights. On April 7th an Italian aviator named Captain L. Robbiano had left in an attempt to beat C. W. A. Scott's record to Australia, and on the day of Lancaster's arrival Jean Batten, in a Gipsy Moth, also took off for Australia. Lancaster's flight would be the third record attempt to start from Lympne in five days.

All next day Lancaster was at Lympne supervising the final overhaul of the Avian, and that night at the Grand Hotel he announced his intention of leaving next day. "Everything is ready," he told reporters, "the aerodrome is a fine taking-off field and I have no fears of making a good start. I used to ferry fighting machines over to France from there during the War and I know every inch of it." He had been warned to expect very bad weather on parts of the route, but he believed the machine could stand up to it and if it was humanly possible he would keep going. "I can't wait for the months that must elapse before conditions are good," he said. Another airman, in fact, was already planning a similar flight. Then he paid tribute to his parents; if he succeeded he would owe everything to them. His father had not hesitated to back him, risking heavy financial loss, while his mother too had supported him magnificently, "believing, as

I do, that I shall be able to make the world forget". The true purpose of the flight was thus publicly expressed.

At five o'clock next morning the Avian was wheeled out of the hangar and loaded with one hundred gallons of fuel. Lancaster was taking a spare propeller and various spare engine parts for running repairs, and also on board he had a two-gallon drum of water which he was compelled by French Government regulations to carry when crossing the Sahara. His only other luggage was a topee, a pair of flying goggles, and his maps.

On arrival at Lympne by taxi from Folkestone he went straight to the tiny control building and learnt that he would be faced with a twenty-mile-an-hour headwind nearly all the way to Oran. This would seriously reduce his ground speed and quite possibly put Oran out of reach without a stop for refuelling. It would be a serious setback, yet he decided to take off just the same. There was always the chance that the wind would change at altitude; and if he allowed himself to be put off by the weather he would never get the record.

Lancaster had assured his parents that he had no intention of taking undue risks; but the whole conception of the flight involved a physical and mental strain of the utmost severity. What condition was Lancaster in to face it? He had done no flying at all for almost exactly twelve months, and for three of those months he had been confined to a cell eight feet by ten. Since his return to England he had suffered bitter disappointments amounting almost to degradation. The self-respect he longed to regain had been denied him. Loyal and selfless as his parents had been, the sacrifices they were making had borne heavily on them, and therefore even more so on him. Now it seemed to the handful of people who gathered in the darkness at Lympne to see him off that, even allowing for a natural tension and eagerness at such a time, he was a pale, nervous, cadaverous ghost of the Lancaster they had known. He was in a hurry all right—too much of a hurry, indeed. To anyone who studied his itinerary it was obvious that his haste, if he was to beat the record, would have to be desperate.

"My most difficult task will be the location of Reggan," Lancaster told the reporters who had gathered to see him off. Then he added: "I want to make it clear that I am attempting this flight at my own risk. I don't expect any efforts to be made to find me if I'm reported missing." Most pioneer aviators said this, and no doubt when they said it they believed it, yet in emergency all looked for help and if it was humanly possible it was always forthcoming. Failure, though, and an ignominious return, was an outcome that Lancaster could hardly contemplate. He had said that this would be his final attempt to re-establish himself in British aviation, so if he failed he would perhaps not wish to survive. On the other hand he had promised his parents and Chubbie, quite independently, that if he was forced down he would stick to the ship; one of the lessons of long-distance flying was that when a plane was forced down in isolated country the best chance for the crew was to stay with it. The machine was easier to find than the man.

Just before half-past five, still in pitch darkness, Lancaster went out to his aircraft. Dressed in flying overalls and a wind-cheater, with a brightly coloured woollen scarf wrapped round his neck and with his maps tucked under his arm, he turned to say goodbye to his mother. She handed him a packet of chicken sandwiches and kissed him, and he climbed into the cockpit of the Avian. He carried no other food except some beef extract and two Thermos flasks, one of water and one of coffee. At the last minute Mrs Lancaster stepped forward again to hand him a bar of chocolate she had forgotten to give him, and then the tiny blue plane turned into wind to begin its take-off run, rapidly disappearing into the early morning mist and gloom. The time was 5.38.

After crossing the Channel Lancaster made a landfall at Le Havre and then continued south across France, aiming to over-fly the Spanish frontier in the eastern Pyrenees. But his ground speed was reduced by headwinds, and long before he reached the Spanish frontier he must have realized that his narrow endurance margin for the Mediterranean crossing had gone; he would have to land at Barcelona to refuel. Besides the inevitable delay that would result, this would take him some distance to starboard of the direct route for Oran. Already, at this early stage of the flight, he was losing valuable time. An English pilot who met him when he landed at Barcelona noted his tension and anxiety; he looked more as though he might be nearing the end of a record attempt than at the beginning.

He finally reached Oran at nine o'clock that evening, fifteen and a half hours after leaving Lympne. Amy Mollison, with a faster plane, no stop, and no headwind, had done it in eleven. More frustrating still, the French authorities at Oran had no knowledge of the insurance he had effected through the agent of the Trans-Saharienne Company in London and refused to let him take off until they received confirmation; the only alternative they offered was that he pay the sum again, and this he could not do. Eventually, after signing a statement that he would fly at his own risk and that he would not expect rescue operations to be mounted if he disappeared, he was allowed to proceed. Meanwhile the servicing and refuelling had also been delayed, and when he finally got away from Oran it was three o'clock on the morning of Wednesday, April 12th, and he had been on the ground for six hours against Amy Mollison's four. That was another two hours to make up. While on the ground at Oran Lancaster learned that Captain Robbiano had disappeared on his flight to Australia.

The delay at Oran had one advantage: on this difficult leg, for which he had always had the greatest respect and where for hundreds of miles there was hardly a pinpoint and nothing to guide him at night, he would shortly be flying into daylight. Meanwhile he completed the crossing of the Atlas Mountains in darkness, striking a match every few minutes to check that he was on course as he had no cockpit lights. One hundred and twenty-five miles to starboard lay Colomb-Bechar and the trans-Saharan motor-track, and as he flew south that track would curve round in a wide arc to meet him. It was nearly five hours after leaving Oran when, in glaring sunlight, he picked out the thin white crease of the motor-track as it converged on his own course from the right. When the road turned south he followed it, and soon afterwards he saw an airfield. The chance of checking his position was too good to miss and at eight-thirty he landed and confirmed his impression that this must be Adrar, a hundred miles north of Reggan.

Fuel was available at Adrar and he decided to fill up; he could overfly Reggan now and make straight for Gao, 800 miles distant and well within range. Forty-five minutes later, at nine-fifteen, he was on his way. He had completed what he had always felt was the most difficult part of the flight, and the short refuelling stop at Adrar had gained him some at least of the lost time. Ahead of him the motor-track ran a reasonably straight course through Reggan and Bidon Cinq to Gao, with "beacons" —small pyramids marking the track—at regular intervals all the way.

The clear early-morning air of the run down to Adrar, however, was now opaque with sand; a severe sandstorm was blowing up and soon visibility was reduced to almost nil. Lancaster tried to keep the motor-track in sight but soon he lost it altogether. When, some minutes later, he picked up what he thought was the same track, he was in fact following a more easterly road heading for Aoulef and In Salah.

At eleven o'clock, aware that he was off course, he landed at Aoulef to fix his position. He had been airborne for 105 minutes since leaving Adrar and he would now almost certainly have to refuel again at Reggan. He took off again from Aoulef within ten minutes, but the sandstorm was still blowing and almost at once he lost his bearings again. There was nothing to do but fix his position a second time at Aoulef and then set course again for Reggan. It was nearly one o'clock when he got there, and he would certainly need to refuel. He had wasted the entire morning.

By this time Lancaster was almost distracted with fatigue and frustration, nervously as well as physically exhausted. M. Borel, head of the Trans-Saharienne Company post at Reggan, persuaded him to rest while the Avian was refuelled and the sandstorm blew itself out, but Lancaster asked to be called within three hours, and he refused food. At four o'clock that afternoon Borel duly woke him, but when he made ready to take off the sandstorm was still blowing and Borel strongly advised him to wait. Even the beacons on the motor-track, he said, would be impossible to see.

The Last Flight

For an hour, two hours, Lancaster waited. His chance of beating the record to the Cape was already almost gone. But there could be no giving up; he would have to keep going while the smallest hope remained. Late that afternoon the wind dropped a little and the sandstorm eased, and Lancaster announced his intention of taking off for Gao. Borel immediately tried to dissuade him. He must at least wait, urged Borel, until the moon came up; he would never be able to follow the motor-track in darkness.

For just over a hundred miles the motor-track roughly coincided with the direct compass course for Gao. Then the track curved away south-eastwards to take in the supply station of Bidon Cinq, after which it pursued a winding but roughly southerly course for 400 miles before turning south-west to meet the direct compass course again about 100 miles north of Gao. If Lancaster found he was unable to see the motor-track—and, as Borel had said, it was not always visible even in daylight, hence the beacons—he would have no choice but to fly the direct compass course. While this would save time, he would be cutting across 500 miles of featureless desert where to be forced down would mean almost certain death.

Lancaster's intention certainly was to follow the motor-track; he hoped that in spite of Borel's warning he would be able to see it. But the alternative he would be faced with if the track was not visible must have occurred to him. He had confidence in his machine, and if forced to fly the direct route he would have to be prepared to do it; that, no doubt, was his attitude. This was not a point, though, on which he took Borel into his confidence.

"We'll give you twenty-four hours," said Borel. "If we don't hear anything of you from Gao by tomorrow evening we'll send a convoy along the track. If you can burn something to light a beacon they'll see you." He gave Lancaster a box of matches and also lent him a pocket torch, and at 6.30 P.M. Lancaster took off for Gao.

It seemed to onlookers that the take-off run was decidedly irregular, almost as though Lancaster was too tired to hold the plane in a straight line. But when the Avian became airborne it flew strongly and steadily and Lancaster turned smoothly on to his southerly heading. Soon the *Southern Cross Minor* became no more than a speck in the failing light, holding its course due south.

Lancaster's estimated time of arrival at Gao was 2.30 A.M. next day, Thursday, April 13th; but they waited for him at Gao in vain. Nothing was seen or heard of him anywhere along the Niger, and at dawn he was officially reported overdue.

There was no great alarm at first. He could have come down to check his bearings, or to wait for daylight. News might come through at any moment, perhaps from one of the innumerable villages north of the Niger. But the silence continued all day. Around the curve of the Niger from Gao to Timbuktu, and northwards to Reggan, wireless messages between French military stations filled the ether. There was still no news. At six o'clock that evening Borel, as good as his word, sent the first car south from Reggan along the motor-track. Next morning the search was taken up from Gao.

The news that Captain Lancaster was missing on a flight across the Sahara reached London later the same day, in time for the afternoon editions. But it was Easter week, the next day was Good Friday, when there would be no newspapers, and the story made little impact. Scares of this kind were frequent; the fellow would probably turn up tomorrow. Everyone was hurrying off to enjoy the Easter holiday. An exception, of course, was Chubbie. She had followed the news of the flight with disappointment and dismay; the stop at Barcelona alone had been enough to make her extremely doubtful of success. Now it seemed that Bill had been forced down somewhere. But there was nothing she could do for a day or so; at any time a report might come through to say he had been found.

When he had been missing for forty-eight hours, Chubbie decided it was time to act. She had kept in touch with the Express group of newspapers, who had telephoned her regularly with news, and that Saturday evening she went to their offices in Fleet Street and asked to see the editor. She was quite prepared to put what little money she had into mounting a rescue flight, but she knew she would need further backing to get such a flight organized in time. She was shown into the office of the editor of the *Sunday Express*, who was sympathetic and pronounced himself ready to help, and next morning a report of her visit appeared on the front page of the newspaper; it included an appeal for help in finding a suitable plane. This, Chubbie knew, would be the greatest single stumbling-block; very few private owners operated machines with the required range. "There are only two or three planes in England that could go to the rescue," she was reported as saying. "I must find one of them." Chubbie herself was prepared to fly it.

Her best chance, she felt, was the Fokker monoplane owned by the Duchess of Bedford, and on Sunday morning she rang Captain C. D. Barnard, the Duchess's personal pilot, and travelled by road to Gerrards Cross to see him and make plans for a rescue attempt. Anxious to help as he was, Charles Barnard could only point out to Chubbie the impossibility of mounting such an expedition in time. The Fokker was laid up and would need several days' work to prepare it for a long flight, and Barnard could think of no other aeroplane with sufficient range that might be available. Desperate, Chubbie went back to London to sound other of her many friends in aviation; but that same day Edward Lancaster, Bill's father, in an interview that was published next morning, expressed the wish that no one should risk their lives in such a problematical search. He was relying, he said, on the French authorities on the spot. "It is not our wish that anyone who doesn't know the terrible flying conditions of the Sahara Desert should go out there to try to find our son," he said. "It would be a futile attempt and very much against all our wishes. Everything that can possibly be done is being done. . . . I have been in constant touch with the Trans-Saharienne Company. They have already sent out a motor-car, and I am told that an aeroplane is joining in the search." Mr Lancaster added that he would not worry unduly for at least another week. "It is my belief," he said, "that my son has been forced down south-east of Gao. He is in splendid physical condition and has enough food and water to last ten days." This estimate, of course, was based on the assumption that Lancaster, like Lady Bailey three months earlier, had come down in the later stages of his flight; a forced landing in the Sahara would be a different matter. The remark about Lancaster's physical condition too was open to contradiction.

The French authorities, in spite of a natural annoyance with Lancaster for taking off against advice, were meanwhile mounting an extensive search. The Nigerian Government had instituted an inquiry, but no one had seen an unidentified plane and the French were reasonably sure that Lancaster had never reached the Niger. Two civil planes reconnoitred the motor-track on Monday, April 17th, but wireless messages intercepted in Algiers reported no news. An intensive search of the whole desert area was clearly beyond the resources of the scattered French outposts, so an attempt was made to concentrate the search in the most likely region, thought to be the area north of Gao as far as Bidon Cinq, the latter stages of the projected flight. The prevailing winds that night—north-westerly—were also taken into consideration, and on April 18th two military aircraft took off from Gao and covered an area 50 kilometres west and 100 kilometres east of the motor-track, but again without success. A further search next day based on Bidon Cinq, covering the surrounding area but orientated mainly south, was similarly unsuccessful.

On April 20th General Georges, commander of the military forces in Algeria, called a conference in Algiers to assess the situation and establish a new search plan in which military stations hundreds of miles apart were to co-operate; but three days later, when two French pilots landed at Algiers at the end of a trans-Saharan flight in which they had combined routine radio tests with a further search for Lancaster, hope was abandoned. One of the pilots, M. Minguet, after tracing the history of Lancaster's navigational mistakes in the sandstorm around Adrar, said: "When Captain Lancaster was ready to resume his flight there was no moon and a strong north-west wind was blowing. M. Borel, the head of the Trans-Saharienne Company at Reggan, told him it was madness to take off when he would not be able to see the day beacons on the motor-track, and when he had no lighting on his instrument board for steering a compass course. Captain Lancaster said he would manage with some matches, and M. Borel gave him a pocket electric torch. Captain Lancaster made a very bad take-off, and that was the last seen of him." The dangers of trans-Saharan flight, especially in sandstorm conditions, were not sufficiently realized, added Minguet. He thought Lancaster might have been flying very low to try to keep the motor-track in sight in bad visibility and flown into a sand dune; it was unlikely that Lancaster could have flown south of Gao without being noticed.

Thus of the three aviators to leave Lympne on record attempts between April 8th and April 11th, 1933, two had disappeared. Only Jean Batten got through.

The tacit assumption that Lancaster was dead was now generally made. Even the Lancaster family were resigned within a month to his death. "I did not want him to go on this last flight," said Mrs Lancaster senior, "but he was promised a job if he succeeded. That is why I let him go. I could not bear to see him unhappy because he could not get work." On May 21st she held a meeting in London to honour her son's memory at which she claimed to have made contact with his spirit, and Edward Lancaster apparently accepted this. "I do not now believe that my son is alive," he said. "Indeed I know he is not. Messages have come to us from the other side. . . . He did not suffer; that is a great relief to his mother and to me. Sooner or later we shall know everything. He and his machine will be discovered in much the same way as Bert Hinkler was found, after an interval. . . . I have been assured that he will be found." Bert Hinkler, missing on a flight to Australia in January of the same year, had been found dead beside his plane on an Italian mountainside four months afterwards.

It was as well that the Lancasters should believe their son had not suffered, and as well too, perhaps, that they did not know how long the interval was to be.

The impression in aviation circles was that, in spite of his father's confidence in his physical fitness, Lancaster after his ordeal in America had been in no state for such a test of endurance. "One can well understand his nervous state," wrote C. G. Grey in the *Aeroplane*. "He regarded this flight as his great chance of reinstating himself in the esteem of the British aeronautical community after his unfortunate experience in America. Since he came back to England he had been trying hard to get a job, without success, and naturally that worried him and wore out his nervous energy. Consequently when he started he must have been already in a state of nervous exhaustion." Grey had noticed the change in Lancaster since his experiences in America, and after paying tribute to his achievements as a flyer, he added: "Also he was a likeable chap, and, when cheerful, very good company." But that had been long ago. These and similar muted tributes confirmed an impression in the public mind that was to gain conviction as the years passed, and even to find confirmation in the writings of aviation specialists: Lancaster had known when he left Reggan that the record was outside his reach and, perhaps with the murder of Haden Clarke still on his conscience, had deliberately flown to his death.

CHAPTER XX

The Diary

THE smell of the breakfast toast was already escaping from the kitchen of a small modern house in a Berkshire hamlet. A teaspoonful of instant coffee covered the base of the coffee-cups, a saucepan of milk was nearing the boil. A slim, petite, dark-haired woman, five feet one and still not much more than seven stone, was lighting a cigarette. Her airline-pilot husband, smelling the toast, was just coming down the stairs into the hall when the telephone rang. The date was Monday, February 19th, 1962.

"Take that call, will you, darling?" called the woman. "Otherwise this milk will boil over."

The phone was in the hall, and the man picked up the receiver to hear the voice of his next-door neighbour, a woman. "Chubbie's in the news," she said. "Do you get the *Daily Mail*?"

"No, we get the *Express*."

"I'll just finish my breakfast and get dressed," said the neighbour, "and I'll bring it over."

"Who was it?" called the woman in the kitchen.

The man told her. "What have you been up to, Chubbie?"

"Not a thing."

"Mary says you're in the news. Have the police pinched you for speeding or something?"

"I haven't done a thing," said Chubbie. "What's she talking about?"

The man took his newspaper from the letter-box and strolled into the dining-room. He began to thumb idly through the pages. "My God," Chubbie heard him say, "here it is." The body of Bill Lancaster, and the wreck of his plane, missing without trace for twenty-nine years, had been found. More than that, for eight days, as he sheltered in the shadow of his plane, waiting for rescue or death, Bill Lancaster had kept a diary. That diary, written in his aircraft log-book, brittle and desiccated, scorched and faded, yet still in a remarkable state of preservation, the early pages written when he was still in pain from injuries, the later pages scribbled despairingly as he died of thirst, held the secret to his disappearance, and perhaps to his life. That diary, the last copyright of Bill

The Diary

Lancaster, was now in the hands of the French authorities at Reggan. All this was recorded briefly in the report. For Chubbie it was a moment of awful poignancy.

It was natural that Bill Lancaster's daughters—Kiki, who had never remarried, had died in 1953—should seek possession of that diary, or anyway seek access to it; and in addition to their natural interest, attractive offers for the right to publish the diary had reached them within hours of its discovery, and within a week both daughters were on their way to Algiers. But Chubbie, who had experience of Bill as a diarist, was at least as interested in what the diary contained as they were, and she too was inundated with inquiries from newspaper-men.

Chubbie by this time was nervous and apprehensive. She feared that the diary, in addition to containing the story of Bill's last flight, and of how he had met his death, might contain revelations of a personal nature. Chubbie, who had remarried in 1936—her second marriage had thus already lasted for 26 years—was determined that this episode from her past should remain forgotten. The attention and publicity she received when the news of the finding of the body reached London was distressing enough; publication of the diary might magnify this tenfold. Fortunately for her, Bill Lancaster had made her the sole beneficiary under his will. Thus the excursion of the Lancaster daughters to Algiers proved abortive; after a frustrating few days the British Consul-General told them he had received instructions from the Foreign Office that all Lancaster's possessions, including the diary, were the property of the former Mrs Keith Miller, and that the Lancaster family had no legal claim. After a long delay caused by the civil war then raging, the diary eventually reached the Foreign Office and was forwarded to Chubbie's solicitor.

It remained for Lancaster's daughters to agree on a final resting-place for their father, Chubbie having indicated through her solicitor that she had no wish to interfere with any decision they might make. Lancaster's body had been buried by the French Air Force in the civilian cemetery at Reggan, interred in a lead-lined coffin so that it could be exhumed and transported elsewhere if that was the wish of the next of kin. After long deliberation the daughters decided not to disturb the body again; the desert in which their father's bones had already lain for twenty-nine years seemed the most fitting resting-place.

It remained for Chubbie to read the diary. One afternoon in April 1962 she collected it from her solicitor, and that evening she began reading it. The French authorities at Reggan had already described it as the most moving document they had ever read. Now Chubbie, turning the pages unbelievingly after so long, was visibly affected, so much so that when her husband asked her what was upsetting her she found herself doing something she had never expected to do—reading passages to him. He was so transported that he insisted on hearing more, and she settled down to reading the entire diary to him, holding back nothing.

When she had finished they were both emotionally overwhelmed. "He was incredibly brave," she heard her husband say. "No whining, no self-pity, no moans about his luck, nothing." Profound admiration for a fellow-pilot had overcome all his natural antipathy. "This story must be told. We owe it to him to have it published, to let the world know."

The diary was published in serial form in October 1962, twenty-nine and a half years after it was written. It is reproduced here in full.

Thursday morning, April 13th, 5 a.m.

I have just escaped a most unpleasant death. Why? My first act was to go on my knees and thank God for it and implore his aid in my dire need. It happened like this—I was flying a due compass course for Gao when something went wrong. The engine spluttered and she died out. It was pitch dark, no moon being up (about 8.15 P.M.) I tried to feel her down but crashed heavily and the machine turned over. When I came to I was suspended upside-down in the cockpit. I do not know how long I had been out. There was a horrible atmosphere in my tiny prison with petrol fumes. By worming my way round and scraping sand away with my nails, eventually I corkscrewed my way out into the open. My eyes were full of blood which had congealed, but eventually I managed to get them open.

My first thought was the water: had it run out? No, thank God. Two precious gallons of it. I can live for a few days. I am naturally feeling shaky but must keep my head at all costs. I hope the French will search for me, but it is going to be difficult to find me as I am away from the track. I thought of walking to the track and prepared to set out, but Chubbie's and my talk about this came to my mind. No: I must stick to the ship.

I am going to ration my water. A week at most I suppose. It will give me time to reflect and write a few notes in this log-book. I wonder where everyone thinks I am. I think mostly of my mother and Chubbie. I love them both. Chubbie is my own sweetheart, but mother is such a darling. They both were

Comment: Lancaster had been forced down the previous evening, Wednesday, April 12th.

proud of me before I set out. Alas I have truly bitten the dust of disappointment.

Here is what I make of my position:

```
Reggan○─────Track──────────
         ‾ ‾ 160 ‾ ‾  ↓ ─ 20 miles ─
                    ✈
                    me
```

Guesswork, of course.

I find I am cut about the nose and above eyes. I hope it does not become an infected wound. The sun is now going up into the heavens and I suppose I must crawl under the lower wing and hide myself until sundown. Am going to try and exist on one pint of water a day. Doubt it rather. I am preparing material from the aeroplane to light a fire tonight. Pray God it will be seen. The Trans-Saharienne Co. send out for me tonight if I am still missing.

I wonder will Chubbie try and get a machine to search. She will get busy I feel sure. Mother will worry, so, too, will my father. Bless them all. I wish they liked Chubbie. I am going to have an anxious time, however long it may be.

I shall keep jotting down in this log what comes into my mind. Old Smithy would not think much of old *Southern Cross Minor* now. I wonder what caused it—petrol failure, I am sure. Poor old Lamplugh. If I ever get back I will tell him how I bowed my head in sympathy. He is the chap who covered me by insurance. Well, it will be a tough job salvaging this bus from the middle of the Sahara.

Later in the morning. There is a certain amount of pain from my wounds. I do not know whether to walk to the track or not. I don't think it can be more than 20 miles and I expect the motor-cars out tonight. I am

Comment: In fact Lancaster was twice as far from the track as he supposed.

Comment: Captain A. G. Lamplugh, underwriter of the British Aviation Insurance Group.

afraid of my wounds getting worse. I cannot spare any water to bathe them. My nose is going to look a sight. I wonder how everyone will bear with me if I ever get back.

What a story! I can just hear my newspaper friends say this. I am glad I am solo this time. I would not wish this anxiety on my worst enemy. Strange if I should pass out in the desert after scoffing at the idea. Lady Bailey must feel for me I know. Pleasant, there is a friendly vulture already circling. I shouted and he flew away a little distance.

10.45 a.m. As hot as blazes even under the shade of the wing. NO!!! I stick to the ship. If I die I hope it will be over fairly quickly. Feel low.

11.0 a.m. The first day is passing like a year. I am a little worried about my wounds as there is much sand in them I know. Find it difficult to fight against taking a drink *but I must*. My very life depends on strict rationing. Hope I don't go blind—the blood is clotting around my eyes. Weird ideas one gets when minutes seem hours. Watching the vulture fly made me wish I could catch him and tame him and leap astride and fly to a pool of water. I would not mind how dirty it was. There is a small brown and white bird a little bigger than a sparrow settled just near me. I wonder how far an oasis is?

Hot and exhausted. Will hold out as long as possible but loss of blood maybe has made me weak.

I can now quite realise this period of agony in the Sahara desert is going to be as long to the mind as my whole life-time. Truly am I atoning for any wrong done on this earth. I do not want to die. I want desperately to live. I have the love of a good mother and father and a sweetheart whom I adore. If anything happens to me Chubbie go back to your mother and think of the good things about me. There must be some because you have so often told me all you think of me.

2.40 p.m. First day. Have been making some rough flares. Cut strips of fabric, rolled them, wired them, and put on the flying wires doubled over. Will put petrol on them and they should burn. Will use one every twenty minutes during the night. Sun intense but occasional breeze helps.

3.00 p.m. About 2 degrees cooler. Have just peeled off all my clothes and am sitting on the pilot's cushion in my vest and drawers, these happily are silk so I am as comfortable as I can make myself. As I was taking off my socks I saw the places which had been beautifully mended by Chubbie. Of course what is going to be a dream is the bar of chocolate given me by mother just as I took off. I have practically no food. The vulture has gone for which I am grateful, so too have the other birds.

3.30 p.m. I am buoyed up with the hope that Chubbie may do something. I don't know how she can do anything, but I seem to have faith in her arousing interest anyway. She said she would the last time I saw the little darling.

4.15 p.m. I have an idea I am going to get dizzy and stupid spells so I must write as much as possible in the beginning in case I am not able to write a final entry. I am going to wrap this in a piece of fabric, tie it with wire and leave it, I hope, to be collected and sent to the two people I love most. Of course, I may be fortunate enough to be rescued. I can last about a week. Oh please Mr Airman bring out your machine and come and find me.

4.30 p.m. I can hardly believe my eyes but I have just seen a sparrow—this cheers me up considerably as I must be within range of the track. *Two sparrows.* The cars are to start at 6.00 P.M. if there is no news of me. I don't believe they can see me from there. They may see a fire or a flare. Let me *pray* so. The day seems never ending and this only the first! If I survive I have made some resolutions I mean to keep. Chubbie how are you? Mother, I miss your care and forethought.

I have found a dental mirror in the first-aid kit and examined my head wound. Just nasty cuts. Have emptied a whole bottle of Mercurochrome over the cuts hoping to stave off blood poisoning. Fancy, another hour to zero when they start to send out the cars to seek me. I expect the London papers will carry news tonight of my being missing. Chubbie in a flat spin and my darling old mother heartbroken and so worried. All I can say is I hope they get busy in London and Paris. I am only about 150–200 miles from Reggan, if that. Strange, I don't remember much before my crash. Perhaps it will all come back to me.

Comment: Wireless messages between French military stations had been intercepted in Algiers and the news that Lancaster was missing reached London that afternoon.

Oh for some bath water, dirty as it might be I'd drink it. Chubbie and my mother have got to make it up and meet. I wish I could feel that they were going to kiss and talk about me if anything happens to me. You bet if I get out of here I'll see to it they do.

5.15 p.m. I had in the way of liquid *two* whole gallons in the back, one Thermos bottle of coffee, and the remains of some water in the other Thermos. I drank this last night after my fight to get out of the cockpit. Today I have been taking a sip of coffee about every half hour—the bottle is not empty yet. I am *going to ration my water. One* Thermos bottle a day which I shall pour from the 2-gallon tank (removed from machine). This latter is nearly full and holds 7 Thermos bottles of water so after 7 days I shall be waterless. If I get fever I may not be able to confine myself to one bottle but I pray for the strength to do this. People who haven't been in the desert have no real idea of *thirst.* It's *hell*! I did not realise it until this moment. It drives a man mad. I have not experienced a tenth of what agony I must endure to survive this.

Please come out soon. Zero hour is 6.00 P.M. Another 40 minutes then step on it boys. I hope you bring some water.

6.30 p.m. Zero hour has begun and a car has started down the track from Reggan about 150 miles away. I will light the fire at 10.30 and flares from then on at half-hour intervals. Am a bit low. Lost a lot of blood. Could not resist a pick-me-up of spirits of ammonia and half-pint water. Tried to eat part of chicken, not successful but managed to swallow small amount of chocolate.

Comment: A car was duly despatched southwards from Reggan.

What a strange and powerful thing is faith. I have faith that someone will come and find me. But I have learned a lot in the past twenty-four hours. I only hope I can get back to

The French patrol finds the wreck of *Southern Cross Minor* with partly buried skeleton (*see inset*) in foreground, February 1962
Photo London Express News and Feature Services

A montage of the wallet and documents found with Lancaster's body

The wallet

mother darling and my little sweetheart Chubbie.

It is going to be quite dark until 10.30. No moon. Will try to sleep. No one can be anywhere near me for five or six hours.

Good Friday! April 14th.

6.00 a.m. Well, I spent a quiet night, not so much pain. My flares were a success, at least they showed a brilliant light for 60 seconds. I burnt one every fifteen minutes to half an hour. No one saw them!!! For I am still under the port wing. I drank a pint during the night so must really limit myself to the one flask until eight-thirty tonight. It is evident to me that I may be further off my course than I anticipated otherwise the car would have seen me in the night. I certainly saw no lights at all. Oh! please send out your aeroplanes now. I am not strong as I have had no real food since I left England. I am, of course, stripping the fabric to make my flares.

9.00 a.m. My eyes are bothering me again. They have practically closed up they are so swollen. I found some "Joncolia", an American sunburn preparation, so I have smeared some of this around my eyes. It is soothing. The sun is heating up gradually, there is a breeze which, hot though it is, is comforting. The contrast in temperatures is ghastly. In the day so hot it's like being in an oven, at night I need every bit of clothing I have with me: vest, shirt, sweater (thick one), coat, flying jacket (light), muffler of wool, trousers, flying trousers over them, socks, underpants. In spite of all this I am still chilly. The water-tank gets cold at night so by morning if I fill the Thermos flask I have an icy cold drink all day. I take a sip every half-hour. Not getting lost in desert much, I don't know the technical method of consuming one's water. *I do know this*: when I lift the flask for my sip I have to fight with all my will-power to prevent my tipping it up and having a good drink, say of half a cup.

I do not know when I shall start to get really weak, not for a couple of days at any rate. While I am strong I am going to prepare some

Comment: Day temperatures of one hundred degrees Fahrenheit in the shade fall to near freezing point at night in the Tanezrouft.

flares from the rolled strips of fabric placed on the ends of the flying wires, which are bent double. [Here Lancaster appended this sketch of himself holding up flare.]

So I want to light one every half-hour or so at night. I counted my matches. I have *eighteen*. I must therefore keep a fire going for most of the night. I shall have to burn bits of the wreck as sparingly as possible. I am going to leave the fabric on the upper wing (bottom of lower wing as machine is upside-down) to show any searching planes.

If machines are sent out from Reggan tomorrow I should be found alive. My thoughts have been of those near and dear to me this morning. I send them my loving thoughts and expressions of endearment. Oh Chubbie my darling, shall I ever see you again? Sweet little mother, for your first-born's sake, take Chubbie to your heart and guide her in the right direction if I die. For if I live I swear this will be my only occupation except for such duties as I must perform for our support. Poor old *Southern Cross Minor*. What an ignominious finish! I bet "Smithy" will be sad about it. She was a nice little bus. And with what loving thoughts did my father and mother send me out in it to make a record. What a failure and what a place to choose to stop in. Feeling exhausted, more later.

10.30 a.m. Have just tried to inspect extent of injuries. The main worry is the cut between the eyes and more over the left eye than the right. I am terribly afraid of blood poisoning setting in. I removed the bandage after some painful work of pulling it away from where it had stuck. Now what to do I don't quite know, whether to cover up or leave to dry up. Lots of sand got into the cuts last night—at least the night before. Of course I am terribly disappointed at not seeing car lights during the night. It is now a matter for *planes*, lots of them.

What a temptation it is to go to the water bottle. What absolute nectar does it contain. It is my only desire for the moment, water, water, water. Mother, what would you think if I were to dash into your bathroom while you were bathing and plunge my head into the water, clean or dirty, and drink and drink and drink?

Just saw a white butterfly and a dragon-fly (no, not dreaming, actually), this gives me hopes I am near an oasis and so near the track. Come on planes! It was strange, I was just as thirsty at night as during the day. Strange this because it is quite cold as I said at night.

Wind has changed from N.E. to S.W. It blows strong and hot. From 10.30 a.m. to 4.30 p.m. is agony!!!

I shall cease writing this book when I find myself getting weak, then I shall tie it up in fabric from the wing and address it to my mother. It is the true account of my thoughts and feelings while waiting for rescue or the END. If the latter please God I pass out like a gentleman.

1.45 p.m. Felt bad owing head pains. Tried little alcohol out of compass, not good. Sprinkled it over head, the evaporation was cooling for a few seconds. My book is not going to interest me more than a couple of days, will be too weak. Thoughts of mother and Chubbie—I love you both.

3 o'clock. Nearly finished flask but will not touch any more from main supply until six. I have enough water for five or six days, *I think* (one consumed), leaving four or five days for them to find me. Have been missing nearly two days.

Comment: The Nigerian Government had alerted all outposts and the French had begun an air search, concentrated along the motor-track and in the area immediately north of Gao. In London, Chubbie waited all day for news.

Saturday April 15th (Third day)

Slept a lot during night, was exhausted and could not keep awake. I must now conserve every bit of energy to keep alive for about three or four days in the hope that I will be rescued. If the planes start searching today I hope for relief. My water will hold three or four days longer—unless I go mad and consume it before. You see, my wounds have made it hard for me as I lost a lot of blood and they trouble me terribly in the day when the sun is up. Mind you I do not unduly complain of my plight. After all I brought it on myself and must call it the luck of the game and play it out to the end.

Chubbie I hope you succeeded in stirring up interest for a search to be made for me. And I suppose, mother my darling, you have urged people to influence the French Government.

There was a tall French pilot I met in Oran who will probably turn out. If there are several machines based at Reggan I should be found from there for I am only about 150 miles away.

The hours from 11 A.M. to 4.30 P.M. are the dreaded ones. The heat of the sun is appalling. That I shall be ill after this even if found is inevitable. But I don't mind as long as I can get water. That is my constant craving. *WATER.*

Comment: This was the day Chubbie called at the *Sunday Express.*

Sunday April 16th (Fourth day)

6.10 a.m. Fourth day commences. Wind has died down. All yesterday afternoon there was a strong wind and sandstorms. All I could do was to completely cover my head with my shirt and lie in the shelter of a wing. Every half-hour I would take a sip of water. I drank 2 Thermos (pint) bottles full yesterday and had to fight hard to keep away from the main water tank. It is now half full so I may be able to last three more days after today. *This will be my limit*, so please planes start your search.

Last night I boiled some water in one of the outer Thermos coverings and melted some chocolate. It was good but I drank it too quickly. I was sick. I had only consumed two-thirds so I waited until it got cold and drank the rest—it was good and it stayed down.

The most tantalising thing happened last night. It commenced to RAIN. Yes really it did. Cold icy raindrops. Alas it was only for a few brief moments and I was unable to gather even a teaspoonful.

Let me go over the actual crash again. I feel clear headed just at the moment. Here it is for a technical report:

I left Reggan at 6.30 P.M. feeling fine to fly to Gao. I intended following the motor-car track. This I did until it got dark. It was a black night so of course I could see nothing on the ground. I flew at 1000 feet. After flying

Comment: Here and in his earlier remark about scoffing at getting lost in the desert Lancaster shows that his own confor one hour and 40 minutes the engine coughed. I had nearly a full load of petrol on board so tried to push up a bit. Nothing happened for five minutes, when she coughed and missed badly. I started losing altitude. Down, down I came. It was impossible to keep my load in the air. I hit the ground before realizing it, bounced 50 yards, hit again and turned over. This was all I remembered at the time. I came to in a terrible shape, bad cuts about forehead etc. Upside-down confined in cockpit. With strength of desperation I dug and clawed my way out.

Now I know I am to the right of my proper course, this fact makes me anxious as they may not suspect this so early in the flight. I can only stick it out until the last. The days when the sun comes up are indescribable. I just lie it seems for years on my back under the shelter of the wing thinking all sorts of mad thoughts.

Undoubtedly I should not have had such a bad time as I have if it had not been for my injuries. I shall drink water for every meal if I ever get out of this. No more smoking. I have not missed cigarettes a bit!

As I said before this morning I am quite clear in the head. I feel weak, so weak, in the body. It is shrivelling up around my stomach and ribs.

Chubbie my sweetheart, and mother my best friend, and father my pal, do not grieve, I have only myself to blame for everything. That foolish, headstrong self of me.

Life after all is only just a very short span in the scheme of things. I wish I had done more good in my time that's all.

There is still hope but I want to get my last message right. You will have to sort out the words in the rough log and put them into sense.

No more probably until tomorrow. God be with you all.

Bill Lancaster.

6.30 a.m. The sun is getting up strength, this is why I cease.
10.15 a.m. Same day. The sun is mounting in the heavens, but still there is a breeze which

fidence in success was unimpaired up to the crash, whatever others may have thought.

Comment: The search, as Lancaster feared, was still concentrated farther south. The *Sunday Express* had published an account of Chubbie's quest that morning and Chubbie had been to Gerrards Cross to see Barnard.

helps. I am sipping the water at half-hour intervals. I cannot help feeling I must be near water because a small bird like a sparrow just flew over to me from the east. If it were not for my promise to Chubbie I would leave the ship tonight and walk east. But that promise stands because I know she will try and do something. Come to me Chubbie but take care in the coming, believe me I shall *never fly over a desert again*. I suppose I can last two or three more days. Then it will be a few hours —madness—and death at last. I pray that it comes quickly if it has to be.

I will wait until the sun goes down. Mother, you have no idea of this heat. Oh that I could just dash into your kitchen and turn on the cold water tap all over me to feel it gurgling in my mouth and the cold liquid pouring all over me—that would be heaven.

Monday April 17th (Fifth day)
6.20 a.m. Morning of the fifth day. Feeling bad this morning and I should not as last night just after dusk I saw a Very light fired some distance away. I immediately answered with my remaining flare—so I assume I am located. I trust so. Water supply will hold out today and tomorrow. Yesterday was a swelter. If today is like it I shall have to drink a little more than yesterday. I cannot stand the hours between 10.30 and 4.00. I think they will come for me.
9.15 a.m. Am suffering mental torment again. I am positive I saw that light last night and the person who fired it must have seen mine, yet nothing has come to support the fact that they have located me. No machines in the sky etc. I wish I had not drunk that extra flask of water last night. I have cut my chance by a day. Things seem very bad to me. If that light last night was genuine I should have thought to see something this morning.
10.00 a.m. Heat is going to be ghastly today. Am thinking of you mother and Chub.
10.20 a.m. Not a breath of air. I am resigned to the end if it has to be. I think I can last until day after tomorrow—but no longer. Oh for water, water.

Chubbie my darling give up flying and settle down and be a comfort to your mother in her declining years. I wish I had been more of a comfort to you mother o'mine. Never mind think of such pleasure as I have been to you. I will still have faith and hope to be rescued.

End of fifth day—that is to say 6.45 P.M. on the fifth day. The *Southern Cross Minor* does not look much now, I have had to tear away a lot of fabric to make flares so she looks like a poor broken-backed duck with lots of feathers missing. I am resigned to my fate, I can see I shall not be rescued unless a miracle happens. Chubbie remember I kept my word, I "stuck to the ship".

Mother darling my thoughts have dwelt a lot on father and you today. How very sweet you both were to me before I left.

I hope it will not be too hard to bear—the end I mean. I have lain gasping with thirst today—but I stuck to my guns and think I can survive two more days. Am getting a bit weak for I have had no food of course. I only feel thirsty. I want this log to be a rational one and remember Chubbie is to have the original or an exact copy.

Mother, see little Pat and Nina Ann for me, kiss them for me and explain what is in my heart. See Kiki, tell her she can now really forget. Am I getting too sentimental? I must this last time for I am by nature a sentimentalist.

I wonder if the pilot will reappear dropping Very lights again. Please permit it fate. It's getting dark, will probably write a few notes in the morning.

The sixth day Tuesday April 18th

6.00 a.m. Much colder night, dozed from 3 to 5, woke up shivering in spite of all my clothes. Certainly can the human body put up with contrasts. Here in the day I lie gasping for want of air and WATER. And at night I shiver and need a tot of rum.

Well, this sixth day I open with a prayer

that something will happen today. It is now almost unbelievable that I shall be rescued.

Again my thoughts turn to those near and dear to me. I feel very badly about the fact that one or two may be suffering mentally. Chubbie and mother and father I feel sure are.

I suppose I must be further off the track than I supposed. Perhaps some more enterprising pilot than the others will venture this far after all.

I am bracing myself for the five hours of hell. Mind you if it had not been for my wounds I should not have suffered quite as much.

I hope to write up in this log tomorrow morning.

Perhaps something *will* happen today. Bill Lancaster.

Comment: The French air search moved northwards and based itself on Bidon Cinq, which was a move in the right direction, but the approaches to Gao remained the chief area of the search.

Sixth day 11.15 a.m. Not a breath of air. Flies bad today. After my poor cut head.

Can last today I feel sure, but doubtful of tomorrow unless things remain same re wounds. Am just listening for noise from engine. It would sound like music to me now.

I want you to get this mother darling so I will wrap it up before final entry as I do not want to get too weak to do this. My last word will be on outside.

The seventh day, Wednesday April 19th

The last day of a week in the middle of the Sahara Desert with a crashed light plane and a can of water.

Chubbie darling I have stuck to my guns re sticking by the ship and I have stayed the course for a week anyway. Of course, the wounds impeded somewhat.

Now my water will give out today. It cannot be made to last longer. It is then just a matter of a few hours and please God a *quick* end.

As this is the last entry I want to say a few words more to all who are dear to me. I have just lain and thought and tried to see all sides of any point.

Chubbie *give up flying* (you won't make

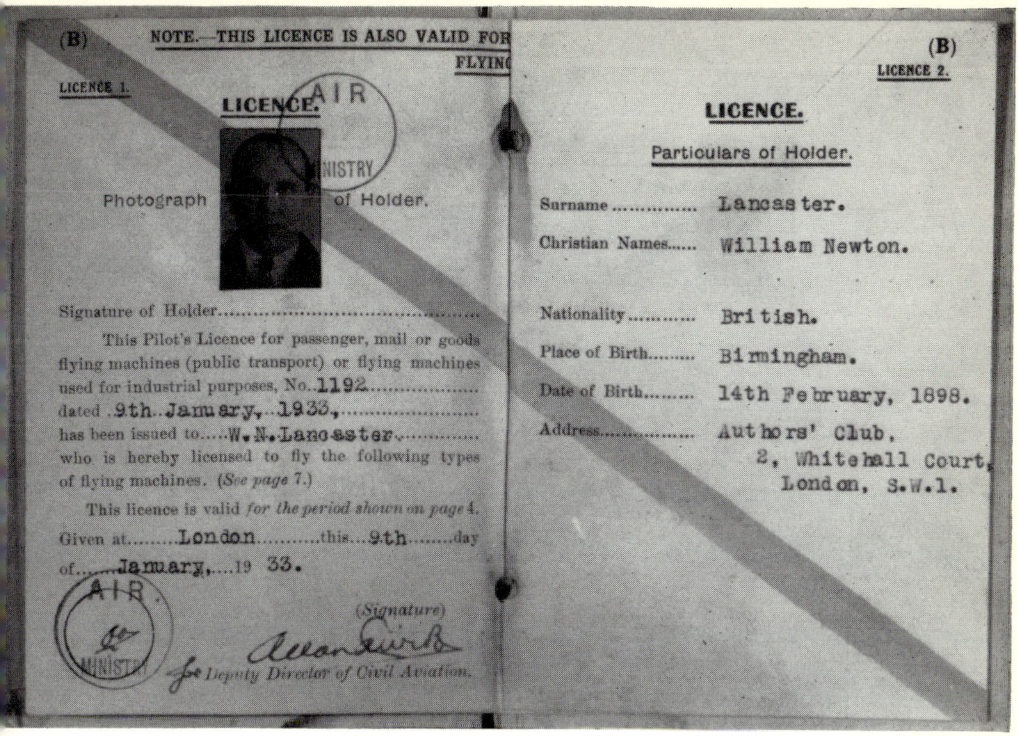
(B) NOTE.—THIS LICENCE IS ALSO VALID FOR FLYING

LICENCE 1.

LICENCE.

Photograph of Holder.

Signature of Holder..

This Pilot's Licence for passenger, mail or goods flying machines (public transport) or flying machines used for industrial purposes, No. 1192................... dated 9th January, 1933,.................... has been issued to.....W. N. Lancaster.............. who is hereby licensed to fly the following types of flying machines. (*See page* 7.)

This licence is valid *for the period shown on page* 4.

Given at.........London...........this....9th........day of.......January,....19 33.

(*Signature*)

for Deputy Director of Civil Aviation.

(B)

LICENCE 2.

LICENCE.

Particulars of Holder.

Surname................ Lancaster.

Christian Names...... William Newton.

Nationality............ British.

Place of Birth......... Birmingham.

Date of Birth......... 14th February, 1898.

Address................ Authors' Club, 2, Whitehall Court, London, S.W.1.

Lancaster's pilot's licence

The aircraft log-book, in which the eight-day diary was kept

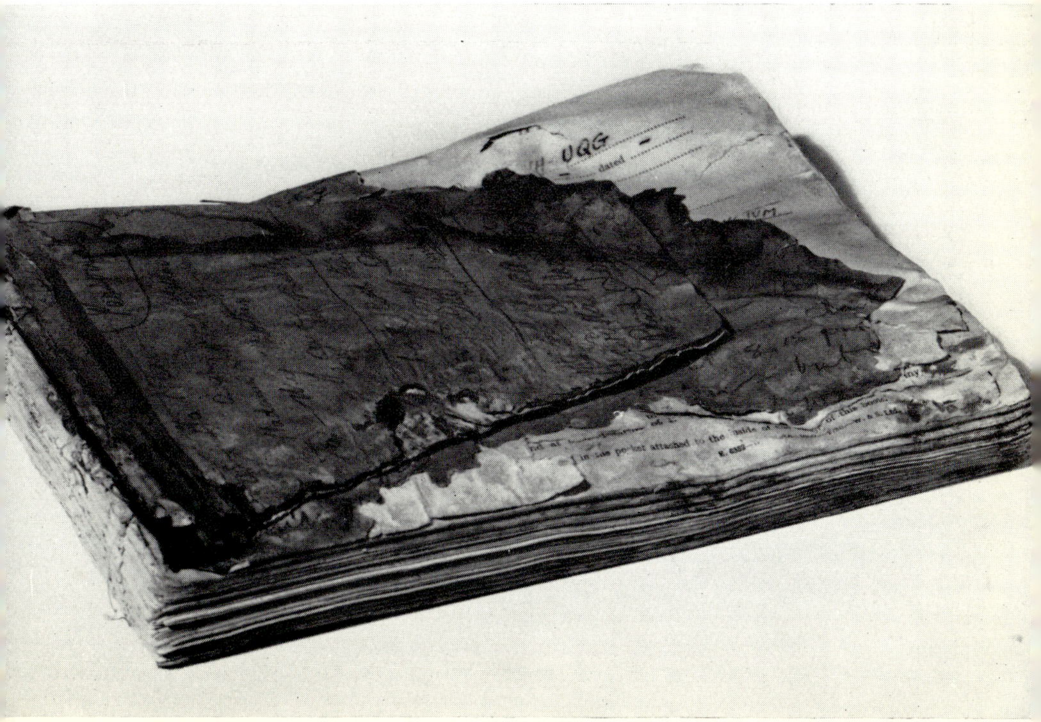

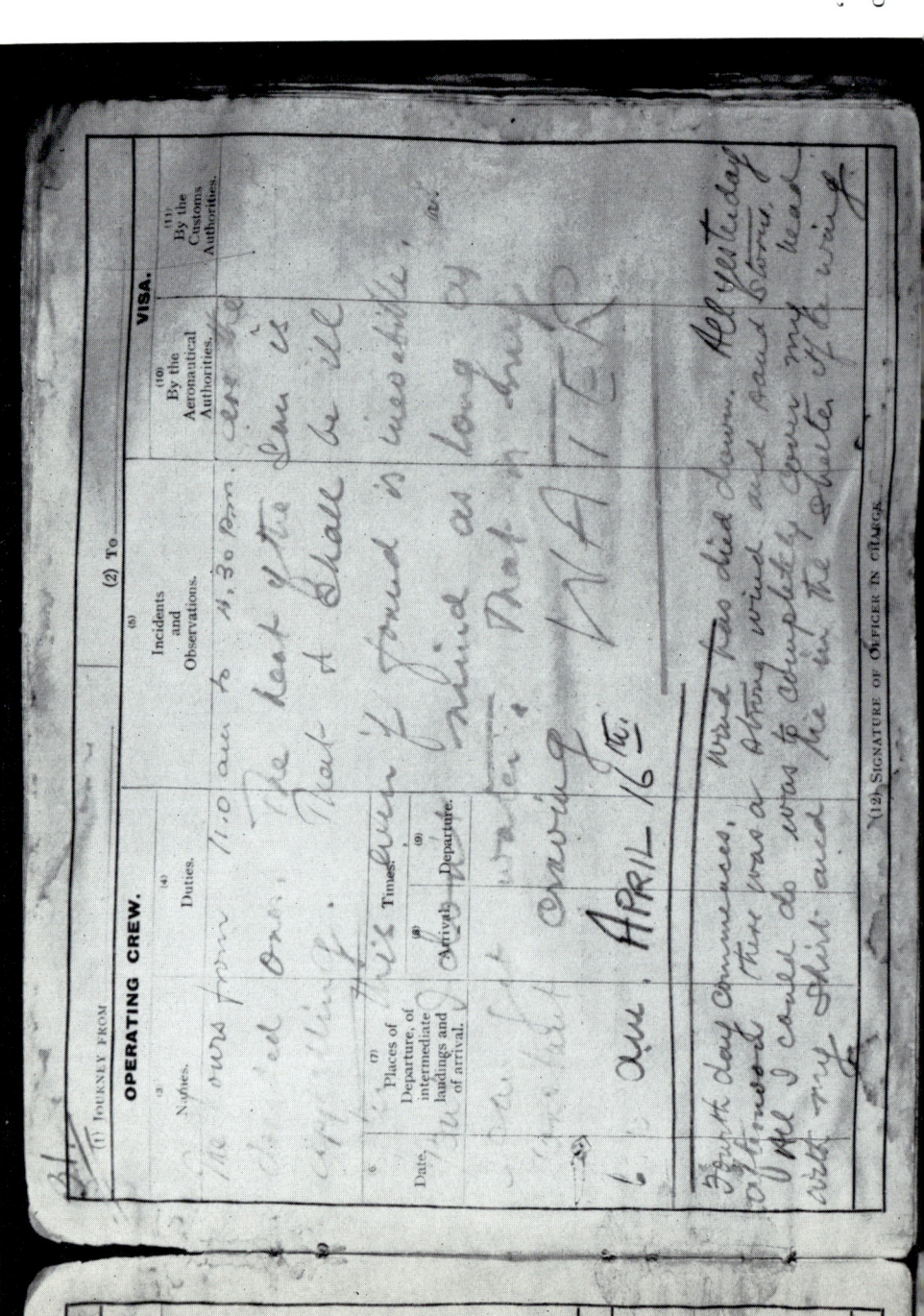

"That is my constant craving. WATER."

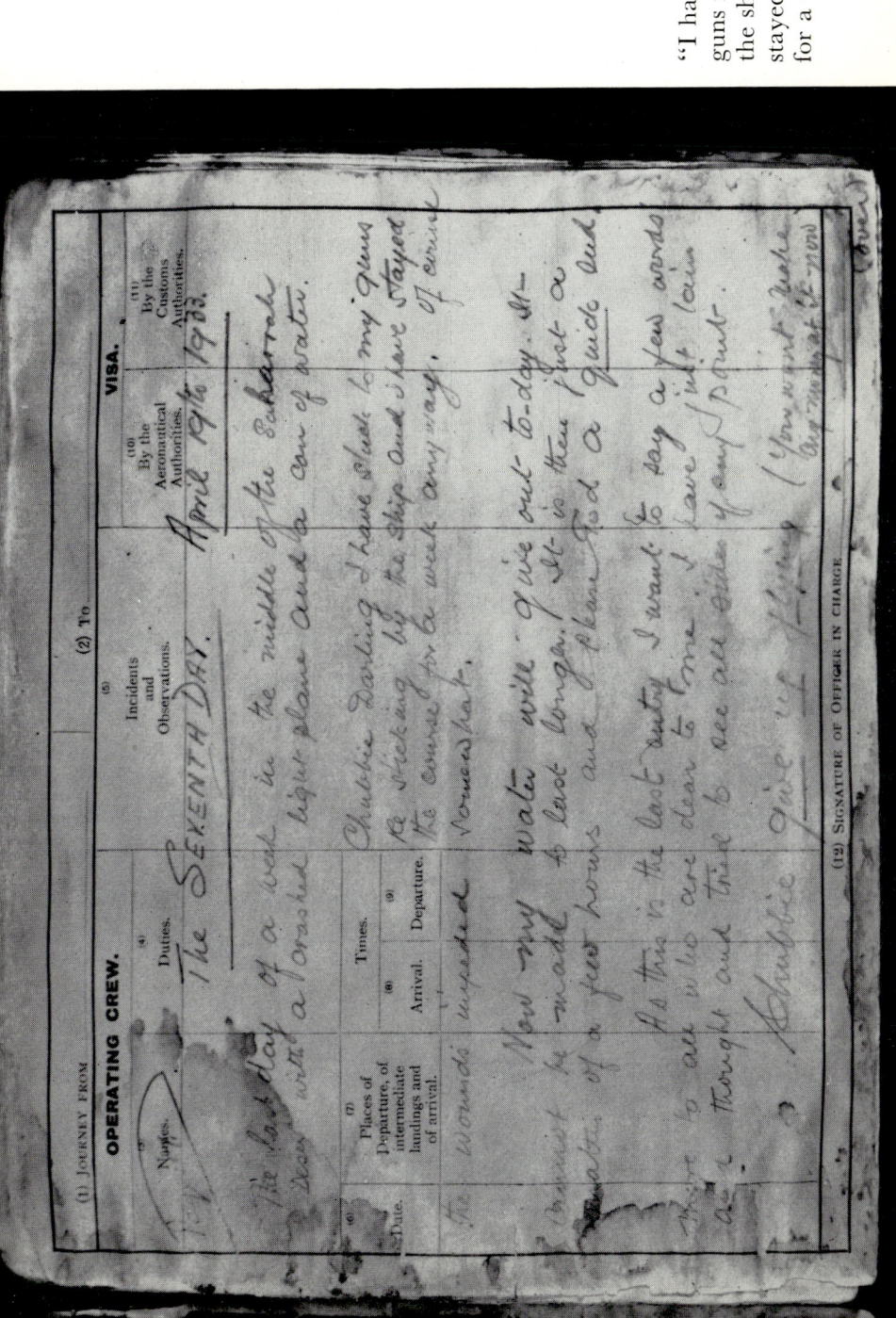

"I have stuck to my guns re sticking by the ship and I have stayed the course for a week."

"The chin is up right to the last"

"So the beginning of the eighth day has dawned"

any money at it now). Collect what money there is available. Pay back my mother and father what is just. Then take a passage for Australia and join your sweet mother. Give her some comfort for the few remaining years of her life. You will always think of "old Bill" as a good scout. Too bad I had to go like this —think of me occasionally and write your book—I'd like to think it would be dedicated to me.

Now my Darling Mother whom I have neglected far too much in my life—I want you darling to see Chubbie and talk everything out with her. Forgive your enemies should be included in your "password". Thank you so much darling for the card of the "Flowers". It gives me great comfort. I no longer scoff at your verse. It's beautiful, Mother. I hope you and Father will be ever so close to each other. Give my brotherly thoughts to Jack when you write.

To my Father—you and I just need a handshake in thought form. We understand.

This accident was in no way my fault, it was just the "luck of the game". Think of me when you have your draught stout. One would be nectar just now.

I made a will before leaving that was not made to hurt anybody but to have my wishes carried out. Isaac has it for Chubbie.

Well, the sun is coming up, soon I must crawl under a wing and wait. I am going to wrap this up in fabric for protection. I hope it is sent home to you safely. Remember this: there must be *no* withholding this log. It is to be read by *both my darling Mother* and *my darling Chubbie*, either separately or together. Old Bill here would like to have them read it together, it's his last wish, remember.

I am now going to tie it up with a note on the outside.

Goodbye to you and God be with you. Bill.

Mother and Chub. If there is another world, if there be something hereafter (and I feel there is), I shall just be waiting. Bill.

Later. I am just going under the wing for the hours of torment ahead of me. Of course, this wreck must be hard to see from the air. It does not look much like an aeroplane.

The chin is up right to the last I hope. Am now tying this up in fabric, will write anything else on strips and push inside wire which will bind the fabric.

Goodbye, Bill.

Inside the front cover of the log-book Lancaster then wrote:

My darling mother, comfort father. See Mrs. K.M. (I love her so. Read this together and both get a better understanding.) Father will get £600 back from machine.   W.

On the outside of the front cover he wrote:
PERSONAL
To: Ma Mère and Madame J. M. Keith Miller.
To: My Mother and Mrs. J. M. Keith Miller.

Please both read this together for my sake.   Bill—my last wish. Mrs. Lancaster, 69 Crystal Palace Park Road, London, England.

His final messages were written on pages of his Shell Fuel Card, as follows:
To my darling mother and my darling Chubbie. I have written a log of the seven days to date, this is written on the seventh day away from Reggan. I hope you get the log and both read it together *for my sake*. No one to blame, the engine missed, I landed upside-down in the pitch-dark and there you are.

See Nina Ann and Pat for me. Kiss them. K will understand. I am tying the main log which has all my thoughts and wishes expressed in it to the strip of the left wing. I hope they find it and give it to you.

Goodbye Father old man. Write Jack [his brother]. And goodbye my darlings.   Bill.

On the eighth day, Thursday April 20th, Lancaster wrote again in the fuel card.

So the beginning of the eighth day has dawned. It is still cool. I have no water. No wind. I am waiting patiently. Come soon please. Fever wracked me last night. Hope you get my full log.   Bill.

Comment: On this day General Georges called a conference in Algiers. Three days later hope was abandoned.

The Diary

In addition to the log book and the fuel card, the following documents and papers were also found, perfectly preserved in a small metal box:
Lancaster's wallet, containing two snapshots of Chubbie and a number of printed visiting cards.
His passport.
His flying licence.
Twenty-five pounds in English money and a similar sum in French francs.

On the cover of a pamphlet about the "Mission of Flowers" which included poems by his mother he had written:

>   Mummy, darling, this was a comfort to me
> in the end.

Epilogue

ALMOST certainly, Bill Lancaster died on that eighth day, Thursday, April 20th, 1933, twelve months exactly after his return to Miami from St Louis. He had outlived Haden Clarke by a few hours less than a year.

Moving as the diary is, the most remarkable thing about it surely is that it is not a depressing document. It is more than merely resigned and philosophic; a kind of contentment, even a happiness, pervades it. While his body shrinks his mind grows in maturity, and he comes to terms with himself and with life.

One by one he ties up all the loose strings of that life. He advises Chubbie to give up flying; he urges her to go back to Australia. He dies with the knowledge that she will always think well of him. His mother and father are to remember the good things and the good times in his life. He relies as always on Kiki's understanding; now at last she can really forget him. He asks that his children shall be told the things that were in his heart.

He knows from the beginning that his chances are small, because the French will never expect to find him so far from the motor-track so soon after the start of his flight. This had come about because he had been unable to see the motor-track and had had to fly a direct compass course for Gao. Thus his first thought is to walk to the track, and he even prepares for it, then remembers his promise to stick to the ship. His life may be forfeit either way, but at least he can keep his promise. By doing so he will give himself serenity of mind, together with perhaps a week in which to reflect on his life, and to write some account of himself for posterity. He prefers these sure advantages to the gamble of setting out for the track. (He was probably right. For the first day or two he was weak from his injuries, too weak to walk forty miles and keep his bearings; and after that he was further weakened by hunger, thirst, and exposure. He had little chance of reaching the track; even if he had got there he would probably have been dead before he was found.)

He never speculates on what might have been if he had made for the track; he abides by his choice.

Epilogue

At first he remembers little about the flight after leaving Reggan, but when he feels clear-headed he sets down the course of events carefully. He blames no one for his plight except himself. As always, he shows no fear of death. "My son had no fear, he has no fear," his mother had said during the trial. And Chubbie, during the Australia flight, had wondered if he knew what fear was. These two women whom he loved knew him best.

There is no trace of any death-wish. "I want desperately to live," he writes. He is still making resolutions for the future. He speculates on what reception he will get if he ever gets back. He never loses hope.

He is conscious of failure, yet that failure is not absolute. He is not cast down by it. He is proud of the way he has held out, and of keeping his promise.

He sets down his last wishes about financial matters. The will he has made in favour of Chubbie is not meant to hurt anyone.

Self-centred as his thoughts are bound to be, he thinks guiltily of those who will be worrying about him. Although it might be natural to wish for company, he is glad in the circumstances that he is alone. He thinks ruefully of "Smithy" and the *Southern Cross Minor*. He even has a twinge of conscience for the man who insured the plane.

As he gets weaker his anxiety to get his last message right grows. His diary shows moments of hallucination soon after he recovers consciousness, but he writes with astonishing clarity near the end.

What should be the final word on Bill Lancaster? There can, perhaps, be no final word, in the sense that some latent doubt of his innocence of murder is bound to remain. The contradictions in his character, too, cannot be wholly resolved. Although an individualist he was not a rebel; intelligent though at times naïve, impulsive yet not impetuous, articulate but not intellectual, he was remarkable mainly for his mastery of or insusceptibility to physical fear. He was not a great flyer, nor was he a great or heroic or even an unusually complex character; but alone with himself at the last he did display a true nobility. "If we can face ourselves," Carson had said of Haden Clarke at the trial, "we can face anyone." Lancaster, while showing consciousness of his faults and failures, faced himself in those last eight days without flinching. His ambitions in life were simple ones, and they remained simple at the end: to keep his word, to leave some account of himself, and to die unafraid. All three were triumphantly achieved.

From his last diary, and from his other writings, it is clear that Lancaster, while capable of self-deception, was neither insensitive nor devoid of moral sense. Yet nowhere in the forty-one pages of log-book that comprise his last diary does he make the smallest mention of the events of a year before. The coincidence that his last physical agonies were suffered hour by hour exactly twelve months after his mental agonies in St Louis does not seem to strike him. In his review of his life, and in the composition of his last message, the death of Haden Clarke has no place.

He sees his sufferings as an atonement, but not for any particular wrong. Forgiveness is something he asks of his mother for Chubbie, not for himself.

What might be the reaction of a guilty man? Wouldn't one expect his final message to the world to contain some boast or revelation, some special plea, some consciousness of the irony of fate, or of retribution, even perhaps some ultimate, reiterated, stubborn denial? What can one make of a man who makes no reference at all? Can he be deliberately shutting his mind to it? He shuts his mind to nothing else. The inference to be drawn, surely, is that Haden Clarke's death was neither on his mind nor on his conscience. And granted—from the other cares and sorrows that occupied his thoughts—that the man had normal sensibilities, may not one deduce from this alone that he was innocent? Is any other explanation tenable?

With such a conclusion, the finding of Bill Lancaster's body by the French patrol, and with it his last diary, would furnish the final missing pieces in the jig-saw, making the picture of the man complete.

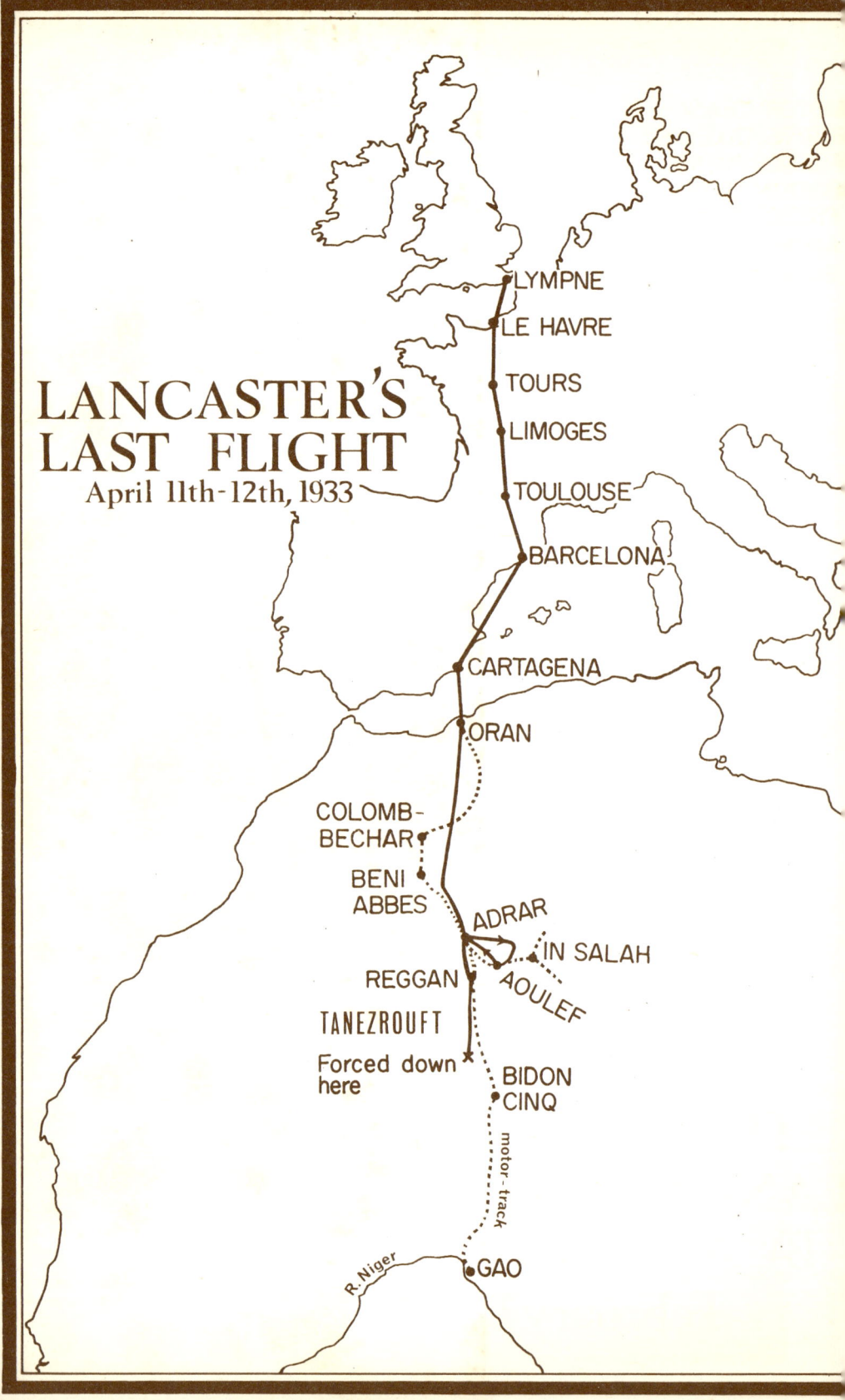